Jesus and Marginal Women

MATRIX
The Bible in Mediterranean Context

∾

Richard L. Rohrbaugh
The New Testament in Cross-Cultural Perspective

Markus Cromhout
Jesus and Identity:
Reconstructing Judean Ethnicity in Q

Pieter F. Craffert
The Life of a Galilean Shaman:
Jesus of Nazareth in Anthropological-Historical Perspective

Douglas E. Oakman
Jesus and the Peasants

Eric C. Stewart
Gathered around Jesus:
An Alternative Spatial Practice in the Gospel of Mark

Jesus and Marginal Women

The Gospel of Matthew in Social-Scientific Perspective

STUART L. LOVE

CASCADE *Books* • Eugene, Oregon

JESUS AND MARGINAL WOMEN
The Gospel of Matthew in Social-Scientific Perspective

Matrix: The Bible in Mediterranean Context 5

Cascade Books
A Division of Wipf and Stock Publishers
199 W. 8th Ave., Suite 3
Eugene, OR 97401

www.wipfandstock.com

ISBN 13: 978-1-59752-803-0

Cataloging-in-Publication data:

Love, Stuart L.

Jesus and marginal women : the Gospel of Matthew in social-scientific perspective / Stuart L. Love.

Matrix: The Bible in Mediterranean Context 5

xvi + 260 p.; 23 cm.

ISBN 13: 978-1-59752-803-0

1. Bible. N.T. Matthew—Social scientific criticism. 2. Bible. N.T. Matthew—Criticism, interpretation, etc. 3. Bible. N.T. Gospels—Criticism, interpretation, etc. 4. Jesus Christ. 5. Sociology, Biblical. I. Title. II. Series.

BS2575.6 .L67 2009

Manufactured in the U.S.A.

For D'Esta
My Beloved Partner and Companion

and
Mark and Jon
My Dearly Loved Sons

and
Zachary
Joshua
Nick
Noah
and
Andrzej
My Much-Loved Grandsons

Contents

Figures

Acknowledgments

THE AUTHOR AND PUBLISHER are grateful to the following journals and publishers for granting permission to use materials from the author's previous publications.

"Gender Status and Roles in the Church: Some Social Considerations." *Restoration Quarterly* 36 (1994) 251–66.

"The Household: A Major Social Component for Gender Analysis in the Gospel of Matthew." *Biblical Theology Bulletin* 23 (1993) 21–31.

"Jesus, Healer of the Canaanite Woman's Daughter in Matthew's Gospel: A Social-Scientific Inquiry." *Biblical Theology Bulletin* 32 (2002) 11–20.

"Jesus Heals the Hemorrhaging Woman." In *The Social Setting of Jesus and the Gospels,* edited by Wolfgang Stegemann et al., 83–91. Minneapolis: Fortress, 2002.

"The Place of Women in Public Settings in Matthew's Gospel: A Sociological Inquiry." *Biblical Theology Bulletin* 24 (1994) 52–65.

"Women's Roles in Certain Second Testament Passages: A Macrosociological View." *Biblical Theology Bulletin* 17 (1987) 50–59.

Abbreviations

ANCIENT

1QM	War Scroll (1QWar Scroll)
1QSa	Rule of the Community (1Q28a)
4QD^d	Damascus Document (4Q269, renumbered 4Q267 or 4QD^b)
4QMMT^b	Halakhic Letter^b (4Q395)
11QApPs^a	Apocryphal Psalms^a (11Q11)
11QTemple	Temple Scroll
Ant.	Josephus, *Antiquities of the Judeans*
Ap.	Josephus, *Contra Apion*
Arch.	Cicero, *Pro Archia*
b.	Babylonian Talmud (*Babli*)
B. Bat.	*Baba Batra*
Bikk.	*Bikkurim*
Conj. Preac.	Plutarch, *Conjugalia Preacepta*
Fact. et Dic.	Valerius Maximus, *Factorum et Dictorum*
Ep.	Pliny, *Epistles*
J.W.	Josephus, *Jewish War*
Ketub.	*Ketuboth*
LXX	Septuagint
m.	Mishna
Meg.	*Megillah*
Mor.	Plutarch, *Moralia*
Ned.	*Nedarim*

Oec.	Xenophon, *Oeconomicus*
Off.	Cicero, *De officiis*
Op.	Hesiod, *Opera et dies* (Works and Days)
Pesaḥ.	*Pesaḥ.*
Q	Sayings Gospel Q
Qidd.	*Qiddushin*
Shabb.	*Shabbat*
Sheq.	*Sheqalim*
Sot.	*Sotah*
Sif.	*Sifre*
Spec.	Philo, *De specialibus legibus*
Sukk.	*Sukkah*
t.	Tosefta
Tim.	Plato, *Timaeus*
Xen.	Xenophon
Yebam.	*Yebamoth*

MODERN

AAASP	American Anthropological Association Special Publications
AB	Anchor Bible
ABD	*The Anchor Bible Dictionary*
ABE	Asociación Bíblica Española
ABRL	Anchor Bible Reference Library
AE	*American Ethnologist*
AJS	*American Journal of Sociology*
AmAnth	*American Anthropologist*
AmEth	*American Ethnologist*
AnBib	Analecta Biblica
APCTS	Annual Publication of the College Theology Society
ARA	*Annual Review of Anthropology*

ARS	*Annual Review of Sociology*
ASR	*American Sociological Review*
ATS	*Anglican Theological Supplement*
AQ	*Anthropological Quarterly*
ANTF	Arbeiten zur neutestamentlichen Textforschung
BA	*Biblical Archaeologist*
BAR	*Biblical Archaeology Review*
BASOR	*Bulletin of the American Schools of Oriental Research*
BEvT	Beiträge zur evangelischen Theologie
BibInt	*Biblical Interpretation*
BIS	Biblical Interpretation Series
BSR	Biblioteca di Scienze Religiose
BT	*Bible Translator*
BTB	*Biblical Theology Bulletin*
BZNW	Beihefte zur Zeitschrift für die neutestamentliche Wissenschaft
CAnth	*Current Anthropology*
CBQ	*Catholic Biblical Quarterly*
CC	Continental Commentaries
CJud	*Conservative Judaism*
CMP	*Culture, Medicine and Psychiatry*
CRINT	Compendia Rerum Iudaicarum ad Novem Testamentum
CSHSMC	Comparative Studies in Health Systems and Medical Care
CSSA	Cambridge Studies in Social Anthropology
CSSH	*Comparative Studies in Society and History*
EncAnth	*Encyclopedia of Anthropology*
EncJud	*Encyclopaedia Judaica*
FF	Foundations and Facets
FMA	Foundations of Modern Anthropology

FMS	Foundations of Modern Sociology
FRC	The Family, Religion, and Culture
FRLANT	Forschungen zur Religion und Literatur des Alten und Neuen Testaments
GBS	Guides to Biblical Scholarship
HBD	*Harper's Bible Dictionary*
HR	*History of Religions*
HTR	*Harvard Theological Review*
HvTSt	*Hervormde Teologies Studies*
HUCA	*Hebrew Union College Annual*
ICC	International Critical Commentary
IDB	*Interpreter's Dictionary of the Bible*
IDBSup	*Interpreter's Dictionary of the Bible, Supplementary Volume*
IESS	*International Encyclopedia of the Social Sciences*
Int	*Interpretation*
IRMS	*International Review of Modern Sociology*
IRT	Issues in Religion and Theology
JAAR	*Journal of the American Academy of Religion*
JBL	*Journal of Biblical Literature*
JJS	*Journal of Jewish Studies*
JR	*Journal of Religion*
JSHJ	*Journal for the Study of the Historical Jesus*
JSNT	*Journal for the Study of the New Testament*
JSNTSS	Journal for the Study of the New Testament Supplement Series
JSOT	*Journal for the Study of the Old Testament*
LAA	Library of Ancient Israel
LCC	Library of Christian Classics
LCL	Loeb Classical Library
MHSS	McGraw-Hill Series in Sociology

MSA	Monographs on Social Anthropology
NHS	Nag Hammadi Studies
NovT	*Novum Testamentum*
NRSV	New Revised Standard Version
NTA	*New Testament Abstracts*
NTL	New Testament Literature
NTM	New Testament Message
NTS	*New Testament Studies*
NTTS	New Testament Tools and Studies
OBT	Overtures in Biblical Theology
PASS	*Publication of the American Sociological Society*
PC	Proclamation Commentaries
PEQ	*Palestine Exploration Quarterly*
PSt	*Population Studies*
RB	*Revue Biblique*
RQ	*Restoration Quarterly*
RSR	*Religious Studies Review*
SANT	Studien zum Alten und Neuen Testaments
SBEC	Studies in the Bible and Early Christianity
SBL	*Society of Biblical Literature*
SBLASP	*Society of Biblical Literature Abstracts and Seminar Papers*
SBLDS	Society of Biblical Literature Dissertation Series
SBLMS	Society of Biblical Literature Monograph Series
SBLSP	*Society of Biblical Literature Seminar Papers*
SBLSymsS	Society of Biblical Literature Symposium Series
SBS	Stuttgarter Bibelstudien
SBT	Studies in Biblical Theology
SG	*Sociologische Gids*
SJLA	Studies in Judaism in Late Antiquity
SJWCS	*Signs: Journal of Women in Culture and Society*

SLP	Studies in Language and Philosophy
SNTSMS	Society for New Testament Monograph Series
SNTW	Studies of the New Testament and its World
SSCS	SUNY Series in Classical Studies
ST	*Studia Theologica*
TDNT	*Theological Dictionary of the New Testament*
ThTo	*Theology Today*
UCP	University of Canterbury Publications
USQR	*Union Seminary Quarterly Review*
WBC	Word Biblical Commentary
WUNT	Wissenschaftliche Untersuchungen zum Neuen Testament.
ZNW	*Zeitschrift für die neutestamentliche Wissenschaft*

1

Introduction

M Y INTEREST IN GENDER studies in the Gospel of Matthew has
spanned the period from 1987 to the present. Throughout that
time I have worked with social-science models to interpret the stories of
women in Matthew. My initial efforts involved the use of *macro*sociology,
a branch of sociology that focuses on human societies themselves in contrast to *micro*sociology, which concentrates on individual components or
features of a particular society. Both approaches are concerned with the
study of individuals, families, classes, and social issues such as crime, race
relations, religion, politics, and gender but *macro*sociology analyzes those
components and others in relation to the larger social systems or societies
of which they are a part.

Put another way, I wanted to understand the topic of gender in
Matthew not in isolation but in association with the polity, economics,
religion, education, and kinship ties of Palestinian society of the first century as they in turn were informed and governed by Rome and the values and socio/political ideology of Greco-Roman society. I believed that
too often, whether right or wrong, gender analysis tended to be isolated
and/or divorced from the greater cultural fabric found within a gospel
like Matthew and its contextual setting within the Mediterranean social
world.

Further, coming from the opposite direction, I wanted to do my
work freed as much as possible from the influences of my own social
world—twenty-first century America, an advanced industrialized society
enmeshed in individualism and a democratic social ideology. In other
words, my purpose was to examine the stories of women in Matthew
from the inside out, that is, to refrain as much as possible from forcing
upon the writing a peripheral template derived from my social world.
When a template was deemed necessary, I wanted to acknowledge its us-

1

age deliberately and to take pains that its contours were consistent with social systems in Greco-Roman society. There is a need to examine both the "trees" and the "forest"—the trees being the social, historical, and literary data relevant to the topic of gender in the Gospel of Matthew and the forest being the social realities of an advanced agrarian society like ancient Rome of which Matthew was an integral part.

My first exposure to macrosociology came from Marvin Chaney at San Francisco Theological Seminary in a doctoral seminar on the origins of early Israel and the rise of Israel's monarchy. Chaney introduced me to the compelling work of Gerhard Lenski, whose interest in societal types was first set forth in his seminal book entitled *Power and Privilege: A Theory of Social Stratification*. Lenski also wrote a textbook, originally coauthored with Jean Lenski, that has gone through ten editions and is now coauthored with Patrick Nolan, titled *Human Societies: An Introduction to Macrosociology*. My reading of Lenski, along with others such as Gideon Sjoberg's *The Preindustrial City: Past and Present*, came to have relevance for my interests in the topic of gender. In the initial stages what stood out was the importance of the Greco-Roman household, the basic social unit of advanced agrarian societies encompassing in ever-widening but interrelated circles families, villages, towns, cities, and empire.

TWO PREVIOUS STUDIES AND THE USE OF A MACROSOCIOLOGICAL MODEL

This background led to the publication of an article in *Biblical Theology Bulletin*, "The Household: A Major Social Component for Gender Analysis in the Gospel of Matthew."[1] In this study I examined gender-specific household behavior in Matthew through three steps: (1) the creation of an advanced agrarian model of the status and roles of women (and men); (2) the application of that model as a comparative index of household data in Matthew; and (3) an examination of exceptional (deviant) examples to the model. I found that the Gospel presupposed a rigid, hierarchical, authority-centered social structure largely based on the paradigm of the ancient Mediterranean household. I also found that exceptional or deviant behavior did exist including Matthew's message about hierarchical authority within the Jesus group, Matthew's emphasis upon the kingdom's

---

1. Love, "The Household."

new surrogate family,[2] and his treatment of women by Jesus. However, I was reticent to label the Matthean community[3] an egalitarian group. That seemed anachronistic. True, there were two actualities that existed: one following advanced agrarian normative behavior and the other the Matthean exceptions (deviant behavior), but it appeared, given that tension, that the writing did not burst the societal boundaries of the household of advanced agrarian societies. The Gospel of Matthew seemed very much at home in its social world.

One facet of the household model included a number of gender expectations related to private and public space.[4] A woman's place primarily was within the private space of the household where she managed that realm through the delegated authority of her husband. Conversely, the public realm was primarily male space which had corresponding social implications in the political, educational, and public religious spheres of advanced agrarian societies. Variations and exceptions to these macrosocial generalizations needed to be taken into account, but in the end a public/private gender distinction remained a legitimate working model for my analysis.

But, could this distinction be identified and hold true in Matthew? Women's roles within the household had been established but what about the place of women in public settings? Was there a way to identify the place of women in public settings? I concluded that there was and subsequently published a second article in *Biblical Theology Bulletin* titled "The

2. Guijarro ("The Family in the Jesus Movement," 115) provides a definition of a surrogate family. "A 'surrogate family' is a group of people that, not having an actual kinship relation, relate to each other as if they did. This type of fictive kinship was and is very common in traditional Mediterranean societies because of the centrality of the family in them. Because of this the majority of significant relationships follow the model of kinship relations."

3. We will use the term "community" rather than "church" (16:18; 18:17) to identify the Matthean Jesus group. This is because the word "church" for most Americans is quite different from churches that existed in the first century. Our choice is to distance the Matthean community from contemporary churches, which in fact derive from Constantine's Nicea. Duling ("Matthean Brotherhood," 164) has chosen the term "brotherhood." His reasoning is similar: "the *ekklesia* translated by English 'church' has become overloaded with Christian content."

4. See Sjoberg, *The Preindustrial City*, especially chapters 1–4, 6; Malina, *New Testament World*; Elshtain, *Public Man, Private Woman*; MacMullen, "Women in Public in the Roman Empire"; Corley, "Were the Women around Jesus Really Prostitutes?"; idem, *Private Women, Public Meals*.

Place of Women in Public Settings in Matthew's Gospel: A Sociological Inquiry."[5]

In this study, I did a gender analysis of the place of women among three character groups: the disciples, the crowds, and the religious leaders as they were taught by Jesus or interacted with him in three representative public places: the mountain in the Sermon on the Mount (5:1—7:28), the boat in the Parables Discourse (13:1–52), and the clash between Jesus and the authorities in the temple (21:12—23:29). To interpret the data I used two gender-specific analogies to provide a social index: a macrosociological model of the public status of women in advanced agrarian societies and a social summary of the public place of women in the culture represented by the Mishna, a legal literature thought by many scholars to have emanated from the Pharisees, Jesus' major opponents in Matthew. I found that the religious authorities paralleled advanced agrarian gender expectations without variation; they were all men reinforced by their orientation to the law and their manner of framing questions and religious issues. The disciples were like and unlike the religious authorities. Like the authorities, they were male and were authority figures, teachers, and leaders in the community (28:18–20). In this respect the disciples followed advanced agrarian norms and mishnaic practice for those who study and teach the law. Unlike the authorities, however, the disciples were not to exalt themselves by seeking places of hierarchical power and titles of honor. Rather, their role was to be characterized by humility, their standard of greatness was to be found in children, and their paradigm for faith and service was found among the women and other marginalized persons scattered throughout the writing. At this point Matthew's community seemed to run counter to the crystallized social stratification of the Jerusalem Temple, the synagogue, mishnaic culture and advanced agrarian societies as a whole. But, it appeared that the disciples in the role of teachers[6] depicted some level of male hierarchy within the community, albeit one that eschewed patriarchal authoritarianism.

Matthew's community worked with two tensions: (1) all were "brothers," but (2) the disciples appeared to have had a special standing as teachers. The third group, the crowds, opened a real but limited alternative for women. Both the women in the crowds and the women who

5. Love, "The Place of Women."

6. The role of teaching is given to the disciples only in 28:20. Before that time only Jesus teaches (7:28–29; 23:8).

4

followed Jesus from Galilee were examples of faith. Jesus acknowledged their presence, considered them worthy, treated them as persons, and received their hospitality and ministry. Their faith and faithfulness was juxtaposed to that of the disciples. Their religious status stood counter to that of women in mishnaic culture. No longer were men the only ones who could come before the Lord. Circumcision had been set aside. No longer were women attached to males for their public religious identity. Jesus, as God's presence within the community was the basis for that significant social change. All persons—men, women, children, and non-Israelites[7]— were invited to the eschatological marriage feast and belonged to God's new household. All were part of an inclusive universalism. No longer was ancestry, family role, religious patronage, or socio/economic status the basis for religious standing before God. All were members of the new surrogate household because what counted was obedience to the word of God. Thus, the writing's treatment drew upon the new as well as the old. The old was the androcentric framework; the new was the inclusion of women and men in the new surrogate community. These two, equally real, social realities seemed to complement one another in an unusual social dynamic tension.

AREAS AND QUESTIONS NOT ANSWERED

However, I was not satisfied with my study to this point. There was uneasiness over whether the two social realities actually complemented one another. Also, there was much more to the topic of women in Matthew than the household and the location of women in public teaching settings. As a result, a flood of questions surfaced as I explored other materials and asked how best to get at that data through the use of social-scientific models. My journey in using other models was helped greatly by the work and guidance of S. Scott Bartchy, Dennis C. Duling, John H. Elliott, Philip Esler, K. C. Hanson, Bruce J. Malina, Jerome H. Neyrey SJ, John J. Pilch, Douglas E. Oakman, Carolyn Osiek, Richard L. Rohrbaugh, and Ritva H. Williams.

For example, what about the women mentioned in the writing's opening genealogy: Tamar, Rahab, Ruth, and the wife of Uriah (Matt

---

7. In this study, we will use the terminology "non-Israelite" instead of "Gentile." Matthew, as possibly all of the New Testament documents, is ethnocentric in character. Israelites considered all others simply as non-Israelite.

1:4–6)? What was their significance within the genealogy and was that significance limited to the genealogy itself? Were these exceptional persons (to borrow the words of Herman Waetjen) an essential "key" to understanding the writing as a whole?[8] Or, what about women healed by Jesus such as Peter's mother-in-law (8:14–15), the girl restored to life (9:18–19, 23–36), the woman suffering from hemorrhages for twelve years (9:20–22), and the Canaanite woman's daughter (15:21–28)? Could social-scientific inquiry assess these stories? If so, what would that mean? Does Matthew's redaction remove us farther from the historical period of Jesus as a healer than Mark as maintained by scholars like H. J. Held?[9] Or, what about the period of the Evangelist forty or fifty years after the death of Jesus; how would these accounts be heard by the Matthean community? Using the language of Ulrich Luz,[10] do the narratives function as "transparencies" of the Matthean community? Certainly during the time of the Evangelist the community was in transition as it clashed with a Pharisaic party following the destruction of the Temple in 70 CE. Old external/internal boundaries had been crossed or were being challenged due to the Matthean community's separation from the synagogue and Pharisaic-led Judaism (21:28—23:39) such as a rejection of the dietary laws of the Pentateuch (15:11) and an acceptance of a mission that called for baptism without circumcision (28:19–20). Internally, the community needed to confront "false prophets" (7:15–23), take into account the faith of the "little ones" (18:6–7, 10–14), face up to the "little faith" of the disciples (6:30; 8:26; 14:31; 16:8; 17:20), deal with community disputes (18:6–20), meet head-on leadership issues (16:18–20), take into account its future (chapters 24–25), and cope with a community made up of good and bad followers of Jesus (13:24–30, 47–50; 22:1–14). But, did those uncharted waters also consist of a social struggle within the community? Was Jesus' millennial vision for "structurally"[11] marginalized persons being carried out? What about the social standing or inclusion of marginal Israelite and non-Israelite women within the community? Before we proceed some thoughts on marginality are in order.

8. Waetjen, "The Genealogy as the Key to the Gospel according to Matthew."

9. Held, "Matthew as Interpreter of the Miracle Stories."

10. Luz, *Matthew 8–20*, 2.

11. Duling describes four different kinds of marginality. Duling, "Matthew as a Marginal Scribe"; also see Billson, "No Owner of Soils."

EXCURSUS ON MARGINALITY

We begin with a definition of "marginality" used among social-science scholars. Gino Germani defines marginality as "the lack of participation [exercise of roles] of individuals and groups in those spheres in which, according to determined criteria, they might be expected to participate." "Lack of participation" in this definition refers to "the inability of persons to conform to expected social roles with respect to sex, age, civil life, occupation, and social life in relation to levels of status in the social system." Duling, building on the work of Germani and Billson, has identified four concepts of marginality: (1) structural marginality, (2) social-role marginality, (3) ideological marginality, and (4) cultural marginality. Of these four concepts, three are applicable to our study—structural marginality, ideological marginality, and cultural marginality. The second concept, social-role marginality, is actually a subtype of "structural marginality" and is as Duling notes "more difficult to demonstrate in antiquity because upward social mobility was often limited or non-existent, with the exception of certain subgroups, for example, the Roman military or in religious sects and voluntary associations."[12] This leads us to an elaboration of the other three concepts.

Structural Marginality

Structural marginality refers to structural inequities in the social system, that is, some persons are in the center and some are on the periphery. It is analogous to vertical social stratification. Persons from any level of the social hierarchy can be considered marginal if they are denied access to the goods and services they might be expected to receive.[13] Usually, however, it is those who are on the margins, the socially and economically disadvantaged or oppressed—the poor, destitute, and expendable peoples, as well as women in certain contexts, who are structurally marginal. Duling refers to this as *"involuntary marginality"* because such individuals and groups—due to race, ethnicity, sex, "underdevelopment," and the like—are not able to participate in normative social statuses, roles, and offices and their obligations and duties. As a result they fail to share in both material

---

12. Duling, "Ethnicity, Ethnocentrism," 137.
13. Germani, *Marginality*, 49.

and nonmaterial resources available to other members at the center of society. They experience themselves as being personally alienated.[14]

Duling identifies an extensive list of examples in Matthew that includes forced laborers, day laborers, some slaves, tenant farmers, the poor, the destitute in need of alms, eunuchs, those who are ritually unclean, lepers, a woman with a hemorrhage, the women who follow Jesus, the diseased and infirm, the blind, the lame, the deaf, the dumb, the deformed, paralytics, demoniacs, epileptics, bandits, and prostitutes.[15] He further believes that the parable of the sheep and the goats (Matt 25:31–46) offers a paradigm for structurally marginal persons.[16] Applicable to our study are the woman with a hemorrhage (9:20–22) and the woman who anoints Jesus' body for burial (26:6–13). We classify the women who follow Jesus (27:55–56, 61; 28:1–10) under two categories—"ideological marginality"[17] and "structurally marginal."[18] This leads us to the second concept, "ideological marginality."

Ideological Marginality

Ideological marginality, following Billson,[19] refers to those who willfully desire to affiliate with a nonnormative group. This marginality concept is derived from Victor Turner's analysis of rites of passage.[20] Persons in this category are initiates "who are temporarily separated (usually physically) from the larger society and its statuses and customs." They are "marginal" or "liminal" (Latin *limen*: "threshold").[21] Following Turner, Duling describes such persons or groups as "status-less, role-less, spontaneous, sexless, and anonymous. They experience a certain egalitarianism and intense comradeship, or what is today called 'bonding,' in part due to their common, temporary separation."[22] Turner designates those who attempt to routinize this concept institutionally as belonging to an "ideological

14. Duling, "Matthew and Marginality," 648; Germani, *Marginality.*
15. Duling, "Ethnicity, Ethnocentrism," 138.
16. Ibid.
17. Reasons for this classification are given in chapter 7.
18. See chapter 7.
19. Billson, "No Owner of Soils."
20. V. Turner, *The Ritual Process.*
21. Duling, "Ethnicity, Ethnocentrism," 137.
22. Ibid, 137–38.

communitas," or "voluntary "outsiderhood."[23] Duling calls this "voluntary marginality" because the individuals and groups do so consciously and by choice. They "live outside the normative statuses, roles and offices of society because they reject hierarchical social structures." He adds, "Though freely chosen, they will eventually share in some of the same conditions as involuntary marginals."[24]

Duling believes that the Gospel of Matthew sets forth several types of groups who possibly represent voluntary marginality. One example is the disciples and the mission charge in Matthew 10:9–15. Another example is the more settled community described in Matthew 23:8–10. Such groups, following Victor Turner's description of liminality, are in limbo.[25] They are "neither here nor there," they are "betwixt and between."[26] Turner characterizes this liminal phase by the term *communitas,* "a status-less, roleless phase marked by spontaneity, concreteness, intense comradeship, and egalitarianism."[27] "Persons in this phase are often considered sexless and anonymous, sometimes symboled by nakedness."[28] Communitas for Turner is also anti-structural, that is, there are no fixed "relationships between statuses, roles, and offices." Anti-structure is marked by "spontaneous, immediate, concrete" relations—persons who "are not segmentalized into roles and statuses but (existentially) confront one another." However, Turner warns that "the spontaneity and immediacy of communitas ... can seldom be maintained for very long. Communitas itself soon develops a structure."[29]

Turner distinguishes among three kinds of communitas: (1) *existential* or *spontaneous* communitas, (2) *normative* communitas, and (3) *ideological* communitas. *Existential* or *spontaneous* communitas is approximately what the hippies were in the 60s—what they would call "a happening," and what William Blake might have called "the winged moment as it flies," or, later, "mutual forgiveness of each other."

---

23. V. Turner, *Drama, Fields, and Metaphors,* 266.

24. Duling, "Matthew and Marginality," 648; V. Turner, *The Ritual Process.*

25. V. Turner (*The Ritual Process*), sets forth a common pattern of three phases of the ritual journey: separation, liminality (marginality), and aggregation. For our developed rite of passage model see chapter 7.

26. Ibid, 95.

27. Ibid, 127, 132.

28. Duling, "Matthew and Marginality," 646.

29. V. Turner, *The Ritual Process,* 132.

Normative communitas, takes place when under the influence of time the need to mobilize and organize resources, and the necessity for social control among the members in pursuance of these goals takes place to the extent that the existential communitas is now organized into a perduring social system. *Ideological* communitas is a label one can apply to a variety of utopian models of societies based on existential communitas.[30]

Voluntary marginal groups in Matthew illustrate *ideological* communitas,[31] but as we will demonstrate in future chapters there are signs of the movement of these groups toward *normative* communitas. In this movement, there are "pressures toward hierarchy—that is, there appear to be "those who are more equal than others." One example, Duling believes, is seen in those labeled as apostles (10:2), prophets (5:10–12; 11:9; 10:40–42; 12:57; 21:11, 23–27; 23:29–36; all of the formula quotations, including Ps 78:2 and 110:11 are from "prophets"), teachers (5:19; 28:20), scribes (13:52; 23:34), righteous men (10:41–42), and wise men (23:34). Another example is the special honor given to Peter by Jesus that suggests a transfer of authority (16:17–19). Duling concludes, "Thus, like its rivals, the Pharisees, the Matthew group is not simply a non-hierarchical communitas, but is on its way toward a hierarchical structure (normative communitas)."[32] If this is so, how do the stories of women, which fit the concept of involuntary marginality, fit into the social realities of this larger voluntary marginal community's transition? Are they included? Do they participate in this state of transition? Do their stories help us "wipe away the fog" so we can see through the text to the author's social historical context?

Who then in Matthew belongs to the category of ideological marginality? Duling suggests the author of Matthew may fit this category. Also, we affirm in chapter 7 that the twelve disciples and the women who follow Jesus choose to do so voluntarily and when other considerations are taken into account we identify them among the "ideologically marginal."

---

30. Ibid.

31. Duling, "Matthew and Marginality," 659–62.

32. Ibid.

Cultural Marginality

Cultural marginality, advanced by Park,[33] Billson,[34] Stonequist,[35] and Schermerhorn,[36] refers to persons or groups who are "condemned" to "live between two different, antagonistic worlds without fully belonging to either.[37] Such persons are 'caught between two competing cultures.' They experience isolation, identity confusion, and alienation." They are "unwittingly initiated into *two or more* historic traditions, languages, political loyalties, moral codes, or religions, one of which is more dominant."[38] Those who are culturally marginal "do not fully assimilate; they are said to be 'in-between,' to have 'status incongruence.'"[39] Duling argues that the Matthean author possibly is a *culturally marginal* scribe in a *culturally marginal* community. "He was between two or more historic traditions, languages, political loyalties, moral codes, and religions."[40] We affirm in chapter 5 that the Canaanite woman (1 5:21–28) fits this category of culturally marginalized persons. However, we believe she also is structurally marginal.[41] Having finished our thoughts on marginality, we return to the narrative of my scholarly journey.

HEALING STORIES OF WOMEN

I focused my attention first on the healing stories of the hemorrhaging woman (an Israelite) and the Canaanite woman (a non-Israelite) (Matt 9:20–22; 15:21–28). To do this I explored what it meant for Jesus to be a healer in Palestine of the first century CE. How was illness experienced and treated in societies like the Roman Empire? Who did Jesus heal? Were those healed primarily from among the "poor"—the farmers, artisans, and

33. Park, "Human Migration and the Marginal Man."

34. Billson, "No Owner of Soils."

35. Stonequist, *The Marginal Man.*

36. Schemerhorn, "Marginal Man."

37. Park, "Human Migration and the Marginal Man." We follow Duling, "Ethnicity, Ethnocentrism," 138.

38. Stonequist, *The Marginal Man,* 3 as cited by Duling, "Ethnicity, Ethnocentrism," 138.

39. Schemerhorn, "Marginal Man," 407, cited by Duling, "Ethnicity, Ethnocentrism," 138.

40. Duling, "Ethnicity, Ethnocentrism," 138. See as well Senior, "Between Two Worlds," 1–23.

41. See chapter 5.

outcasts? Where did Jesus's healing activity take place? Was it primarily located in rural environs? Or, did different kinds of illness or bodily affliction make a difference? Matthew recounts that Jesus healed or restored to life lepers, paralytics, demon possessed persons, the dead, a woman with a blood flow, blind persons, deformed and lame persons, and one who was moonstruck (epileptic).

Further, did Jesus's method of healing make a difference? Some he touched; others he healed by his word or command. Did the location of a healing make a difference? For example, were there divergent social implications if a healing took place in a house, in a synagogue, in open space, or among the tombs? For example, Peter's mother-in-law was healed in the private space of Peter's house (8:14–17). Similarly, the ruler's daughter was restored to life in the private space of the ruler's home (9:18–19, 23–26). But, the stories of the woman with hemorrhages and the Canaanite woman were located in open/outdoor space without the accompaniment of male intermediaries or representatives. Did the healing of women in open, public space have political import? Or, for that matter, would the healing of any woman have had political consequences for Jesus? If so, what would this possibly have meant for the period of Jesus or the time of the Evangelist?

Armed with these questions I first examined Matthew's version of the hemorrhaging woman, concentrating on the period of Jesus. Did Matthew's redaction of Mark's account lead one closer to or farther away from the historical Jesus? To do this I utilized two social-scientific models in addition to the advanced agrarian model of my earlier work: healing in non-Western societies, and a taxonomy of illness based on degrees of impurity. Further, I worked with what social-science scholars refer to as four foundational social domains—politics, economics, religion, and kinship (family). These four social spheres, especially politics and kinship, proved useful in examining the location of the woman's healing in open space. This helped demonstrate that there were political implications for Jesus even though his healing work was primarily within the folk sector of Palestinian, Israelite society.

Both models were set within the wider social context of the pivotal value of Mediterranean society of the first century, honor and shame. The healing model, a systems-theory approach, was designed to answer the question as to how illness was experienced and treated in societies such as the social world of Jesus, a system quite different from the biomedical approach largely operative in societies such as the United States and northern Europe. This model demonstrated that sickness was connected to two broader phenomena: religious/cosmological forces and social relationships/interpersonal conflicts. Patients and healers in the Palestinian culture of Jesus were embedded in a cultural system in which the whole system, one that included witchcraft, sorcery, and spirit aggression, was the basis of healing. The second model, a taxonomy of impurity, depicted how purity rules pertaining to the body had a much wider symbolic meaning that could include pollution boundaries related to the public, Israelite, social domain. The results of this study were published in English under the title "Jesus Heals the Hemorrhaging Woman."[42]

Using the two models, I concluded that Matthew's redaction of the woman's story, located entirely in public open space, originated in the time of Jesus' activity. My hypothesis was demonstrated in a combination of the woman's faith, her identity as an Israelite outcast, the location of the healing in open space, and the violation of the Second Temple's purity boundaries. Those factors coalesced to validate the woman's identity as a structurally marginal Israelite in need of healing (Matt 10:1–16)—the heart of Jesus' theocratic mission to Israel. This made a number of significant differences for both the woman and Jesus.

In the study of the Canaanite woman and her daughter, published under the title "Jesus, Healer of the Canaanite Woman's Daughter in Matthew's Gospel: A Social-Scientific Inquiry,"[43] I used the same two social-scientific models. I found that Matthew's version of this story, rather than being an account laden with "Christian missionary theology and concerns" and therefore the "creation by first generation Christians,"[44] also originated with Jesus. My major argument, based on the insights of the political and kinship social domains and the model of impurity, centered on Jesus' statement to the disciples, "I was sent only to the lost sheep of the house of Israel" (15:24). From a social-scientific perspective that statement had historical probability because it made direct and immediate political sense of Jesus' mission to establish an Israelite theocracy (10:5; 15:24). Jesus, accordingly, faced a purity dilemma: a non-Israelite woman had made her appeal to him based on the core value of God's

---

42. Love, "Jesus Heals the Hemorrhaging Woman."

43. Love, "Jesus, Healer of the Canaanite Woman's Daughter."

44. Meier, *A Marginal Jew*, 660–61.

mercy, probably the central value of Jesus' mission to Israel.[45] By doing so, the woman challenged the weaker purity boundaries of Jesus' inclusive strategy only to Israel.

This study examined the social location of the woman, as well. Was she a prostitute? To answer that question I created a model of prostitutes in advanced agrarian societies and found that probably the woman was a prostitute, especially in light of other gender data in Matthew. Beyond that question, I pursued three more questions:

1. What did it mean in social terms for her daughter to be healed?

2. What did it mean for her to penetrate dangerous social-political boundaries, open space, male territoriality, and the ethnocentric barriers that separated Canaanite and Israelite heritages?

3. What did it mean for her in the end to give praise to the "God of Israel," whose healing power had been mediated through an Israelite healer?

Matthew's redaction complicated the heart of Jesus's theocratic mission in that as an Israelite healer Jesus had served as a patron or benefactor of an outcast non-Israelite woman. By acknowledging the woman's "great faith" Jesus placed her alongside the Israelite woman who had suffered from hemorrhages.

HEALING STORIES AND THE EVANGELIST'S COMMUNITY

However, those two studies did not address the period of the Evangelist. How might they have functioned as "transparencies" of the Matthean community? Did the stories supply a social window that possibly depicted an internal community's struggle over the standing and inclusion of structurally marginal Israelite and non-Israelite women? Again, utilizing the same two models I re-examined the accounts. The process and results of those studies were presented as papers at professional meetings of the Context Group and the Society of Biblical Literature and now are integrated into the materials of this volume.

I found that the hemorrhaging woman served as an example (along with others in the healing stories of Matthew chapters 8 and 9) of the

---

45. Matthew's consistent appeal is that Jesus' mission is legitimated out of the prophetic tradition of Hosea, "'I desire mercy not sacrifice'" (9:13; 12:7).

continued need of pastoral instruction within the Matthean surrogate kinship group regarding the standing and inclusion of marginalized Israelites. The community apparently was not adequately following the Evangelist's vision of Jesus' healing activity. Like Jesus the community was to welcome impartially those marginalized persons labeled as examples of the lost sheep of Israel (10:6; 15:24)—"helpless" Israelites without a shepherd (9:36). This was so because the woman's story, based on the deeds and words of Jesus, constituted an example of great faith and discipleship for the community.

Similarly, I found that the Canaanite woman's story also served as a social transparency that required corrective behavior within Matthew's community. The memory of Jesus's cutting encounter with this strong and wise woman held up a new authoritative social norm that not only disclosed pollution within the community but also rendered pastoral instruction to Matthew's surrogate household. The Evangelist's community needed to address whether and how it would include persons like this woman within the community. She was an example of a solitary non-Israelite bereft of male agency in a society that devalued both women and daughters. Most probably she was among the poorest of the poor, probably a prostitute; most surely she was an outcast in a society that, organized along purity lines, carefully avoided contact with such persons. Further, her story appeared to advance the social irregularities of the non-Israelite women of Matthew's genealogy (1:3–6). In addition, her communication with Jesus probably identified her as a capable and worthy woman of wisdom, a foreigner who gave praise to the God of Israel.

Like the foreigners spoken of by the prophet Isaiah who had joined themselves to the Lord (Isa 56:6), this woman should also receive "an everlasting name" (Isa 56:7; Matt 21:13) in the kingdom's community. Her example, therefore, was decidedly different from that of the centurion (8:5–13) who, as a respected male household leader, carried the freight of the anticipated non-Israelite mission.[46] The woman's example did not even hint of that mission. However, if Matthew's community was a

---

46. We recognize that the centurion possibly is an Israelite auxiliary officer. A scholarly debate exists over the meaning of the term *ethnē* in Matthew. Often, it designates a group of non-Israelites. But that is not always the case. For example, David C. Sim argues that in Matthew's final mission statement (28:18–20), Jesus sends his disciples to all Israelites among non-Israelites. See Sim, *The Gospel of Matthew and Christian Judaism*. For the opposite point of view, see Senior, "Between Two Worlds."

prosperous, mixed congregation of Israelite and non-Israelites still struggling over non-Israelite inclusion, it would be one thing to socially embrace
an established, respected householder like the centurion, but quite another matter to receive non-Israelite women with dubious, polluted social
credentials. The vision of the Evangelist's surrogate kinship group called
for the practice of the God of Israel's core value of mercy, as Jesus did. This
meant that it, too, needed not only to maintain weak structural boundaries but to broaden those boundaries as it followed an inclusive strategy
that welcomed structurally marginal non-Israelite women of "great faith"
(15:28). Such social behavior probably would have engendered criticism
by the synagogue which in turn would have heightened the socio-political
separation of the two groups. Thus, this woman's story provided a transparency of a community struggling over a radical non-Israelite inclusion
essential to the vision of Jesus' new surrogate household.

THE GIRL WHOM JESUS RESTORES TO LIFE

At that point my investigation of the two healing stories was complete,
except for the girl that Jesus restored to life (9:18–19, 23–26). This account was different from the previous healing stories in that its location
was not in public/open space but in the private location of a household.
Accordingly, even though I continued to use the model of degrees of impurity I examined the girl's restoration to life only from the perspective
of the Evangelist's community, a surrogate group belonging not to the political social domain but to the kinship social domain. This decision was
reinforced by Matthew's redaction. Instead of connecting the ruler's story
to Jesus' return to Galilee after the healing of the Gerasene demoniac as in
Mark (5:21) and Luke (8:40), Matthew instead associated it with the earlier banquet scene that also was located in the private space of the house
(9:10; see 9:9–17). Matthew's redaction opened and closed the material
from 9:10 through 9:26 featuring private/household space with the exception of the incident with the hemorrhaging woman who was healed not in
the house but in open public space. Matthew's concern, therefore, from an
anthropological perspective was for the community, a matter reinforced
as well by his identification of the father as a "ruler" and not as a "leader of
the synagogue" as did Mark (5:22) and Luke (8:41).

The ruler's need for Jesus' mercy in behalf of his daughter was so
great that he was willing without invitation to cross the boundary of a

private banquet attended by Jesus, his disciples, and moral and social outcasts. That social reality, as well as the healing of the hemorrhaging woman, would be heard in tandem by Matthew's community. Further, the community would know that the ruler and the woman were polar opposites—a respected household leader and an outcast woman. These two entwined but divergent recipients of God's mercy would serve as visionary examples of the radical inclusion of Israelites whose new home was Jesus' surrogate household.

Light was also cast on the two women, the girl and hemorrhaging woman, because both were addressed by Jesus as "daughters," a reminder to the community that belonging to the surrogate kin group of the kingdom entailed a significant social leveling. All persons of this alternative group had parallel standing because all were recipients of God's gracious patronage. Social disparities did not matter whether the reason for marginalization was illness, death, age, male agency, or lack thereof. The community, like Jesus, should be committed to the healing, restoring of life, and including of all.

THE WOMAN WHO ANOINTS JESUS AT BETHANY

After the healing stories I then turned to the account of the woman who anointed Jesus at Bethany (Matt 26:6–13). In this story Jesus was the unexpected recipient of a grateful client. By anointing Jesus at Simon's house the woman crossed the frontier of public to private space and that action portrayed a difficult and controversial navigation among several forbidden and/or marginal boundaries. The story's setting was important because it was situated between two scenes located in public locations: (1) the plot to kill Jesus by the Judean religious leaders in the palace (26:3-5) and (2) the agreement between Judas and the religious authorities in the temple to betray Jesus (26:14–16). From another perspective, the woman's story involved four points of view concerning Jesus' death: (1) the chief priests' and the elders' who conspired to arrest Jesus by "stealth and kill him," (2) the woman's who out of devotion to Jesus engaged in a positive honor challenge by pouring an alabaster jar of ointment on his head as he reclined at table, (3) the disciples', who, angered by the woman's act, believed the ointment should have been sold and its considerable proceeds given to the poor, and (4) Judas' who betrayed Jesus before the chief priests. The woman's story, therefore, did not stand alone. It was situated in a larger and most vital social context. However, because it did take place in the private kinship domain and not in the public, political sphere, I treated the story at the level of the Evangelist's *Sitz im Leben*.

To interpret the story I carried forward insights related to the political and kinship domains. In addition I utilized two social-scientific models: (1) patronage and (2) a taxonomy of degrees of impurity understood within the "pivotal value of Mediterranean society of the first century"—honor and shame.[47] This was the first time I had used a patronage model but it was justified in light of the obvious patron-client ties of Jesus and the woman. Jesus, I affirmed, had been and was presently broker of the kingdom's resources to her. We do not know the exact form of the good she previously received. But as a grateful client she anointed Jesus. I then applied the models to the four groups, but with each application I emphasized the woman's position in relationship to the religious-political elite, the disciples, and Judas.

Following the purity model, I found that the woman was probably a marginal person, perhaps a woman of "questionable reputation." Following the patronage model, I affirmed that the woman's "good work" substantiated her client relations with Jesus. Her lavish deed honored her broker and solidified the dyadic bond between them even as it riled the disciples. Finally, Matthew's Jesus interpreted the woman's anointing as a prophetic work that prepared his body for burial (26:12). This was significant because Matthew's later redaction omitted that the women went to the tomb to anoint Jesus's body. Matthew, therefore, treated the deed as a singular prophetic act and the woman as a prophet. As a prophet and client of God, she was juxtaposed to the religious elite and the city of Jerusalem which killed the prophets. As a prophet she was harassed by the disciples and treated without honor within Jesus' surrogate family. At the same time, however, she was approved of and defended by Jesus. As a prophet she belonged to the heritage of prophets cited fourteen times by Matthew that included Isaiah, Micah, Jeremiah, David and Zechariah. Thus, as the Canaanite woman most probably was a woman of wisdom who taught Jesus, this woman was a prophet who, although she never spoke a word, taught the disciples by her prophetic deed. Prophets and sages were two significant ways of beholding women in a writing that apparently stressed the leadership of teachers, wise persons, and prophets.

---

47. Malina and Rohrbaugh, *Synoptic Gospels*, 269–72.

If the teachers are males, it should not be forgotten that marginal women served as examples of wisdom and prophecy, which implied also the role of teaching.

THE WOMEN AT THE CROSS AND TOMB

The final inquiry involved a social-scientific reading of the three references to women as followers of Jesus in Matthew's passion and resurrection narratives (27:55–56, 61; 28:1–10). The first citation (27:55–56) stipulated "many women" were present, "looking on" at Jesus's crucifixion "from a distance." Among the "many" three were identified: Mary Magdalene, Mary the mother of James and Joseph, and the mother of the sons of Zebedee—James and John. All of these women followed Jesus from Galilee and ministered to him. The second reference (27:61) at the tomb of Jesus narrowed the number to two, Mary Magdalene and the other Mary, and identified them alongside a wealthy male from Arimathea named Joseph. The third and more extensive account at the tomb comprised only the two women who had witnessed Jesus's burial, Mary Magdalene and the other Mary. They came "to see" the tomb (28:1) but not to anoint Jesus, because that had been accomplished by the woman at Simon's house in Bethany. Guided by the angel, the women were instructed to hasten and tell his disciples that Jesus was resurrected and that he would precede them to Galilee where they should meet him. Leaving the tomb the women were greeted by Jesus who reiterated their unique task given by the angel. The striking exclusion from all of these scenes was the twelve male disciples who had deserted and betrayed or denied him but who now became the object of the women's mission.

For this material I did not set aside such previous models as honor and shame and degrees of impurity, but I employed as my central comparative paradigm a rites of passage model, a combination initiation/death ritual, because I believed that it best illumined why the women suddenly and inexplicably appeared in Matthew's narrative and provided an essential linkage between Jesus and his disciples after his resurrection. The disciples, following this model, were in transition (state of *liminality*). This state began at the time of their call by Jesus (state of *separation*) and would last ultimately until the return of the Son of Man—but more immediately until they were recommissioned (state of *aggregation*) as teachers by Jesus for a universal mission (28:16–20). The temporal (from call [4:18–22] to commission [28:16–20]) and geographical (from Galilee [4:12] to Galilee [28:16]) lines of this transitional process were broken and/or interrupted decisively shortly before the death of Jesus (26:56). At that critical juncture, the disciples' desertion, a break in their initiation as Jesus' neophytes took place. That break created a vacuity that was filled by the women who alone provided the indispensable temporal and geographical connections to the disciples' aggregation on the mountain in Galilee. Within that initiatory process the women also underwent their own *liminal* transition and aggregation.

Beginning with the disciples I drew upon seven characteristics of the *liminal* state as set forth by Arthur van Gennep, Victor Turner, and Terence Turner. Those characteristics were

1. Death to the world

2. An occasional loss of names

3. An engagement in tasks that involved prohibitions, pain, humiliation, and risk

4. An inter-structural association marked by simplicity

5. Participation in a "structureless realm" in which sexual distinctions did not apply

6. The participation in sacred places of concealment that link the initiates with the deity, and

7. Dangerous boundary ambiguities involving purity infractions.

I then applied the seven characteristics to the women who followed Jesus and found that these women probably underwent six of the seven characteristics, the exception being a changing of their names, an attribute that applied only to Peter. Thus, in their role as Jesus' neophytes the women at the cross and the tomb demonstrated in their own right their faithful and complete initiatory preparation as Jesus' followers. In doing so, they finished the interrupted temporal ("from that time," 4:17; 16:21) and geographical (Galilee) lines of the ritual process due to the male disciples' desertion. In other words, they alone supplied the vital and indispensable bond for the realization of Matthew's purpose (28:16–20). That transformative initiation at the pivotal moment of Jesus' crucifixion, however, began with the woman who anointed Jesus at Bethany. It was then carried forward by the women and especially by Mary Magdalene and the other Mary in their newly appointed task to communicate with the disciples to join Jesus in Galilee.

REASSESSMENT LEADING TO MY THESIS

My investigation of the stories of the women called for a reassessment of aspects of my earliest studies of the household and women in public locations. Before I saw the agrarian household and Jesus' surrogate household as standing in tension but ultimately complementing one another due to the pervasive social reality of the "agrarian mould." I now see that the Matthean community most probably was being challenged by what Max Weber identifies as a routinization of charisma.[48] Would Matthew's community regress to the gender and social stratification realities indigenous to the larger Palestinian and Greco-Roman societies? The Evangelist, accordingly, in telling the stories about women (and others as well) was rekindling for the Jesus group the unconventional vision of the new surrogate family of God that stood diametrically opposed to the values and structural lines of the larger society. The community needed this pastoral instruction.

How else could one see the social/political position of Jesus as an Israelite healer? The hemorrhaging woman that he healed was a structurally marginal Israelite. The outcast Canaanite woman was not only a structural/cultural marginal—*doubly* so, a woman and a non-Israelite[49]— but also a *wise* woman who became Jesus' teacher. The girl was restored to life and her father signified the opposite pole of the household in agrarian societies, but their story paralleled that of the hemorrhaging woman. Social leveling among those who followed Jesus ran deep and wide. Within Jesus' surrogate family outcasts without households were lifted up and traditional elite households were brought down so that there might be social/religious reciprocity within the community due to the universal experience of God's mercy. That same message was carried forward in the story of the woman who anointed Jesus. In the end an unnamed outcast woman was designated a prophet by Jesus because her preparations of his body for burial constituted a prophetic act. This was so in spite of the disciples' criticism of her lavish anointing. By her visionary behavior she

48. See Weber, *Economy and Society.*
49. Anderson, "Matthew: Gender and Reading."

taught the disciples, but they apparently were not ready or willing to see the meaning of her prophetic example as interpreted by Jesus. Finally, the women at the cross and tomb not only displayed faithful discipleship but uniquely functioned to fill the void of the male disciples' desertion of Jesus. They alone finished the interrupted lines of the ritual process of the male disciples and supplied a vital and indispensable bond to the realization of Matthew's purpose. The *Gestalt* configuration of these four women's stories heard within the larger tapestry of the writing served to warn a relatively wealthy, urban community not to capitulate to the magnetic, powerful influences of gender differentiation and stratification so pervasive to advanced agrarian social norms.

PREVIOUS GENDER STUDIES OF THE GOSPEL OF MATTHEW

A number of studies have been done on gender in Matthew that have contributed to this field of inquiry and that have greatly benefited my own work. The unique contribution I bring to this topic is the analysis of most of the Gospel data through the use of multiple social-scientific models that provide an in-depth study of the stories of women in the Gospel.

Antoinnete C. Wire employs macrosociology to explore "the meaning of gender in Matthew's Gospel," by reconstructing "the gender roles characteristic of scribal communities within advanced agricultural societies,"[50] and her analysis provides a basis for "evaluating how Matthew's gender construction is congruent and/or deviant within its social world."[51] Her conclusion, that the Matthean community exhibits deviant behavior but that conduct is couched within a pervasive patriarchal worldview, is similar to mine concerning the household. However, she does not address in depth the stories about women nor does she use multiple models to interpret the data.

Feminist rhetorical literary-critical analysis is applied to the Gospel in two studies by Judith A. Anderson, the first of which is an analysis of the writing as a whole, and the second is an investigation of the birth narratives in Matthew and Luke.[52] Anderson, by exploring the symbolic power of gender, discerns a pervasive androcentric perspective within

50. Wire, "Gender Roles in a Scribal Community," 87–121.

51. Ibid.

52. Anderson, "Matthew: Gender and Reading"; and idem, "Mary's Difference."

Matthew that she believes is couched in a "patriarchal social, political, religious, and economic" world view. For her, "the presence of such a view is not surprising given the pervasiveness cross-culturally of a male ideology that defines male as the norm, as "self," and female as "different," "anomalous," or "other." This binary opposition appears homologously in oppositions such as culture/nature, order/disorder, and public sphere/domestic sphere."[53] Mary and other women of the Gospel fulfill extraordinary roles, Anderson holds, while remaining in subordinate and auxiliary positions to men.[54] Matthew's exceptional treatment of women is played out within the boundaries of a patriarchal worldview.[55] Anderson and Wire, through the use of different methodologies, arrive at similar results. Their commendable efforts, however, do not probe the stories of women. Neither do they ask whether the Evangelist's community is struggling over Jesus' social vision of a new surrogate family.

Writing from a theological perspective, Jane Kopas surveys examples of women in the Gospel. The Gospel struggles "to incorporate women moving from the periphery to greater public involvement and from being victims and survivors to being disciples and leaders."[56] In a redactional study, Maria J. Selvidge examines Matthew's treatment of women against the violent background of the Matthean community.[57] Both Kopas and Selvidge utilize the text of the Gospel to provide contemporary theological insights. They see Matthew as an ally for human rights and the dignity and authentic existence of women today.[58]

A leading feminist reading of Matthew is the work of Elaine Wainwright. Her initial study, *Towards a Feminist Critical Reading of the Gospel according to Matthew,* is carried forward in her treatment of women in Matthew in the feminist commentary, *Searching the Scriptures, Volume 2.* Her most recent expansion of the theme is found in *Shall We Look for Another: A Feminist Re-reading of the Matthean Jesus.* These works advance a "*basileia* vision" of Jesus for a new age by utilizing Matthew's first-century image of the scribe who is "trained" for the implementation of the

53. Anderson, "Mary's Difference," 183.

54. Ibid, 185.

55. Love, "The Household."

56. Kopas, "Jesus and Women in Matthew," 13.

57. Selvidge, "Violence, Woman, and the Future."

58. See Tolbert, "Introduction."

"*basileia* vision," an image that provides "a key to the narrative and theo-logical worlds which the Matthean Gospel constructs."[59] She recognizes that her work is not complete—in fact using her own words, "it has barely begun."[60] Unfinished is the "difficult task of reconstructing the history of the Matthean community so that it is a history of women and men . . ."[61] My study carries forward another step in this journey. Not to be forgotten is Wainwright's publication of Jesus as a healer titled, '*Women Healing/ Healing Women': The Genderisation of Healing in Early Christianity.*

Useful for my work is the study by Sharon Ringe, "A Gentile Woman's Story" located in the *Feminist Interpretation of the Bible,* edited by Letty M. Russell. Ringe identifies the Canaanite woman as an outcast prosti-tute, a finding that parallels my research. She also treats Matthew in the first volume of *Searching the Scriptures,* jointly edited by Ringe and Carol Newsom.

A book-length study by Parambi Baby, titled *The Discipleship of the Women in the Gospel according to Matthew,* asks whether it is possible "to speak of a discipleship of women" in the Gospel.[62] Baby contends that male religious Catholic exegesis has tended to underplay the signifi-cance of women in the gospels, whereas feminist studies, both Catholic and Protestant, have resulted in "forced exegesis." Baby seeks to offer "a balanced and systematic approach to the question of the discipleship of women."[63] Whether that is accomplished along with the purposes of opening new frontiers and addressing issues about discipleship in the early community remains problematic.

Significant gender or family analysis of Matthew within larger works include Kathleen Corley's chapter in *Private Women, Public Meals: Social Conflict in the Synoptic Tradition,* families in Matthew within the larger tapestry of *Families in the New Testament World* by David Balch and Carolyn Osiek, and the treatment of Matthew by Elizabeth Schüssler Fiorenza in her well-known work, *In Memory of Her.* Balch and Osiek set their study within the Mediterranean cultural value of honor and shame. Not to be forgotten is an article by Celia Deutsch, "Wisdom in Matthew:

59. Wainwright, "The Gospel of Matthew," 67.

60. Ibid.

61. Ibid.

62. Baby, *The Discipleship of the Women,* 9.

63. Ibid, 10.

Transformation of a Symbol." Most of these studies are not social-scientific in nature and the one that is, works only with macrosociology in the formation of a working model. My work, therefore, fills a distinct place in a growing body of literature.

APPROACH

Having set forth the journey and thesis of my research and a review of the literature I now encourage the reader to examine the development of my analysis. Chapter 2, "The Household in Matthew," introduces what is meant by social-scientific modeling and is followed by an examination of gender-specific behavior in Matthew by means of a macrosociological model of the household.

Chapter 3, "Women and Men in Public Settings in Matthew," extends and deepens the findings of the household model set forth in chapter 1 by examining the place of women among three character groups: the disciples, the crowds, and the religious leaders as they are taught by Jesus or interact with him in three representative public settings: the mountain in the Sermon on the Mount (5:1—7:28), the boat in the Parables Discourse (13:1–52), and the temple in the clash between Jesus and the religious authorities (21:12—23:29). In addition to the household model in advanced agrarian societies, I add a parallel microsocial index of women in mishnaic culture. These two chapters set the stage for the four stories about women.

However, before those stories are examined, the reader is introduced in chapter 4 to three additional models that are utilized more than once in the stories about women—(1) honor and shame, (2) healing in non-Western societies, (3) a native taxonomy of illness—degrees of impurity.

Three other models, (1) patronage, (2) prostitutes in advanced agrarian societies, and (3) an initiation/death rites of passage are employed but once, and their constructions are reserved for the particular story in which they are used.

The models used in each chapter are set forth in the following diagram.

CHAPTERS AND THE MODELS THEY EMPLOY

Chapter 4—"Three Essential Models"—three models used more than once are described:

1. Honor and shame,

2. Healing in non-Western societies,

3. A native taxonomy of illness—degrees of impurity.

Chapter 5—"Jesus Heals the Hemorrhaging Woman and Restores a Girl to Life" employs the three models constructed in chapter 3.

Chapter 6—"Jesus heals the Canaanite Woman's Daughter" employs the three models set forth in chapter 3. In addition a fourth model is employed: a macrosociological model of prostitutes in advanced agrarian societies.

Chapter 7—"'Why do You Trouble the Woman?' The Woman Who Anoints Jesus at Bethany" employs the models of (1) honor and shame and degrees of impurity. In addition a patronage model is utilized.

Chapter 8—"Jesus and the Women at the Cross and Tomb" employs only an initiation/burial rites of passage model.

After chapter 8 I summarize my findings and engage in hermeneutical reflection concerning how the Gospel of Matthew's treatment of women might be used profitably today.

Finally, I am indebted to many who have patiently helped my research over a twenty-year span. But most of all I am grateful and indebted to my wife, D'Esta, whose insights, suggestions, and inspiration have helped me far beyond what words convey.

2

The Household in Matthew

An advanced agrarian household:

> [5] When he entered Capernaum, a centurion approached him, asking him [6] and saying, "Lord, my son is lying at home paralyzed, in terrible distress." [7] And he said to him, "Shall I come and heal him?" [8] The centurion answered, "Lord, I am not good enough to have you come under my roof; but only speak the word, and my servant will be healed. [9] I also am a man under authority, and I have soldiers under me; and I say to this one, 'Go,' and he goes, and to that one, 'Come,' and he comes, and to my slave, 'Do this,' and he does it." (Matt 8:5–9, author's translation)

Jesus's new surrogate kinship group:

> [46] While he was still speaking to the crowds, behold, his mother and his brothers stood outside, seeking to speak to him. [47] But someone told him, "Behold, your mother and your brothers are standing outside, seeking to speak to you." [48] But to the one who had told him this, he replied, "Who is my mother, and who are my brothers?" [49] And he held his hand over his disciples and said, "Behold, here are my mother and my brothers! [50] For whoever does the will of my Father in heaven is my brother and sister and mother." (Matt 12:46–50, author's translation)

INTRODUCTION

OUR STUDY OF THE four stories of women in Matthew is social-scientific in nature, which means that conceptual social models are employed. But what are such models? What do they achieve? Social-scientific models are used to expand horizons, to sharpen insight, to provide greater comprehensive understanding of connections and processes previously unperceived in a one dimensional, one disciplinary view.[1] Models are employed to help alert scholars to the limitations of their received exegetical wisdom, hone their perceptions, and deepen their understanding of early Christian texts; they are used to heighten awareness of behavioral patterns, pivotal values, social structures, cultural scripts, and social processes of the biblical world. Ultimately, models provide a more systematic means for organizing biblical material as a whole (in this case the women's stories of the Gospel of Matthew) and evaluating that data through social analysis; that is, they provide "cognitive maps" of the social behavior, structures, and processes set forth in Matthew and its social setting within the more extensive social world of first-century Greco-Roman society.

Models come in various sorts and sizes (maps, mannequins, toy trains, scale art models and architecture; range in size, complexity, and degree of abstraction). Care must be given, therefore, in defining them. The term "model" can refer to an assortment of synonyms that fail to provide a systematic meaning.[2] For example, as John H. Elliott notes, a model is like a metaphor: both "compare similar properties and stimulate imagination in order to advance understanding from the more well known to less well known."[3] But a model also differs from a metaphor "in terms of its comprehensiveness and complexity and often its intended function."[4]

What then is a model? T. F. Carney observes that models are *selective* representations that focus on *major* components of interest and their *priority* of importance.[5] Carney then clarifies what this means,

> a model is something less than a theory and something more than an analogy . . . A theory is based on axiomatic laws and states general principles. It is a basic proposition through which a variety of observations or statements become explicable. A model, by way of contrast, acts as a link between theories and observations. A model will employ one or more theories to provide a simplified (or

1. Elliott, "Social-Scientific Criticism," 2.

2. Ibid., 3. Elliot lists the following terms associated with the word "model": *metaphor, example, exemplar, analogy, image, type, reproduction, representation, illustration, pattern, parallel, symbol,* and *paradigm.*

3. Ibid., 4.

4. Ibid.

5. Carney, *The Shape of the Past,* 7, as noted in Elliott, "Social-Scientific Criticism," ibid., 4.

an experimental or a generalized or an explanatory) framework which can be brought to bear on some pertinent data.[6]

For Bruce J. Malina, a model is "an abstract, simplified representation of some real world object, event, or interaction constructed for the purpose of understanding, control, or prediction."[7] Models are, in Elliott's thinking, "conceptual vehicles for articulating, applying, testing, and possibly reconstructing theories used in the analysis and interpretation of specific social data."[8] Patrick Nolan and Gerhard Lenski assert that modeling "helps us in analyzing societies and in constructing theories about them" that in turn expresses "hypothesized cause-and-effect relationships in a detailed and explicit manner." Nolan and Lenski then state, "'Modeling compels us to be precise about the relationships involved in a theory—more precise than we might otherwise be."[9] Therefore, as Elliott points out, a model is "*consciously structured* and *systematically arranged* in order to serve as a *speculative instrument* for the purpose of organizing, profiling, and interpreting a complex welter of detail."[10]

In this book we shall use several models for different reasons but only one will be developed in this chapter, a social scientific macro-sociological model of households in advanced agrarian societies. *Macro*-sociology is concerned with establishing a broad cross-cultural comparative social analysis through an empirical delineation of societal types (in contrast to *micro*-sociology that builds a deep base of empirical data).[11] Broad in scope, *macro*-sociology studies relations among the basic components of human societies. Each major institutional system brings together people, culture, the material products of culture, and social organization and then seeks to understand these in light of a society's polity, religion, economy, education, kinship, and other major elements.[12] Based on the primary mode of subsistence of human societies, Nolan and Lenski identify ten basic categories: hunting and gathering, simple horticulture, advanced

6. Carney, *The Shape of the Past*, 8.

7. Malina, "The Social Sciences and Biblical Interpretation," 231.

8. Elliott, "Social-Scientific Criticism of the New Testament," 5.

9. Nolan and Lenski, *Human Societies*, 17.

10. Ibid.

11. See Chaney, "Systematic Study," 53–76; Lenski and Lenski, *Human Societies*, 1982, 1987; Sjoberg, *Preindustrial City*; Parsons, *Societies*.

12. See Nolan and Lenski, *Human Societies*, 24–43.

horticulture, simple agrarian, advanced agrarian, industrial, fishing, maritime, and herding. Over the course of human history people have lived principally in six of these societal types—hunting and gathering, simple and advanced horticulture, simple and advanced agrarian and industrial societies.[13]

The applicable societal type for the Roman Empire of the first century is referred to by ethnologists as "advanced agrarian,"[14] that is, an agricultural society based on the technology of the animal-drawn and iron-tipped plow.[15] Marvin L. Chaney defines agrarian societies as those in which "their principal means of subsistence was a tillage of fields which knew the plow but not that concatenation of inanimate energy sources whose use in production denotes industrialization."[16] Ester Boserup states, "The advent of the plough usually entails a radical shift in sex roles in agriculture; men take over the ploughing even in regions where the hoeing had formerly been women's work."[17] By the first century "advanced agrarian societies were firmly established in the Middle East (ancient Near East), throughout most of the Mediterranean world, and in much of India and China."[18]

Our model establishes a broad cultural setting for comprehending gender-specific behavior in Matthew. Antoinette C. Wire, as one example, achieved this when she explored "the meaning of gender in Matthew's Gospel" through the use of macro-sociological analysis for the purpose of reconstructing "the gender roles characteristic of scribal communities within advanced agricultural societies."[19] In our analysis a macro-sociological model is constructed to explore gender-specific behavior in household and public/private social settings. We believe that it is against this larger societal backdrop that the four women's stories can be better understood.[20]

13. Ibid., 62–64.

14. Lenski and Lenski, *Human Societies*, 1982, 1987.

15. Ibid., 176; Aitchison, *A History of Metals*.

16. Chaney, "Systemic Study," 60.

17. Boserup, *Women's Role in Economic Development*, 33.

18. Lenski and Lenski, *Human Societies* (1987), 176.

19. Wire, "Gender Roles in a Scribal Community," 87–88.

20. In chapter 3 other models are created including the following: (1) honor and shame, (2) healing in non-Western societies, and (3) a native taxonomy of illness involving degrees of impurity. These models are developed together because they are used

The model will have two essentially related foci: (1) the place and role of the household in determining societal and family structure and (2) the social effect of the household upon gender status and behavior in the private and public realms.

AN ADVANCED AGRARIAN MACROSOCIOLOGICAL MODEL

Male Hierarchy and Social Stratification

There are many interrelated features of advanced agrarian societies. One that has special bearing upon the status of women is a crystallized, hierarchically ordered, mostly male dominated, stratified social order.[21] It is linked to a corresponding authority centered view of knowing (epistemology) and thinking (ideology) that underpins and sustains the society's world view.[22] To neglect this insight fails to note the import of what the Lenskis (and Nolan) refer to as the "agrarian mould."[23]

Social stratification is most complex in advanced agrarian societies, with two leading cleavages: (1) the ruling class above and over all others, both city and country, and (2) the city over rural areas, but the former dependent on agriculture for its survival. In the Roman example, urban wealth resides mostly in rural land holdings. The urban aristocratic Roman politician and orator Cicero states, "Of all the sources of wealth farming is the best, the most fruitful, the most agreeable, and the most suited to a

---

more than once in the four stories about women. The model of honor and shame sets forth the most pivotal core value of the ancient Mediterranean world. The model of healing in non-Western societies is designed to understand illness, healing, and healers in a social-cultural perspective different from the biomedical approach largely operative in advanced industrialized societies like the United States and northern Europe. The purity/impurity taxonomy model facilitates insight as to how the human body, in which purity issues are manifest, is a microcosm of the social body. The purity/impurity model is used as well to interpret the story of the woman at Simon's house in Bethany (26:6–13). Three other models are utilized but once. They are (1) prostitutes in advanced agrarian societies, (2) patronage and clientage, and (3) rites of passage or status-altering rituals. The first model helps answer the identity question as to whether the Canaanite woman is a prostitute. The patronage-and-clientage model casts light on our reading of the woman who anoints Jesus (26:6–13). The rite-of-passage model assists us in reading passages concerning the women at the cross and the tomb (27:55–56, 61; 28:1–10).

21. For the subordination of wives to their husbands in Greco-Roman society see Elliott, *1 Peter,* 554–59.

22. Lenski and Lenski, *Human Societies* (1987), 166–70.

23. Ibid., 202–4.

free man" (*Off.* 1.151). Rabbi Eleazar affirms, "Anyone who owns no land is no proper man" (*b. Yebam.* 63a). In the Roman example, slaves, whose social status depends on their masters, are the primary source of energy to work the land and to serve the needs and desires of the ruling class.[24] The subordinate status of women[25] must be understood not only by the interrelated components of the advanced agrarian societal structure, but most specifically by certain widespread marriage practices related to the extended family or household. Plutarch, a contemporary of the New Testament period, observes in his *Advice to Bride and Groom*: "If they (wives) subordinate themselves (*hypotattousai*) to their husbands, they are commended, but if they want to have control, they cut a sorrier figure than the subjects of their control" (*Conj. Praec.* 33, *Mor.* 142D).

Although family ties are no longer "the chief integrating force" in this societal type, the family remains significant for individuals, especially in the political and economic realms.[26] A difference in family size usually exists between the elite on the one hand and the urban poor and peasant families on the other, the latter most often having significantly smaller families because of higher infant mortality rates.[27]

Elite households are extended households. They may include a man and his wife (occasionally, but rarely, wives), unmarried children, married sons including their wives and children, other relatives such as family widows or sisters of the "patriarch," slaves, patrons who were former employees, and occasionally business associates or tenants.[28] In the rural Roman example, poverty often forced large groups to live together.

24. Carcopino, *Daily Life in Ancient Rome,* 70.

25. Elliott (*1 Peter,* 554) affirms, "Subordination of wives to their husbands was universally regarded in ancient patriarchal society as being dictated by the differing physical and mental characteristics allotted by nature to males and females." By nature females were inferior to males physically, intellectually and morally, and were therefore consigned by nature to the authority, tutelage, and protection of the males (Hesiod *Op.* 695–705; Plato *Tim.* 42AB, 91a; Xen. *Oec.* 3:11–14; 7:4–8; Plut. *Conj. Praec.* 48; *Mor.* 145 C–D). Aristotle states, "As between the sexes, the male [*to arren*]; he is the ruler [*to archon*] and she, the one ruled [*to archomenon*]" (*Pol.* 1.2.12; 1254b; cf. also 1:5.1–2; 1259a; 1.5.6; 1260a).

26. Lenski and Lenski, *Human Societies* (1987), 199–200. For the family in first-century Galilee based on archaeology see Guijarro, "The Family in First Century Galilee." Guijarro offers charts on family types. See also Talbert, "Miraculous Conceptions and Births in Mediterranean Antiquity."

27. Fei, "Peasantry and Gentry," 4–5; Freedman, *Lineage Organization in Southeastern China,* 28; and Dube, *Indian Village,* 133.

28. Meeks, *First Urban Christians,* 30; Orenstein, *Gaon,* 35–36.

In Roman Egypt, says social historian Ramsey MacMullen, as many as twenty-six people lived in only a portion of an adobe house, but the more common rural phenomenon was to find nuclear families usually numbering a half-dozen members.[29] A similar picture appears to have been the case in Galilee. Santiago Guijarro has shown, based on archaeology, which due to economic pressures families could not keep all their children close. He designates these families as "nucleated families."[30] However, a typical urban elite family living under one "roof" could number over fifty people.[31] Sjoberg offers comparative information. He cites a Chinese family numbering fifty-one persons, "joint" families in India numbering over a hundred members, and households of similar size among the elite of current Middle Eastern cities. A large Chinese extended family embraces, according to Sjoberg, a girl's parents, eight brothers and their families living in separate apartments with servants, and in addition eight unmarried brothers and sisters, each with two servants and about twenty cousins, some with their own families and servants. The Chinese example includes house servants such as cooks, bearers, and gardeners, some having their own personal assistants.[32]

Household members belong to an interconnected structure of two kinds, vertical and horizontal. First, within the family there is a hierarchical, mostly one-sided nonegalitarian role arrangement and, second, between (or among) families there are bonds of kinship and friendship. Further, extended households, which most often form the basic social unit of the city and of the society,[33] are largely patrilineal (descent through a single male ancestral line) and patrilocal (living in or near the patriarch's house). This is true for both rural and urban households. With respect to the Roman rural setting, MacMullen states, "A typical household will however consist of no more than a half dozen people under a clearly marked head, the father."[34] Accordingly, some degree of obedience is

---

29. MacMullen, *Roman Social Relations,* 13, 27. See Guijarro, "The Family in First Century Galilee."

30. Guijarro, "The Family in First Century Galilee."

31. Meeks, *First Urban Christians,* 30; Wong and Cressy, *Daughter of Confucius,* 10–11, 88; Tsai, *Queen of the Dark Chamber,* 27–29; and Chao, *Autobiography of a Chinese Woman,* 9.

32. Sjoberg, *Preindustrial City,* 157–58.

33. Meeks, *First Urban Christians,* 29.

34. MacMullen, *Roman Social Relations,* 16.

given by all members to the household head, who is almost always a male. Identity and family longevity are bound up in the father's name to the extent that when a daughter marries, she goes to the home of her husband. Marriages often take place at an early age. In the Roman society, girls can be married at nine to twelve years of age.[35] Marriage contributes to a family's well being and serves as a rite of passage.

The primary function of a family is to survive (subsist), and each member exercises a defined *productive* economic role.[36] In ancient Israel, the household is made up of "as many sets of childbearing adults and their dependents as is necessary for the entire group to feed and protect itself."[37] In turn, the family is its own welfare agency, protecting its members against poverty, natural disasters and the impact of war.[38] Security is within the family, and provision and protection are therefore primary responsibilities of the family head, usually a father and/or husband. In Israel, the father exercises the power of life and death in the household and his primary responsibility is for his wives and their sons and daughters.[39] The family counts, and individuals are consequential because of the family and for its sake.[40] Malina calls a person who is less individualistic and constantly participating in such "other directed" interrelatedness a "group-oriented personality."[41] He states, "Every individual is perceived as embedded in some other, in a sequence of embeddedness, so to say."[42] If this is true of individuals, how much more is it so for wives! A wife's embedded status to her husband is illustrated in Matthew by the statement, "If such is the case of man with his wife." (Matt 19:10), or, in Ephesians by the statement, "He who loves his wife loves himself" (Eph 5:28). The religious beliefs and values of the household head usually are shared throughout the family for the sake of the family's stability, possibly with

35. Hopkins, "The Age of Roman Girls at Marriage."

36. Lenski and Lenski, *Human Societies* (1982), 340.

37. Matthews and Benjamin, *Social World of Ancient Israel*, 7. See Stager, "The Archaeology of the Family in Ancient Israel," 22; de Geus, *The Tribes of Israel*, 133–35; Gottwald, *The Tribes of Yahweh*, 285–92.

38. Sjoberg, *Preindustrial City*, 159–60.

39. Matthews and Benjamin, *Social World of Ancient Israel*, 9.

40. Lenski and Lenski, *Human Societies*, (1982) 207–08.

41. Malina, *The New Testament World*, 60–67; while he still uses "dyadic personality" as in earlier editions, he seems to prefer "group-oriented" or "collectivist."

42. Ibid., 62.

differing degrees by individual members, but usually within the inclusive worldview of the family authority.[43] Exceptions may exist, but when they do, the family's stability can be threatened.

More specifically, throughout advanced agrarian societies most men and women pursue relatively fixed gender roles. Marriage is the normal expectation and within the marriage relationship women are usually subordinate, unequal, and inferior to men, possess few rights, are born to delight their fathers, are married to serve their husbands, bear and rear children, and are widowed to be cared for by their sons.[44]

Anthropologists often distinguish public space from private space. In an advanced agrarian society like the Roman Empire public space is reserved mainly for men (political contexts such as the senate, the forum; official religion); private space is mainly, but not exclusively, the province of women (household management; domestic religion). Within the larger social order and household structure there are definite public and private spatial gender expectations.

Private Spatial Expectations

Gender roles are characterized by a basic division of labor.[45] A woman's place primarily is within the household. In the Roman society example, concerning household occupations, Hierocles states, "They should be divided in the usual manner; namely, to the husband should be assigned those which have to do with agriculture, commerce, and the affairs of the city; to the wife those which have to do with spinning and the preparation of food, in short, those of a domestic nature." ("On Duties," *Household Management*, 4:28.21—5.696, 15). Xeneophon advocates a gender-based division of labor for husbands and wives. Outside work is for men; inside work is for women because men are physically stronger. Xenophon grounds his ideology in the nature of God and what is honorable. "Thus to the woman," Xenophon states,

---

43. Lenski and Lenski, *Human Societies*, (1982) 163–79; Balch, *Let Wives Be Submissive*, 109; Yarbrough, *Not Like the Gentiles*.

44. Whyte, *The Status of Woman in Preindustrial Societies*, 156–66; Martin and Voorhies, *Female of the Species*, 276–322; Kendall, *The Yorkist Age*, 364–73, 403–5, 411, 430; Salzman, *English Life in the Middle Ages*, 253–60.

45. Whyte, *The Status of Women in Preindustrial Societies*, 156–66.

it is more honourable to stay indoors than to abide in the fields, but to the man it is unseemly rather to stay indoors than to attend to the work outside. If a man acts contrary to the nature God has given him, possibly his defiance is detected by the gods and he is punished for neglecting his own work, or meddling with his wife's. (*Concerning Household Management*, 7:3—10:13)[46]

Each sex has a God-given space and task. Neither sex is to dwell or meddle in the other's sphere.

Through the delegated authority of her husband a wife manages her own realm including the rearing, training and education of children, both sexes at an early age, and daughters until they leave home. Childbearing confers status to a woman, especially in times when the need to produce more children is critical, owing to war, famine, disease, and epidemics. The domestic care of the household is a wife's own world, her realm of authority,[47] through which she pleases her husband by preparing food and clothing, so enhancing his standing among his peers. A productive wife usually is an economic, social, and political asset. Sjoberg states, "Figuratively, the husband is a 'god' who requires unswerving obedience."[48] Consequently, since a wife is embedded in her husband she often lacks authority to intrude into the economic and property decisions outside the household, since, as already noted, it is the husband's primary responsibility to provide for and to protect his family.[49] A wife's proper

46. Hierocles also argues for a gender division of tasks based on the greater strength of men even in the domestic realm. "For in other domestic works, is it not thought that more of them pertain to men than to women? For they are more laborious, and require corporal strength, such as to grind, to knead meal, to cut wood, to draw water from a well" (*On Duties*, 5.689.13–20). For additional data and bibliography see Balch, *Let Wives Be Submissive*, 23–26, 33–38.

47. In the Israelite example, Sarah casts out Hagar and her son Ishmael (Gen 21:10); the Shunammite woman extends kindness and hospitality to Elisha (2 Kgs 4:8–10); Rebekah perpetrates Jacob's deception of his blind father Isaac, which resulted in the wrongful bestowal of his brother Esau's blessing on Jacob (Gen 27:11–17). The last example suggests that trickery and deception may have been necessary, even admirable, qualities in a woman living in a male-dominated society. See Craven, "Women Who Lied for the Faith."

48. Sjoberg, *Preindustrial City*, 164. Nolan and Lenski state "Within families, male dominance was the rule and unquestioning obedience to the wishes of father or husband were generally held to be the prime virtue in a woman," *Human Societies*, 166.

49. This is not to say that a woman's household role is without economic implications. In the Israelite example of the "ideal wife" (Prov 31:10–29), this particular woman is involved in a variety of household roles that are economic in nature. However, she is

response is to honor that obligation. Wage earning by a wife among the elite most likely would bring public dishonor to her husband.[50] Nolan and Lenski state,

> Husbands were "generally regarded as quasi-guardians" of their wives; in English Common Law, a woman's husband "acquired extensive rights to the administration and ownership of her property, including full ownership (with no obligation even to given an accounting) of any moneys she received," while in India, under Hindu law, the only property of which a woman was absolute owner consisted mainly of wedding gifts and gifts from relatives.[51]

Further, a woman's "salvation" is through bearing children, many if possible, and especially sons. In ancient Israel, "The mother of the household was authorized not only to bear sons and daughters for her household, but also to see that all the other women in her household regularly bore sons and daughters as well."[52] Therein she gains honor from her husband and standing within the family. Childless, she is the brunt of social reproach since it is her husband's responsibility to procreate, and in him she largely finds her status and honor.[53] Children help protect a wife against divorce.

Public Spatial Expectations

If a woman's place is within the household, the public realm primarily belongs to men.[54] Women, especially unmarried daughters among the elite,

---

not a peasant. The elegant garments of her household are described as follows: "All her household are clothed in crimson. She makes herself coverings; her clothing is fine linen and purple" (Prov 31:21–22). Peasant women engage in crafts such as basket making, spinning, and weaving tapestries and mats. Tamar is portrayed as kneading dough, making cakes, and baking them (2 Sam 13:8). The daughters of the priest of Midian fill the troughs to water their father's flock (Exod 2:16). Women build fires, make cheese and yogurt, milk the sheep and goats, grind grain into flour, work in the fields (Ruth 2:21–23), tend flocks (Gen 29:9), and act as professional mourners (Jer 9:17). See King and Stager, *Life in Biblical Israel*, 50–51.

50. Malina, *New Testament World*, 30–56.

51. Nolan and Lenski, *Human Societies*, 234.

52. Matthews and Benjamin, *Social World of Ancient Israel*, 25.

53. Sjoberg, *Preindustrial City*, 163–64.

54. Ibid., especially chap. 1–4, 6; Malina, *New Testament World*, 46–48; Elshtain, *Public Man, Private Woman*; MacMullen, "Women in Public in the Roman Empire"; Corley, "Were the Women around Jesus Really Prostitutes?"

may live in semi-seclusion in homes having special corridors, rooms, and doors designed to sequester a woman's existence, especially when the husband entertains guests.[55] When a woman appears in public, however, she often reflects her husband's standing among his peers through her dress, coiffure, jewelry, makeup, and self-adornment. Among the upper classes respectable women are often restricted to the home.

Because of the separation of the public and private realms, women do not usually participate (or have major roles) in political, educational, or public religious functions. For example, in the political realm, says Elshtain, Greek linguistic usage shows a contrast, the *polis*, "the reality of a structured body politic," and the *oikos*, the private household which includes a "world of familial and economic relations."[56] In the Roman society example, marriage is important for a man who seeks public involvement because a wife enables a husband to go out from the house to study and/or pursue political affairs. Antipater states, "For the gentleman who wishes to have leisure for study or political affairs, or both, (married life) is absolutely necessary. For the more he goes out from the house, the more he ought to take to his side someone to take care of the house and make himself free from everyday cares" (*On Marriage*, 256–57). Pliny the Younger in a letter to Capurnia Hispulla extols his wife for her private interest in his public presentations. At one point Pliny describes his wife as being "concealed behind a curtain." "When at any time I recite works," Pliny states, "she sits close at hand, concealed behind a curtain, and greedily overhears my praises" (*Ep.* 4.19). Valerius Maximus believed women should have nothing to do with a public assembly. He asks, "What have women to do with a public assembly? If old-established custom is preserved, nothing" (*Fact. et Dic.* 3.8.6). Public debate is unbecoming behavior for women. Wives are not to speak unless their husbands are present. Plutarch states concerning bold women who take part in debate, "But Numa ... nevertheless enjoined great modesty upon them, forbade them all busy intermeddling, taught them sobriety, and accustomed them to be silent; wine they were to refrain from entirely, and were not to speak, even on the most necessary of topics, unless their husbands were with them" (*Lycurgus and Numa* 3.5). Roman philosophers and moralists uphold a public/private, gender-specific spatial dichotomy.

55. Meeks, *First Urban Christians*, 30.
56. Elshtain, *Public Man, Private Woman*, 12.

In the educational sphere, emphasis upon women's education differs somewhat among cultures, but largely fosters limited literacy for domestic purposes.[57] Sjoberg states, "Few girls ever learn to read and write, and those who do, receive this training at home and for a few years at most."[58] However, there is now some evidence for female scribes because of their beautiful handwriting.[59] Formal, advanced education often is provided through the male dominated religious institutions among the upper classes of the urban centers, and is largely designed to "socialize the student into the basic values of the social order and . . . to ensure that the rising officialdom is fully indoctrinated into the society's ideal norms."[60] Duling states, "As educated and literate, scribes tended to come from the elite classes and thus to serve the political establishment . . . Yet scribes in Judaism had a special prestige or honour captured in their specifically 'religious' functions over long periods of Jewish history."[61]

The areas of study "buttress the already concrete like authority structure."[62] Sometimes, teachers and students develop a teacher/mentor relationship over a number of years, "forming cliques in the governmental bureaucracy and other non-academic realms."[63] Finally, in the religious structure (which also may possess variations) the public/private dichotomy tends to prevail. Homes often have private worship shrines where wives assist their husbands at the family altar. Orenstein states, concerning an Indian example:

> The household was conceived to be a community of worship as well as a social and economic entity. Each household had associated with it a number of deities, intended to be worshipped twice a day by the household head. On important occasions he was as-

---

57. Ferguson, *Backgrounds of Early Christianity*, 83–87.

58. Sjoberg, *Preindustrial City*, 298.

59. Duling, "Matthew as a Marginal Scribe in an Advanced Agrarian Society"; nevertheless, "full" illiteracy of the Roman Empire under the principate is almost certain to have been above 90 percent. See Harris, *Ancient Literacy*, 22. Advanced education is a privilege of the urban elites, and *paideia* takes place principally in the philosophical schools (Duling, "The Matthean Brotherhood," 175–77).

60. Sjoberg, *Preindustrial City*, 301.

61. Duling, "The Matthean Brotherhood," 176. See Lemaire, "The Sage in School and Temple."

62. Sjoberg, *Preindustrial City*, 301.

63. Ibid., 306.

sisted by his wife, who touched his hand at appropriate parts of the sacrifices, thus participating in the offerings.[64]

Leadership and participation in public worship settings (synagogue/ temple) is largely a male affair. Contributing factors include the general lack of formal education on the part of women, practices of female seclusion, the close relationship of religion to the political order among the elite, and the dyadic nature of the husband/wife relationship. The husband, the superior member of the dyad, represents his wife and family in public matters.

Throughout the description of this model care has been given to use such language as "most," "mostly but not exclusively," "usually," "primarily," and "emphasis . . . differs among cultures" for two reasons. First, societal typology recognizes variation and the exceptional. Second, more specifically, recent studies concerning the public place of men and the private place of women have rightly warned against making overly simplistic correlations.[65] For example, older studies emphasized the differences between men and women. Hobbs[66] cites more recent research that emphasizes "the element of complementarity in relationships between the sexes and sex roles."[67] Rogers,[68] for example, develops "the notion of an informal public power" on the part of women, the use of gossip, which "indirectly affects male political decisions and behavior."[69] Benjamin and Matthews observe that "The mother of a household in the Bible had significant power and authority over decision-making and problem-solving for both land and children."[70] Hobbs cites Friedl,[71] who in a study of the rural Greek community of Vasilika found a continuum of tasks related to the household linking men to the agricultural fields, women to the house, but both sexes to the house compound. Admittedly, social expectations in rural areas are not as crystallized as among the urban elite. Moreover, Balch

---

64. Orenstein, *Gaon*, 36.

65. Dubisch, "Culture Enters through the Kitchen." See Hobbs, "Man, Woman, and Hospitality—2 Kings 4:8–36," 93.

66. Ibid.

67. Herzfeld, "'As in Your Own House.'"

68. Rogers, "Female Forms of Power and the Myth of Male Dominance," 736.

69. Hobbs, "Man, Woman, and Hospitality," 93.

70. Matthews and Benjamin, *Social World of Ancient Israel*, 23.

71. Friedl, "The Position of Women; Appearance and Reality," 47–48.

and Osiek show that ancient Roman women, as contrasted with Greek and Israelite women, are more public and thus Roman households are somewhat more fluid.[72] A public/private gender distinction nonetheless remains a legitimate working model for gender analysis in advanced agrarian societies.

THE HOUSEHOLD AND GENDER-SPECIFIC BEHAVIOR IN MATTHEW

Having set forth the model, an analysis of the household[73] as a social reality and metaphor[74] in understanding gender-specific data can now be made in Matthew.[75] Three lines of evidence are taken into account: (1) the household as the basic social unit of the society, (2) actual households within the Gospel, and (3) the use and portrayal of the household in Jesus's teaching.

The Household—the Basic Social Unit of the Society

The household in Matthew, like the household in advanced agrarian societies, seems to function both in reality and in metaphor as the basic hierarchical social unit for the kingdom, nation, city, village and family.[76] For example, when Jesus states in the Beelzebul controversy, "Every kingdom divided against itself is laid waste, and no city or house divided against itself will stand" (12:25), the terms *kingdom*, *city*, and *house* that signify the negative effects of social division are ranked in a greater/lesser hierar-

72. Balch and Osiek, *Families in the New Testament World.*

73. See the basic studies by White, "Domus Ecclesiae-Domus Dei: Adaptation and Development in the Setting for Early Christian Assembly"; Verner, *Household of God*; Michel, "Oikia/Oikos"; and Filson, "The Significance of the Early Christian House Communities."

74. Sapir and Crocker, eds. *Social Use of Metaphor*, chap. 2; Winter, *Liberating Creation*, 6–10; *Elements for a Social Ethic*, 18–33; McFague, *Metaphorical Theology*, 40; Crosby, *House of Disciples*, 10–12.

75. Greco-Roman bibliographic guides and recent studies include Balch, *Let Wives Be Submissive*, 141, n. 1; Kraemer, "Women in the Religions of the Greco-Roman World"; Pomeroy, *Women in Hellenistic Egypt*, 317–72; Skinner, ed., *Rescuing Creusa*; Kraemer, ed., *Maenads, Martyrs, Matrons, Monastics*; Gardner, *Women in Roman Law and Society*; Yarbrough, *Not Like the Gentiles*; Corley, "Were the Women around Jesus Really Prostitutes?"

76. MacIver, "The Family as Government in Miniature," 7–11; Meeks, *First Urban Christians*, 30; Tidball, *The Social Context of the New Testament*, 70; Elliott, *A Home for the Homeless*, 175–80; Crosby, *House of Disciples*, 23–32.

chical sequence. Elsewhere, household imagery informs the language and ideas describing both the kingdom of heaven and the kingdom of Satan. Beelzebul is called "master of the house," and those who serve him belong to "his household" (10:25). Satan's kingdom is a house (12:25–29) that can be despoiled only if the strong man of the house is first bound. In the kingdom of heaven, non-Israelites are included as they "sit at table" with the patriarchs Abraham, Isaac, and Jacob, while "the sons of the kingdom" are cast out and punished (8:11, 12). In the parable discourse (13:1–52) the disciples are likened to scribes who, having been trained for "the kingdom of heaven" are like a "householder who brings out of his treasure what is new and what is old" (13:52).

In other settings, the kingdom is likened to a king who "settles accounts with his servants" (18:23), a household responsibility; or entrance into the kingdom demands that potential disciples become like children (18:1, 4; 19:14), who are the least or inferior members of the Israelite family, a striking reversal of greatness. Kingdom household images of master, servants, sitting at table, sons, a father, a householder, and children are all illustrations of social realities compatible with advanced agrarian households. Further, when the twelve are commissioned and taught concerning their mission to Israel (chap. 10), Jesus instructs them to go only to the lost sheep of the house of Israel (10:6) which means entering Israel's cities, villages (10:11), and houses (10:12). Four observations about this last passage can be made. First, Israel not only is designated as a house, but the disciples enter that house by way of its cities, villages, and homes. Second, as they go, they are to proclaim, "The kingdom of heaven is at hand" (10:7). Third, the language sequence once again is not only connected but ordered from the greater to the lesser—nation, city, village, and house, the first and last members of the sequence being identified explicitly by the term "house." Fourth, when not welcomed, the disciples are to "shake off the dust" from their feet as they "leave that house or town" (10:14). True, in the sequential chain cities and villages are not compared to households. They are, however, bracketed by the nation and family, which are households. Cities and villages, accordingly, are middle terms in a unified sequence which depicts four hierarchically ordered and interrelated elements of the social order. It appears that Matthew assumes the household to be a part of a hierarchical social structural foundation: *nation*, city, village, and *family*.

The Household in Matthew—Advanced Agrarian Families and Gender Relations

When the focus is narrowed to actual families, a number of social parallels rooted in the household structure of advanced agrarian societies can be detected.

The Household of Jesus (1:1—2:23; 12:46–50; 13:55–56)

First, the genealogy that introduces the birth narrative and possibly functions as a key to understanding the Gospel[77] is cradled in advanced agrarian expectations. Whether preserved in written form or through oral tradition, Israelite genealogies were highly treasured.[78] They were traced through a single line, that is, they were unilineal (other relatives are omitted [cognatic descent]) and that line was male, from father to son, thus patrilineal. The Gospel therefore opens by tracing the patrilineal ancestry of Jesus Christ through a highly stereotypical formula, "A was the father of B." It is divided into three sets of fourteen generations that set forth the patriarchal and royal ancestry of Jesus: 1) Abraham to King David, 2) King David to the Babylonian exile, and finally, 3) the Babylonian exile to "Joseph, the husband of Mary of whom Jesus was born, who is called Christ" (1:16). Thirty-nine times the phrase "the father of" appears with proper male names coming before and after—e.g., "Abraham was the father of Isaac." The phrase "the mother of" never appears. Yet, four women other than Mary, Joseph's wife who bore Jesus, are mentioned, but never as "the mother of a son." Rather, their inclusion is secondary and identified: *ek tēs* ("out of"), that is, "out of Tamar" (1:3), "out of Rahab" (1:5), "out of Ruth" (1:5), and "out of the wife of Uriah" (1:6). Even Mary is not referred to as "the mother of Jesus." Instead, Joseph is said to be "the husband of Mary, of whom Jesus was born" (1:16). This is not to say the women's inclusion is unimportant. Two explanations that link the four women to Mary are that there was either something "extraordinary or irregular" in the union of the women with their partners, or that the women "showed initiative or played an important role in God's plan and so came to be considered the instrument of God's providence or of His Holy Spirit."[79] The role of

---

77. Waetjen, "The Genealogy"; Hood, "The Genealogies of Jesus"; Johnson, *Purpose of the Biblical Genealogies*.

78. Stendahl, "Matthew," 770; Waetjen, "The Genealogy"; Josephus *Life* 1.6. See Phil 3:5.

79. Brown, *Birth of the Messiah*, 71–74; Stendahl, "Matthew," 771.

the five women is therefore very significant. Moreover, in spite of the male line, as Judith Anderson emphasizes, "Jesus has no male progenitor."[80] Yet, even though there is no fleshly father for Jesus because Joseph is not the physical progenitor, Joseph, as Stendahl points out, does acknowledge "his son's paternity which in Jewish tradition closed all questions."[81] Benjamin and Matthews state:

> At the time a child was born, the father had to decide whether or not to adopt it into the household. In the world of the Bible, life began not with a viable birth, but only with adoption. Regardless of the status of the newborn at the moment of delivery, without adoption it was considered stillborn. If the father did not adopt the child the midwife took it from the birthing room and left it in an open field to declare it eligible for adoption by another household.[82]

Thus, the remote possibility of a genealogy through Mary is impossible since it is only through the father's family that a viable ancestry is established. A rabbinic statement puts it well: "The family of the father is regarded as the proper family, but the family of the mother is not regarded as proper family" (*b. B. Bat.* 109b).

Second, within the birth narrative (1:18—2:23), Joseph, the central patrilineal figure,[83] is depicted as the superior member of the marriage dyad while Mary is portrayed as belonging to Joseph either as his betrothed or his wife. Further, the story dramatically turns on Joseph because divine revelations are made to him through dreams that precipitate decisions and actions on his part that affect his wife and son. Accordingly, Joseph without fear takes Mary to be his wife (1:19–24), flees with his wife and son to Egypt for safety (2:13–15), returns from Egypt with the child and his mother after the death of Herod (2:19–21), settles in Nazareth rather than Bethlehem (2:22–23), and names his son "Jesus" (2:25) according to the angelic directive (1:21). Joseph with "the child and his mother" is the chief protagonist of the narrative. Joseph is the family head.

Two additional observations correspond to advanced agrarian expectations. First, emphasis is upon the birth of a son (1:21, 25; 2:15).

---

80. Anderson, "Matthew: Gender and Reading," 9.

81. Stendahl, "Matthew," 771.

82. Matthews and Benjamin, *Social World of Ancient Israel*, 10–11. See Patai, *Sex and Family*, 135, 127; Stager and Wolff, "Child Sacrifice at Carthage," 50; Qur'an 16:58–59.

83. Anderson, "Matthew: Gender and Reading," 7.

Interestingly, when the child and his mother are mentioned together, the child is mentioned first (2:11, 13–14). And second, during the pregnancy Joseph has no conjugal relations with Mary (1:25), no doubt a theological emphasis by the author, but plausible sociologically since sex in advanced agrarian societies usually has a single purpose: procreation. Mary is pregnant. Sexual intercourse is socially inappropriate.

Third, beyond the genealogy and infancy narrative, members of the family of Jesus—his mother, brothers, and sisters—are mentioned on two occasions (12:46–50; 13:55–56). In the first instance (12:46–50), Jesus's mother and brothers seek to speak with him. The omission of Joseph possibly indicates that Joseph is dead, which would make Jesus (the eldest son) the male leader of the family. Another omission, not uncommon or insignificant to public settings in advanced agrarian societies, is the absence or nonrecognition of Jesus's sisters by name (see 13:55–56). Mary's presence is possibly sanctioned by her widowhood, by the presence of Jesus as the first son, and possibly by the accompaniment of Jesus' brothers. Thus, Jesus' physical family is employed as a foil for Jesus to speak of the new surrogate family of God. In this household, the father is "my Father in heaven" (cf. 23:9), and other members are "my brother, and sister, and mother." Belonging is based on a commitment to do "the will of my Father in heaven" (12:50). This family, not based on physical lineage, is exceptional but foundational for an understanding of the Matthean community.

In the second instance (13:55–56), four elements of Jesus's family (Jesus, his mother, four brothers, and sisters) are mentioned in a descending order. First, the highest position is given to Jesus possibly suggesting that Mary is a widow. The phrase "the carpenter's son" may simply identify the occupation of the father, Joseph being known by his economic role. But emphasis seems to be as well upon the son in relationship to the occupation of the father as a carpenter. If so, another possibility from the community's perspective is that Jesus is the eldest son and thus the proper son to fulfill the status and economic role as "the carpenter's son." In advanced agrarian societies, a family's status often is bound up in the economic role fulfilled by a family head. Therefore, Jesus would not be accepting his status or carrying out his proper role. At any rate, the phrase "the carpenter's son" does not appear to be accidental (contrast Mark 6:3, "the carpenter" in reference to Jesus with no implication about Joseph). Second, Mary the mother of Jesus is named. Third, the brothers of Jesus are mentioned by name (James, Joseph, Simon, and Judas). Last and least, sisters are identified without acknowledgement of number or name as noted.

The genealogy, the behavior of Joseph in the birth story, the later absence of Joseph and its implication for the status and role of Jesus in the family, the absence of the sisters in a public setting but their later anonymous inclusion in a family hierarchical list set forth family relations compatible with advanced agrarian households.

The Household of Zebedee (4:21; 10:2; 21:20; 26:37; 27:56)

Little is said of the household of Zebedee, but the bits of social information regarding Zebedee the father, his sons, his spouse, and the unnamed mother seem significant. First, in all four family references the father's name, Zebedee, is honored by being mentioned even though the father never takes an active part. Second, when the brothers are named, James is mentioned first (4:21; 10:2), his name alone being linked to Zebedee the father, as in "James the son of Zebedee and John his brother." A superior/inferior gender status may stand behind the stated order of the father/mother and brother/sister dyads. For example, when the terms father and mother are mentioned together, the term father is mentioned first (15:4, 5; 19:5, 19, 29) and when the terms brothers and sisters are used together, the term brothers is spoken of first (12:50; 13:55; 19:29). Simon and Andrew are treated similarly (4:18; 10:2) without mention of their father's name. The specifically ordered language probably indicates the status of James as the eldest son and accordingly as the superior member of the brother dyad. Third and last, the mother is referred to twice (20:20; 27:56) but never by name. This is not to imply that her function in the Gospel is unimportant. To the contrary, the mother appears at two significant moments: in the first instance (20:20) she asks Jesus to "command" hierarchical positions for her sons in his kingdom, and in the second instance she is one of the women who observe the crucifixion (27:56). Her anonymity may be due simply to the fact that her name is unknown. However, since in each instance the father, Zebedee, is also mentioned by name, social deference seems to be given to the superior/inferior positions of the husband/wife dyad by leaving the mother unnamed.

The Household of the Centurion (8:5–13)

Several details of the healing of the centurion's son/servant reflect household relations of a military officer in an advanced agrarian society. First, social ranking: the officer treats Jesus as one who is greater than himself. He is not worthy to have Jesus "come under [his] roof" (8:8). Jesus, the greater one, should not stoop to enter the house of an inferior. Second, military occupation and chain of command: the officer's behavior grows out of the reality that he himself is a man "under authority" (8:9) with soldiers and slaves under him (8:9) who obey his commands. In short, the officer's worldview is hierarchical, over and under, a perspective that shapes his career, his household, and his relations with others. Jesus does not attack the officer's social-organizational perspective but sees within his response an expression of significant faith.

The Household of Peter (8:14–15)

Finally, Matthew briefly mentions the healing of Peter's mother-in-law by Jesus in Peter's house. After her healing, the woman rises and serves Jesus, a typical gender-specific domestic function.[84] The text is silent concerning the circumstances surrounding the presence of the mother-in-law in Peter's house. It would be unusual for her to be a permanent resident, since normally she would be cared for by her husband or, if widowed, by her sons. In their absence, she would most likely return to her father's house. Possibly, she is a guest, or the relationship is exceptional. Actually, domestic scenes are not plentiful in Matthew. In the parable of the leaven a woman mixes yeast in a large amount of flour (13:33).[85] At the end of time, two women will be grinding at the mill (24:41). The women from Galilee who minister to Jesus (27:55) probably perform a domestic type of service in an itinerant setting.

---

84. In contrast to Mark, who concludes the story with the statement "the fever left her, and she began to serve them," Matthew changes the wording to the singular, "to serve him." Thus, Matthew has a christological emphasis—Peter's mother-in-law ministers to Jesus. For the debate over whether she "serves" or "ministers" to Jesus, see Schottroff, *Lydia's Impatient Sisters*, 79–90. The issue is probed more in chapter 7—the women at the cross and the tomb who earlier ministered to Jesus or made provision for him (27:55).

85. It should be noted, however, that her work is apparently paired with that of a man who sows mustard seed. Also, a male audience "sees" a woman's task that is usually invisible. Balch and Osiek state, "Here a woman's work, usually invisible, is paired with that of man who sowed mustard seed. Her work is transparent for God's; in the hands of a woman baking bread, one can perceive the creative hands of God" (*Families in the New Testament*, 136.)

The Household in Jesus's Teachings

Advanced agrarian household practices are found as well in the teachings of Jesus. For example, the "cost of discipleship" passage divides families along gender-specific lines. A man (son) is set against his father, a daughter against her mother, a daughter-in-law against her mother-in-law, and "a man's foes," the enemies of a family head, are "those of his own household" (10:35–36). Further, the controversy over the question of the resurrection (22:22–33) concerns the legal provision of "levirate" marriage (see Deut 25:5–10 as well as the story of Judah and Tamar in Gen 38)—that if brothers live together and one of them dies leaving no son, another brother is to marry the widow. Although the practice is otherwise undocumented in Israelite marriage practices of the first century, it was an institution not only of Israel's past, but also of other Semitic peoples,[86] and is consistent with marriage and property preservation practices of advanced agrarian societies.

A number of household examples are found in the parable teachings. In the parable of the unforgiving servant, the property status of a slave and his wife and children is described. Since the slave is unable to pay his debt, not only is he to be sold, but also are his wife, his children, and all that he has (18:25). In the parable of the laborers in the vineyard (20:1–16), the kingdom is compared to a male householder who hires laborers for his vineyard. The parable of the two sons (21:28–32) emphasizes the greater/lesser status of being either the first or second son with a parallel drawn to the religious leaders and to the tax collectors and harlots. In the parable of the wicked tenants (21:33–46), a male householder plants a vineyard and lets it out to male tenants who harm and kill the male servants and, finally, the son. In the parable of the marriage feast (22:1–14), all of the characters are male: a king, his son, the servants, and the attendants. Even the person removed from the feast for not having a wedding garment probably is male (22:11). If the male householder had known when the thief was coming, he would have watched (24:42–44). A faithful and wise male servant is placed over his master's household to provide for the servants' needs (24:45–51). In the parable of the talents (25:14–30), a man goes on a journey and entrusts his property to male servants who engage in business for the purpose of making a profit for their master. The parable

---

86. See Baab, "Marriage," 282; Mace, *Hebrew Marriage*, 107–15; Patai, *Sex and Family*, 92–93.

of the ten maidens (25:1–13) appears to be exceptional, but the maidens and the bridegroom behave according to advanced agrarian social norms as the maidens await the arrival of the bridegroom, and as the bridegroom comes to the home of his wife's parents to fetch his bride and to take her to his own.

Finally, the property and/or embedded status of wives in their husbands may be suggested in such phrases as "his wife" or its equivalent (5:31, 32; 18:25; 19:3, 5, 7, 9). References not found in Jesus's teachings may suggest the same (1:24; 14:3; 22:25; 27:19), as may be the case when children are mentioned in parallel fashion with lands (19:29). Passages on divorce (5:31–32; 19:3–12) assume that divorce is a male privilege and that wives belong to their husbands. Jesus's radical teachings on the topic prompt an astonished but typical male response from the disciples: then, it is "not expedient to marry" (19:10).

Thus far, the pervasive position of the advanced agrarian household in the Gospel has been demonstrated. It is manifest in a variety of social details of actual family examples. It is a familial/political metaphor that cuts across the society from the *oikos* to the *polis*. And it is one of the significant images used by Jesus in his teachings concerning the kingdom and discipleship, especially in the parables. The household functions both as a social reality and as a social metaphor. At both the macro- and the microlevels of the society it seems to predominate. Accordingly, its place and function in the Gospel parallel advanced agrarian social structures and practices.

EXCEPTIONS TO THE MODEL

Exceptions, that is, examples of deviancy, are twofold: (1) the reversal of hierarchical authority in Matthew's community concomitant to Jesus's new surrogate family of God, and (2) the place of women in the gospel narrative along with their treatment by Jesus that emphasizes their dignity and worth.

Hierarchical Authority and the Matthean Community

Matthew's Jesus opposes leadership authority (20:25) that "lords it" over others in the community. Instead, he advocates a reverse leadership paradigm (bottom/up) based on the servant model of the Son of Man (20:28). This paradigm, consistent with the passion predictions (16:21–23; 17:22,

23; 20:17–19) and the teaching on discipleship (10:24–25; 11:29), stands opposite to a typical advanced agrarian leadership pattern (top/down) illustrated by the request of the mother of the sons of Zebedee (20:21).

Some scholars believe that Jesus's critique of advanced agrarian household structural practices specifies that the new surrogate family of God is organized along egalitarian lines. Representatives of this position include Elizabeth Schüssler Fiorenza, John Dominic Crossan, Gerd Theissen, Annette Merz, and Richard Horsley.[87] For Schüssler Fiorenza and Horsley, Jesus's demand to break with one's own family is addressed to all of the disciples, and his sayings about breaking away from the family, therefore, contain a criticism of the patriarchal family.[88]

Others such as Stephen C. Barton emphasize that the household ethic of Jesus' new surrogate family is "afamilial" or "suprafamilial," that is, Jesus supports almost an antifamilial position.[89] Warren Carter asserts that Jesus' passion prediction (20:20–28) and the ensuing struggle of the disciples for hierarchical superiority associated with Jesus's critique of household relationships in chapter 19 demonstrates that advanced agrarian (patriarchal) leadership structures are to be abandoned by Matthew's community—jettisoned as remnants of its past.[90]

Carter affirms that Jesus advanced several thoroughgoing proposals for a new household structure and family relations model. For example, Matthew's Jesus critiques Israelite marriage and divorce practices (19:3–9), promotes a single lifestyle ("eunuchs") for males after divorce (19:10–12), blesses little children (19:13–15), and indicts the rich man whose identity is defined by his wealth and possessions (19:16–22). Conversely, he blesses the disciples' response that they have left houses to follow him, that is, they

87. Advocates of the egalitarian perspective include Schüssler Fiorenza, *Discipleship of Equals*; idem, *In Memory of Her*; Crossan, *The Essential Jesus*; idem, *The Historical Jesus*; idem, *Jesus: A Revolutionary Biography*; Theissen, *Sociology of Early Palestinian Christianity*; idem, "'We Have Left Everything . . .' (Mark 10:28)"; Theissen and Merz, *The Historical Jesus*; Horsley, *Jesus and the Spiral of Violence*. For additional references, see Corley, "The Egalitarian Jesus," 291nn. Critics of the egalitarian position include Elliott, "Jesus Was Not an Egalitarian"; Duling, "'Egalitarian' Ideology"; idem, "The Matthean Brotherhood"; D'Angelo, "Theology in Mark and Q"; Levine, "Second Temple Judaism, Jesus and Women"; Corley, "The Egalitarian Jesus."

88. Schüssler Fiorenza, *In Memory of Her*, 151–54; Horsley, *Jesus and the Spiral of Violence*, 231–45.

89. Barton, *Discipleship and Family Ties*, 13, 69, 176–77, 191, 222. We follow Balch and Osiek, *Families in the New Testament*, 133, 263.

90. Carter, *Households and Discipleship*.

have given up a wealth-based status (19:27), a matter consistent with the values of the household of the kingdom (12:46–50) that shares in God's life and sets aside conventional hierarchical structures (19:29–30). Thus, those who desire greatness and power in Matthew's community must be "servant" (*diákonos*) (20:26), and those who seek to be first must become slave (*doulos*), 20:27).

This "paradigm reversal"—turning accepted norms upside down—is epitomized for Carter when Jesus places a child (a subordinate and inferior member within the Israelite family) in the midst of the disciples (18:4) to answer the question "Who is the greatest in the kingdom of heaven?" (18:1). Children for Matthew constitute a metaphor for the "little ones," perhaps the ordinary members of the Christian community (18:6, 10, 14; cf. 10:42). The example of the child in chapter 18 is carried forward in chapter 19.[91] There, Jesus blesses the little children, the least powerful and most dependent members within an advanced agrarian household. In doing so, he affirms that children are representative examples of those who make up heaven's kingdom.

Further, Carter, working with V. Turner's model of liminality, contends that Matthew's story sets forth "antistructure," that is, egalitarian relationships that are qualitatively different from the dominant contemporary society.[92] He uses the term "egalitarian" carefully, however, knowing that often it is used anachronistically by scholars who superimpose twenty-first century values about egalitarian households upon ancient Greco-Roman households. He does note that the rare adjective "equal,"[93] ("put on the same footing" with an emphasis on "equality of treatment, dignity made manifest and recognized") is used in the parable of the laborers in the vineyard (20:1–16; see 20:12) but that it is doubtful that the term can be applied to all aspects of household relationships within the pericope. As Balch and Osiek point out, "Carter is wise occasionally to use the expression 'more egalitarian.'"[94] As a result, he differentiates between household relations in Matthew 20 qualitatively from household management instructions in such writings as Ephesians and 1 Peter that feature

91. Ibid.

92. Carter's use of Turner and permanent liminality is based on Duling's, "Matthew and Marginality." See Balch and Osiek, *Families in the New Testament*, note 127, 264.

93. *Isos* is used in Matt 20:12; Mark 14:56; Luke 6:34; John 5:18; Acts 11:17; Phil 2:6; and Rev 21:16 in the New Testament.

94. Balch and Osiek, *Families in the New Testament*, 132.

household codes.[95] For example, in 1 Peter, Christ's passion is used as a model, but it is placed within the slave component of a household code (1 Peter 2:18–25). Also, in 1 Peter slaves are to obey harsh masters but in Matthew those in powerful positions are to serve somehow as slaves as Christ did in his death.[96] Other examples could be cited, but Carter affirms that Matthew's household values appear to be qualitatively different from those in 1 Peter. This is significant because, as Elliott indicates of 1 Peter (and perhaps by extension of other Christian writings that carry forward Greco-Roman household relationships),

> Within the household the roles, relationships and responsibilities of its various members—husbands, wives, parents, children, masters, slaves, the married, the unmarried or widowed, the elder, the younger, the heads of the household and their subordinates—are exemplified through the use of traditional patterns of household conduct, the so-called Haustafeln or "household codes." . . . It is also likely that the household structure of authority influenced not only the roles but also the eligibility for leadership in the Christian community, especially at the local level.[97]

Apparently, it is precisely Elliott's description that Carter believes is not the case in Matthew. However (and this is important to Carter) the Evangelist's vision is not sufficiently evident within the Evangelist's communities. He addresses this issue by contrasting the implied audience and the real one.

> Matthew's actual audience would be familiar with a call to an alternative household structure [e.g., from the Gospel of Mark], but the reality of that structure was not as evident among the actual first-century audience as the First Evangelist wished it to be, especially now that a new situation vis-á-vis the synagogue has developed. The hierarchical and androcentric pattern of the surrounding society has not been sufficiently abandoned, and the new structure,

---

95. Ephesians and 1 Peter can be dated at about the same period. Both Matthew and 1 Peter are "Petrine." See Carter, *Households and Discipleship*, 191, and Balch and Osiek, *Families in the New Testament*, 134.

96. Balch and Osiek, *Families in the New Testament*, 134.

97. Elliott, *Home for the Homeless*, 189. Elliott also affirms in his Anchor Bible commentary that the writing both accords with and differs from conventional perspectives on male-female relations; see Elliott, *1 Peter*, 550–59.

which the presence of the reign of God required, was not properly visible.[98]

Casting the net a bit wider, truths concerning God's reign are hidden from "the wise and understanding" (the greater) and revealed to "babes" (the lesser) (11:25). In contrast to the religious leaders, the disciples are not to be called "rabbi," "father," or "master" since they have one teacher, Jesus (23:8), one Father, who is in heaven (23:9), and one master, who is Christ (23:10). Greatness once again is modeled by service (23:11), and Jesus warns the disciples that whoever exalts himself will be humbled, and whoever humbles himself will be exalted (23:12). The Evangelist's surrogate household, called through baptism to follow Jesus, is to be a "brotherhood" of the sons of God.[99] But is it realistic in an advanced agrarian society to flatten hierarchy? More to the point, does the evidence of Matthew support such a notion?

It is true that on several occasions household imagery is used to describe or allude to the surrogate family of the kingdom in a different way from social expectations of advanced agrarian family life. The Pharisees and Sadducees, for example, are called to repentance by John (3:7–10) because their physical heritage with Abraham is not a ticket into the kingdom. God is able to raise up children to Abraham from "these stones" (3:9). Further, the disciples' mission (chap. 10) divides families in their relationships (10:34–39). Matthew cites a Q passage (10:34–36) and concludes it with a phrase from Micah 7:6, "one's foes (enemies) will be members of one's own household" (10:36). Accordingly, a man is set against his father, a daughter against her mother, a daughter-in-law against her mother-in-law (10:35).[100] These three "against" statements are followed in a citation of another Q passage (10:37–39) with three parallel statements emphasizing the phrase, "is not worthy of me": "Whoever loves father or mother more than me *is not worthy of me*; and whoever loves son or daughter more than me *is not worthy of me*; and whoever does not take

98. Carter, *Households and Disciples*, 213.

99. For "sons of God," see 5:9, 45; 13:38; for "brotherhood," see 12:49–50; 18:35; 23:8; 25:40; 28:10. See Duling, "Matthew 18:15–17"; and idem, "The Matthean Brotherhood."

100. Renunciation sayings of this kind should not be interpreted as a critique of the family as such. They illustrate, as Elliott states ("Jesus Was Not an Egalitarian," 79), "Jesus' call for exclusive allegiance to and unconditional trust in God, and a prioritizing of commitments given the urgency of the time and of Jesus' mission. They involve no explicit critique of the family as such."

up the cross and follow me *is not worthy of me*."[101] Loyalty to Jesus is paramount (8:18–22). It not only solidifies the community, it also receives its own reward (10:42).

However, Jesus' call for exclusive allegiance to God that in turn leads to internal family conflict is not, we believe, a summons to societal egalitarianism or a condemnation of the advanced agrarian family structure per se. Jesus is not calling for, as Elliott states, a "disbanding of the family or a termination of family loyalty, but rather he is calling for a loyalty to himself beyond that of loyalty toward members of the biological family."[102]

As Balch and Osiek point out, these statements should not be interpreted as a "social program,"[103] because in other pericopes Jesus' teachings on divorce (5:27–32; 19:2–12) and the care of one's parents, that is, the fifth commandment (19:19; see 15:4), regulate family life. Jesus does not condemn the biological family. Neither does he seek to abolish the family as such. Instead, his purpose is to transform the relationships within it.[104] For Elliott, Jesus

> in fact embraced the family as a model of both commitment to God and life in community. This surrogate family which Jesus established, as Bruce Malina has pointed out, would have been absolutely necessary in this collectivist, group-oriented culture where "survival in society after the negation of family integrity would require that a person move into some other actual or fictive kin group."[105]

Therefore, reversals of status are not synonymous with the doing away of hierarchy or status. Rather, they are "radical inversions of status, of high and low rankings, of first and last positions."[106] Elliott elaborates:

> To the contrary, their dramatic punch requires the continuation of the reality of high and low, first and last positions in the social order. Patron-client relations, for example, are not eliminated altogether but rather reversed: conventional patrons are reduced to clients and clients, raised to the status of patrons. Similarly, the reciprocal roles and statuses of children and parents are not elimi-

101. Kingsbury, *Matthew,* 105, italics original.
102. Elliott, "Jesus Was Not an Egalitarian," 79.
103. Balch and Osiek, *Families in the New Testament,* 131.
104. Elliott, "Jesus Was Not an Egalitarian," 78.
105. Ibid, 79. See Malina, "'Let Him Deny Himself,'" 114.
106. Elliott, "Jesus Was Not an Egalitarian," 81.

nated altogether but rather reversed: children, more than parents, are the object of God's concern; children, more than parents, illustrate the nature of life in the kingdom of heaven.[107]

Jesus's surrogate group is composed of and identified by those who do the will of the heavenly Father (12:49–50). The creation of this new kin group, however, does not destroy advanced agrarian family structures. Neither does it reorder the family along egalitarian lines. Rather, it redefines this social group according to its faithfulness to do God's will (see 4:18; 8:21–22) as it discerns Jesus' identity and follows him. Matthew places this unit (12:46–50) in a context of discipleship and kinship relations (12:49) that prepares his readers for what follows in the chapter on parables (13). In turn, the parables illuminate the identity of Jesus' surrogate family who do "the will of my Father in heaven" (12:49). What Jesus first tells the crowds (13:2) is then told in a "house" (13:36), where, as Balch and Osiek indicate, "the Matthean communities would be hearing the Gospel read."[108] Elliott states about Matthew 12:49:

> This saying as it stands ... shows Jesus' positive conception of the family as an institution appropriate for defining life under the reign of God. What the saying expressly affirms is not a restructuring of the family along egalitarian lines, but rather a redefinition of the identity of the family of Jesus and the basis for membership—not blood or marriage but obedience to the will of God. In Jesus' collectivist society this new surrogate family makes available to those who have renounced their natural families a form of community essential to their personal and social existence. [109]

There are those who left (at least temporarily) family, occupations, and possessions to accompany Jesus. But there are also those of the new surrogate community who did not renounce their "homes, property, and possessions, but rather put them at the disposal of those on the move ... evidence not of a general equality among Jesus followers but of continuing social and economic disparity in the Jesus faction."[110] The disciples were sent into towns, villages, and households to announce the good news of the kingdom (Matt 10:5–15). Jesus celebrates Passover with his

107. Ibid.
108. Ibid., 78.
109. Ibid., 82. See Malina, "'Let Him Deny Himself.'"
110. Elliott, "Jesus Was Not an Egalitarian," 79.

disciples, a meal that is fundamentally a family celebration. Guijarro states, "the fact that Jesus celebrated it with his disciples indicates that the group understood itself according to the model of family relationships."[111]

Further, even though the householder in the parable of the laborers in the vineyard (20:1–16) pays all of the day-laborers equally (20:11–12—one denarius to all the laborers) the point of the parable does not involve social or economic equality relationships within the early Jesus movement. Neither is it a demonstration of Jesus's egalitarianism. Rather, it is an issue of unfair treatment.[112]

Finally, all believers are "brothers" (23:8–10), but brothers "can be quite unequal in terms of position or privilege (as affected by age, birth mother, strength etc.)."[113] Duling allows that Matthew 23:8–10 expresses "a limited egalitarian ideology," but then affirms that this egalitarian ideology "was in tension with social reality" and that the Matthean gospel on the whole reveals a movement toward "institutional hierarchy."[114] The "Matthean brotherhood," he believes, has moved beyond a "coalition" of the "faction" type. He believes that it also is moving beyond the "sect," especially if one thinks of a "reformist sect." Duling states, "Thus in Matt. 23:34 we find 'prophets,' 'sages' and 'scribes' linked. In 10:40–42 'prophet' is listed with 'righteous one' and 'little ones.' If apostle is added to the list (10:2) . . . there are at least six terms for functional leaders within the Matthean brotherhood."[115] Duling agrees with Wire that "Matthew and his reading audience represent a classically educated, self-sufficient scribal group that dominates a mixed community."[116] Care should be given, therefore, not to flatten hierarchy when affirming a reversal of hierarchical leadership for the new surrogate community of Jesus.

Our observations of the Matthean texts parallel the social-scientific perspective that "the conception of equality as a possibility for all human society did not arise until the eighteenth century with its altered economic, social, and political conditions and its secular optimism concerning the

---

111. Guijarro, "The Family in the Jesus Movement," 115.

112. Ibid.

113. Ibid., 82.

114. Duling, "'Egalitarian' Ideology," 134. See also Duling, "The Matthean Brotherhood," 165–66.

115. Duling, "The Matthean Brotherhood," 179.

116. Ibid., 179–80. See Wire, "Gender Roles in a Scribal Community," 92.

possibility of social transformation."[117] That historical process, according to A. H. Halsey, involved "basic equality of membership in a society" in the eighteenth century, "political rights in the nineteenth century and certain social rights in the twentieth century."[118] Ancient societies like the Roman Empire were "not 'egalitarian' in the modern Enlightenment, individualist, political-philosophical sense in which equality is a self-evident human right and/or social goal for everyone."[119] The claim by Schüssler Fiorenza[120] that ancient voluntary associations were egalitarian in their structure and behavior has been refuted by Thomas Schmeller.[121]

It is evident that disagreement exists among Matthean scholars over the structure of the kingdom of heaven's new surrogate kin group. We believe this is so because Jesus' disciples who may serve as a transparency of the Matthean community are in a liminal (marginal) state.[122] One of the characteristics of the liminal stage is that of inter-structural association marked by simplicity. Victor Turner states, "between instructors and neophytes there is often complete authority and complete submission; among neophytes there is often complete equality,"[123] as opposed to the intricate networks, hierarchical arrangements, rights and duties "proportioned" to "rank, status, and corporate affiliation" elsewhere in the larger society outside the group. However, after the liminal phase is over, those who have undergone the liminal training return to society albeit with a changed status. Could this possibly cast light on the differences between the views of Carter and Elliott? If so, both are right. Their disagreements are due to a failure to distinguish between the last two stages of a rite of passage, liminality, and aggregation. In the liminal stage there can be equality among neophytes but in the stage of aggregation they return to the social realities appertaining to the larger society—in this case, an advanced agrarian society.

117. Elliott, "Jesus Was Not an Egalitarian," 77.

118. Halsey, "Equality," 261–62.

119. Duling, "'Egalitarian' Ideology," 126.

120. Schüssler Fiorenza, *Discipleship of Equals*; and idem. "The Oratory of Euphemia and the Ekklēsia of Wo/man," 3–31.

121. Schmeller, *Hierarchie und Egaltāt*.

122. See the introduction under the section on "Excursus on Marginality." See also chapter 7, which views the disciples through the lens of the liminal or marginal phase of a rite-of-passage model.

123. V. Turner, *The Forest of Symbols*, 99-100.

As depicted in the previous chapter under the section on "Excursus on Marginality" V. Turner distinguishes among three kinds of communitas: (1) existential or spontaneous communitas, (2) normative communitas, and (3) ideological communitas. When Carter perceives the community as anti-structural and tending toward egalitarianism it appears that he sees the group as an "existential or spontaneous communitas," that is, where the disciples are in their liminal journey. But, following Carter, the disciples are at a dangerous juncture. Will they abandon their "spontaneous communitas," and revert to the hierarchical patterns of power and male dominance so indigenous to advanced agrarian societies? Certainly, this is an important question. Duling, on the other hand, apparently views the disciples and the community as not being a "spontaneous communitas" but as a "normative communitas," that is, the community has now become (or is in the process of becoming) a perduring ordered social system. Turner acknowledges that "the spontaneity and immediacy of communitas" eventually develops its own structure.[124] We believe the evidence tips in favor of Duling's position. In either case, it is difficult to spell out the nature of this more permanent social order whose singular structural characteristic is a reversed hierarchy. The danger for contemporary scholars, however, is to read the Gospel of Matthew through egalitarian eyes.

At this point we offer an anthropological suggestion, and merely a suggestion, for understanding the Matthean community's social structure. Victor Turner has observed that all human societies implicitly or explicitly refer to two contrasting social models.[125] The first is "a structure of jural, political and economic positions, offices, statuses, and roles in which the individual is only ambiguously grasped behind the social persona."[126] The second is a "communitas of concrete idiosyncratic individuals, who, though differing in physical and mental endowment, are nevertheless equal in terms of shared humanity."[127] The first, he maintains, is a "differentiated, culturally structured, segmented, and often hierarchical system of institutional position."[128] However, the second "presents society as an undifferentiated, homogenous whole, in which individuals confront one

124. V. Turner, *The Ritual Process,* 132.
125. Ibid., 177.
126. Ibid.
127. Ibid.
128. Ibid.

another integrally, and not as 'segmentalized' into statuses and roles."[129] Malina describes Turner's first model as one that "focuses upon the person in terms of what he or she does by way of social functions and social roles." In turn Turner's second model features "the person in terms of who he or she is as a person, personhood being something accepted in and for itself."[130]

These two dissimilar social models apparently are not only replications of bisexual humanity but serve also as models of the social body; the social body has male and female sides that produce contrasting social roles. Malina points out, "This can be seen in a number of strong group societies in which the patrilineal side is the structured, segmented side, the repository of rights and obligations (a male side), while members of the matrilineal side deal with each other in non-structured, and non-jural terms (a female side; 'jural' here means on the basis of legal and legitimate rights and obligations)."[131] The bond of *uterine descent* is based on a personal bond and not the material, jural kind of structure. As Fortes notes, "it unites individuals only by ties of mutual interest and concern not unlike those that prevail between close collateral kin in our culture."[132] Fortes observes that this uterine line does not "create corporate groups competing with the agnatic lineage and clan." Instead, the uterine line carries. "only a spiritual attribute" and "cannot determine the jural and political-ritual solidarity of the patrilineal lineage."[133] Interpreting Fortes, Turner observes, "Here we have the opposition patrilineal/matrilineal, which has the functions dominant/submerged." He continues, "The patrilineal tie is associated with property, office, political allegiance, exclusiveness, and, it may be added, particularistic and segmentary interests. It is the 'structural' link par excellence. The uterine tie is associated with spiritual characteristics, mutual interests and concerns, and co laterality." Turner concludes: the uterine tie "is counterposed to exclusiveness, which presumably means that it makes for inclusiveness and does not serve

129. Ibid.
130. Malina, *Christian Origins and Cultural Anthropology,* 155.
131. Ibid., 156. See also Fortes, *Dynamics of Clanship,* 32.
132. Fortes, *Dynamics of Clanship,* 32.
133. Ibid.

material interests. In brief, matrilaterality represents, in the dimension of kinship, the notion of communitas."[134]

If so, greater attention should be given to male roles in the non-dominant sides of family groups. We include at this point an email exchange with Bruce J. Malina that describes the non-dominant side. Malina writes, "Here I refer to the mother's brother or uncle on the mother's side (called 'Em' in medieval English, 'Oheim' in medieval German, plus appropriate Latin and Greek names). These are males in the nondominant, non-jural side of society, much like the mother's brothers cited in anthropological literature." He then illustrates the matter among leaders in early Christianity:

> Christian leaders who founded communities as well as the leaders or managers who succeeded those founders (either bishops, or a group of elders called presbyters, or the Christian body as a whole—or a combination of the three) basically DID NOT wield power within the group. Rather what they had at their disposal was commitment activation or loyalty, revealed in the care and concern typical of maternal uncles in dominant patriarchal and patrilineal societies. Thus early Christianity was marked by maternal-uncle-archy, or emarchy rather than patriarchy.[135]

To what degree did the First Evangelist emphasize the feminine side of the social order as a basis for leadership in the Matthean community? Diane Jacobs-Malina argues that the roles recommended by Jesus for his potential leaders arise out of typical women's roles in first-century Palestinian society.[136] It is in the domestic domain, she maintains, where God's standards allow a woman's traditional role to be equally appropriate for both men and women, because of their shared belief in God as Father that binds them to the care and nurture of his children and the stewardship of his creation. If so, the Matthean community is not to follow the patriarchal, male-dominated power structure of the larger society. Ultimately, this is at odds with the uterine line of the family. But, neither could it be egalitarian because such is a social anachronism. Its power, if our suggestion is correct, is centered in its uterine tie and all that "matrilaterality represents, in the dimension of kinship, the notion of communitas."[137]

---

134. V. Turner, *The Ritual Process*, 114.

135. This is based on an e-mail exchange with Malina.

136. Jacobs-Malina, *Beyond Patriarchy*.

137. V. Turner, *The Ritual Process*, 157.

We will demonstrate in ensuing chapters that what the Evangelist wants for his community, rooted in the social ideology and structures of an advanced agrarian society, is to envision an alternative world/social reality that is based on the ideology, values, and leadership paradigm of the surrogate family of the kingdom of heaven. However, it was necessary for that alternative vision to be played out within the social structural realities of an advanced agrarian society.

THE GOSPEL'S TREATMENT OF WOMEN— EXAMPLES OF SOCIAL DEVIANCY?

Finally, even though Matthew is written from "an androcentric perspective," and the number of women and their roles within the writing are not major, women do have "symbolic significance."[138] Accordingly, even though Mary is not the central character in the birth story, she illustrates how God "has acted in a radically new way"[139] in making her the mother of Jesus without male assistance. The woman with the hemorrhage (9:20–22) and the Canaanite woman (15:21–28), members of marginal groups (the crowds and non-Israelites, respectively), are treated as women of faith and serve as foils to the Judean leaders and disciples.[140] The woman at Bethany (26:6–13) and the women at the cross and tomb (27:55–56, 61; 28:1–10) "play important roles the disciples should have played."[141] Furthermore, Jesus attacks his male auditors in the Sermon on the Mount for their treatment of women over the issues of adultery and divorce (5:28, 32; cf. 19:3–9). Such examples serve as instances of deviancy from advanced agrarian expectations. Anderson, casting this reality in patriarchal terms, states: "The important roles of women and Jesus' response to women supplicants strain the boundaries of the Gospel's patriarchal worldview."[142]

CONCLUSION

We have not provided a comprehensive treatment of gender-specific roles in the Gospel of Matthew, but by viewing those roles through the image of the household and against the backdrop of Matthew's social setting

138. Anderson, "Matthew: Gender and Reading," 6–7.

139. Ibid., 10.

140. Ibid., 10–17.

141. Ibid., 17–21.

142. Ibid., 21.

we have sufficiently demonstrated that the writing is at home in its social world, an advanced agrarian society. Clearly, Matthew's community is ensconced within the societal realities of an advanced agrarian society.

However, the exceptional data documents as well two social actualities at work within the writing that stand in a dynamic tension—a Christian household deeply surrounded and embedded in advanced agrarian norms, but also a surrogate Christian household guided by alternative social and ideological criteria based on Matthew's vision of Jesus' mission. Accordingly, care must be given not to view the Evangelist's actual *Sitz im Leben* as an egalitarian group either ideologically, structurally, or both. This is so first because Jeffersonian democracy did not exist in Rome, Athens, Alexandria, Jerusalem, or Syrian Antioch. Further, this is so because even though Matthew portrays Jesus as one who attacks hierarchical, authoritarian leadership identified by title and rank, such leadership structures may still exist within the Christian community quite typical of the type of marginality identified as "ideological marginality." Finally, this is so because the two social actualities substantiate, we believe, a social/religious identity struggle within and without the community. Therefore, to neglect either actuality prevents one from understanding adequately the social setting or the social struggle that is taking place within Matthew's community.

What then does this say about the four stories about women? This is the question we shall ask of future chapters. Nonetheless, the following can be stated in prospect. The women's stories demonstrate both the new surrogate vision of the kingdom's family as well as a number of challenges existent within at least some surrogate groups to which the Gospel was written. Most of the women's stories are located outside the kinship domain in outdoor, public space, a dangerous location for women subsisting in an agrarian social world. In reality, open, public locations would further marginalize most of these women and pose problems for a community in transition. Can new wine be put into fresh wineskins in such a way that both new and old are preserved (9:17)?

In the next chapter we shall examine women (and men) among three character groups: the disciples, the crowds, and the religious leaders. Jesus teaches these new social relationships in the public settings of the mountain (5:1—7:28), the boat in the Parables Discourse (13:1–52), and Jesus's confrontation with the religious authorities in the temple (21:12—23:29). This will be achieved through the use of two social indices: a macro-index of women in public settings in advanced agrarian societies (already set forth) and a micro-index of Israelite women in mishnaic culture. The Matthean data will show that only among the crowds is there a real alternative for women in public settings, a matter that has considerable significance, we believe, for the four stories of women as well as for the character group designated as "the disciples."

3

Women and Men in Public Settings in Matthew

[1] When he saw the crowds, he went up the mountain; and after he sat down, his disciples came to him.... [20] "For I tell you, unless your righteousness goes beyond that of the scribes and Pharisees, you will never enter the kingdom of heaven." (Matt 5:1, 20, author's translation)

[1] On that same day Jesus went out of the house and sat down beside the sea. [2] And great crowds gathered around him so that he got into a boat and sat there, and the whole crowd stood on the beach.... [36] Then he left the crowds and came into the house. And his disciples came to him, saying, "Explain to us the parable o f the tares in the field." (Matt 13:1–2, 36, author's translation)

[23] And when he entered the temple, the chief priests and the elders of the people came to him as he was teaching, and said, "By what authority are you doing these things, and who gave you this authority?" ... [1] Then Jesus said to the crowds and to his disciples, [2] "The scribes and the Pharisees sit on Moses's seat; therefore, practice and observe whatever they teach you; but do not do according to their deeds. For they say one thing and do another." (Matt 21:23; 23:1–2, author's translation)

INTRODUCTION

IN THE PREVIOUS CHAPTER we found that there are two households in Matthew—the typical household of an advanced agrarian society and the surrogate household of the kingdom of heaven. The advanced agrarian example is a familial/political social reality and metaphor that cuts across both the macro and micro levels of the larger society and seems to parallel advanced agrarian social structures and practices. Nearly on every page of the Gospel there is household data that demonstrates how the writing is at home in its social world: an advanced agrarian society.

Conversely, Matthew also advances a familial ideology of the household of the kingdom of heaven, a surrogate kin group that does not stand against the advanced agrarian family per se, but sets forth a model both of commitment to God and life in the community within the social realities of family structure so essential to survival in an advanced agrarian society. His critique is a reversal of hierarchical power, not the doing away of hierarchy as such; a reversal in which those of low rank are made high and those of high standing are made low; in which those of first positions become last and those of last positions become first. His critique, therefore, does not call for the redoing of the family along egalitarian lines. Instead he redefines his new surrogate group according to its faithfulness to do God's will as it discerns Jesus' identity and follows him. Elliott sums up the matter well when he comments on Jesus' statement in Matthew 12:49, "And pointing to his disciples, he said, 'Here are my mother and my brothers!'"

> This saying as it stands . . . shows Jesus' positive conception of the family as an institution appropriate for defining life under the reign of God. What the saying expressly affirms is not a restructuring of the family along egalitarian lines, but rather a redefinition of the identity of the family of Jesus and the basis for membership—not blood or marriage but obedience to the will of God. In Jesus' collectivist society this new surrogate family makes available to those who have renounced their natural families a form of community essential to their personal and social existence.[1]

Accordingly, even though Matthew is written from "an androcentric perspective" and the number of women and their roles within the writing are not major, women do have "symbolic significance."[2] Mary is not the central character in the birth story, but she illustrates how God "has acted in a radically new way"[3] in making her the mother of Jesus without male assistance. The woman with the hemorrhage (9:20–22) and the Canaanite woman (15:21–28), members of marginal groups (the crowds and non-Israelites, respectively), are treated as women of faith and serve as foils to

---

1. Elliott, "Jesus Was Not an Egalitarian," 82; see Malina, "'Let Him Deny Himself.'"
2. Anderson, "Matthew: Gender and Reading," 6–7.
3. Ibid., 10.

the Israelite leaders and disciples.[4] The woman at Bethany (26:6–13) and the women at the cross and tomb (27:55–56, 61; 28:1–10) "play important roles the disciples should have played."[5] Furthermore, Jesus attacks his male auditors in the Sermon on the Mount for their treatment of women over the issues of adultery and divorce (5:28, 32; cf. 19:3–9). Such examples serve as instances of deviancy from advanced agrarian expectations because they involve doing "the will of my father in heaven." These social/religious norms go against and/or stand in tension with significant gender-specific social expectations of women in advanced agrarian societies.

The purpose of this chapter is to extend and deepen the findings of the previous chapter by examining the place of women among three character groups: the disciples, the crowds, and the religious leaders as they are taught by Jesus or interact with him in three representative public settings: the mountain in the Sermon on the Mount (5:1—7:28), the boat in the Parables Discourse (13:1–52), and the temple in the clash between Jesus and the authorities (21:12—23:29). What can be learned about the place of women among these groups within these public settings? We will show that the Matthean data demonstrates that only among the crowds is there a real alternative for women in public settings, a matter that will have considerable significance not only for the four stories of women but also for the character group Matthew designates as "the disciples."

In the previous chapter, a macro-social model of the lack of public status of women in agrarian societies was created. Now, without setting aside the previous exemplar, a micro-index is employed of the public place of women in legal writings of the ancient rabbis, the Mishnah. This analogy is legitimated by the following: (1) the mishnaic materials provide a Judean example of an advanced agrarian society; (2) although Matthew's community toward the close of the first century makes contact with the larger non-Israelite social world, its roots remain within its cultural heritage;[6] (3) those roots are either still tied to the synagogue[7] or have been broken by the time the Gospel was written;[8] and (4) even

4. Ibid., 10–17.

5. Ibid., 17–21.

6. Meier, "Matthew, Gospel of," 625.

7. Barth, "Matthew's Understanding of the Law"; Davies, *The Setting of the Sermon on the Mount*; Hummel, *Die Auseinandersetz zwischen Kirche und Judentum im Mattäusevangelium*.

8. Strecker, *Der Weg der Gerechtigkeit*; Trilling, *Das wahr Israel*; Frankemölle, *Jahwebund und Kirche Christi*; Hare, *The Theme of Jewish Persecution*.

though the Pharisees before 70 CE cannot be identified with the rabbis at Yavneh, points of continuity between the two have been demonstrated.[9] Antoinette Clark Wire states of the Pharisees:

> Their reinterpretation of the revered literary tradition is not carried out in writing, but reference to past interpreters is common by the century's final decades; and the eventual reshaping of their work into a fixed form by the end of the second century as found in the Mishnah shows the extent to which interpretations were being orally retained.[10]

Any "radical discontinuity," Wire continues, "is belied by the reappearance of the same leaders, the same stories, and the same focus on resurrection, tradition, and meticulous observance of tithing and purity laws, as well as by an increased spotlight in the late century on the Pharisees' significance before the war."[11] Ulrich Luz's discussion of the scribes of Matthew's community seems to parallel Wire's insight.

> Thus behind the Gospel of Matthew, Jewish-Christian, partly scribal circles become evident, circles which were interested in Q, the Gospel of Mark, other Jesus traditions, and the Bible. It is my opinion that such traditions must not be shunted aside and the Evangelist must not be placed apart from them. Not only his own language, which repeatedly demonstrates contact with contemporary rabbinic Judaism, or his conservative attitude toward the law which is evident in 5:17–19 and multiple other texts, but also the whole contour of his Gospel, which resembles closely the Semitic world, point to the contrary.[12]

The findings of these two indices, one macro- and one micro-, are then evaluated as they contribute to a possible understanding of the social setting of the Matthean community and the significance of the four women's stories within that setting.

---

9. Cohen, "The Significance of Yavneh: Pharisees, Rabbis, and the End of Jewish Sectarianism"; Wire, "Gender Roles in a Scribal Community"; Saldarini, *Pharisees, Scribes, and Sadducees*; Neusner, *From Politics to Piety*, 81–100; idem, *Oral Traditions in Judaism*.

10. Wire, "Gender Roles in a Scribal Community," 96.

11. Ibid., 96, n. 38.

12. Luz, *Matthew 1–7*, 78.

WOMEN IN THE PUBLIC SPHERE—TWO SOCIAL INDICES

A Macro Index—Women in Public Settings in Advanced Agrarian Societies

The reader is encouraged to review the major contours of women in public settings in this chapter. Prominent features are as follows:

1. Sociologists designate the applicable societal type for the Roman Empire of the first century as "advanced agrarian," that is, an agricultural society based on the technology of the animal-drawn and iron-tipped plow.[13]

2. Social stratification is most complex in advanced agrarian societies. No major societal type has a more crystallized, hierarchically ordered, male-dominated social order marked by social inequality.[14]

3. Throughout advanced agrarian societies, gender roles are characterized by a basic division of labor.[15]

4. A woman's place and power are mostly but not exclusively within the private sphere of the household.

5. The public realm, centered mostly in the political, educational, and religious societal structures, is the primary but not the exclusive sphere of activity and power for men.[16] In the political sector the *polis* is public domain, dominated by men; the *oikos* is the private sphere, the primary location of women's activity and influence.

6. In the educational sphere, emphasis upon women's education differs among various cultures. Formal, advanced education often is provided through the male dominated religious institutions among the upper classes of the urban centers and is largely designed to "socialize the student into the basic values of the social order and

---

13. Lenski and Lenski, *Human Societies*, (1987) 176; Harris, *Rise of Anthropological Theory*, chap. 2; Nisbet, *Social Change and History*; Childe, *Man Makes Himself*; Boserup, *Women's Role in Economic Development*.

14. Lenski and Lenski, *Human Societies*, (1987) 202–4.

15. Whyte, *Status of Women in Preindustrial Societies*.

16. Sjoberg, *Preindustrial City*, especially chaps. 1–4, 6. Pitt-Rivers, *Fate of Shechem*, 126–71; Elshtain, *Public Man, Private Woman*.

... to ensure that the rising officialdom is fully indoctrinated into the society's ideal norms."[17]

7. And finally, in the religious structure, leadership and participation in public worship settings is largely a male affair due to several contributing factors including the general lack of formal education on the part of women,[18] practices of female seclusion, the close relationship of religion to the political order among the elite,[19] and an ideology of the household that involves the dyadic nature of the husband/ wife relationship in which the husband, the superior member of the dyad, represents his wife and family in public matters. A wife is embedded in her husband.[20] The Greek example perhaps best contrasts the *polis*, "the reality of a structured body politic," and the *oikos*, the private household that includes a "world of familial and economic relations."[21] It also illustrates that limited literacy largely for domestic purposes was fostered among women.[22] Roman society apparently was somewhat less male dominated than the Greek and Israelite examples.[23] Even so, our model of women in the political, education, and religious structures remains a viable working model.

A Microwitness—The Mishnah

Evidence for the "advancement" of the status and roles of women within Judaism during the period near the first century is well known.[24] Some Israelite women obtained the right to divorce,[25] were "leaders," "elders," and

---

17. Ibid., 301.

18. Ferguson, *Backgrounds of Early Christianity*; Sjoberg, *Preindustrial City*.

19. Lenski and Lenski, *Human Societies* (1982).

20. Malina, *The New Testament World*, 42, 48, 145, 149.

21. Elshtain, *Public Man, Private Woman*, 12.

22. Ferguson, *Backgrounds of Early Christianity*, 83–87.

23. Balch and Osiek, *Families in the New Testament*, chap. 2–3.

24. The notion that women in general in advanced agrarian societies are considered to be property must be questioned. In the Israelite example Bird states that, "although wives were included among a man's possessions, they were not reckoned as property ("Women [OT]," 956); see Meyers, *Discovering Eve*, and Trible, *Texts of Terror*. The creation stories in Genesis make clear that both men and women are created in God's image (Gen 1:27), with no suggestion of subordination (Gen 5:2). See King and Stager, *Life in Ancient Israel*, 49–50.

25. Brooten, "Jewish Women's History in the Roman Period," 25.

"mothers of synagogues,"[26] although the data are problematic concerning whether their social and religious privileges included a liturgical function.[27] Apparently, they also prayed (silently) in synagogues[28] and a few were educated in philosophy.[29] Some Greek and Roman women became proselytes to Judaism[30] and Israelite women and children were present at the Passover Seder meal.[31] Within the *Therapeutai* Society women studied philosophy and shared communal meals with men.[32] Documentation by Philo (*Spec.* 3.169–72) and Ben Sira (31:12—32:9), conservative if not misogynist males, suggests some women had moved beyond stereotypical practices.[33]

With respect to the public domain such advancements apparently were not the norm within the early rabbinical movement. Indeed, Judith Wegner establishes that even women independent of male authority never won full equality with men because the sages of the Mishnah conspired to exclude them all from the public domain.[34] What then was the mishnaic disposition and practice toward women in public religious settings?

Mishnaic law concerning the status of women in the public sector was rooted primarily in the Priestly Code of Leviticus and Numbers, where a far-reaching subtle but major gender distinction governed those

26. Ibid., 26; Kraemer, "Hellenistic Jewish Women"; idem, "Non-Literary Evidence for Jewish Women in Rome and Egypt"; idem, "Monastic Jewish Women in Graeco-Roman Egypt."

27. Applebaum, "The Organization of the Jewish Communities in the Diaspora," 464–503; Safrai, "Jewish Self Government," 412–17; Tomson, *Paul and the Jewish Law*, 134.

28. Tomson, *Paul and the Jewish Law*, 134.

29. Brooten, "Jewish Women's History," 26; Kraemer, "Hellenistic Jewish Women"; idem, "Non-Literary Evidence for Jewish Women"; and idem, "Monastic Jewish Women in Graeco-Roman Egypt."

30. Balsdon, *Roman Women*; Cantarella, *Pandora's Daughters*; Brooten, "Jewish Women's History in the Roman Period," 27; idem, *Women Leaders in the Ancient Synagogue*, 144–47.

31. Corley, "Were the Women around Jesus Really Prostitutes?" 514–15; *Private Women, Public Meals*, 69; Stein, "The Influence of Symposia Literature," 29–33; Smith, "Social Obligation in the Context of Communal Meals," 178; Bahr, "The Seder of Passover and the Eucharistic Words," 181.

32. Kraemer, "Monastic Jewish Women in Graeco-Roman Egypt," 347–48, idem, *Her Share of the Blessings*, 113–17.

33. Corley, "Were the Women around Jesus Really Prostitutes?" 518–19.

34. Wegner, *Chattel or Person?* 145.

qualified to come before the Lord. Only men (note the exception of the case of an unfaithful wife in Numbers 5:11–31) could do so (Lev 15:14). Women, instead, brought their offerings "to the priest at the entrance to the Tent of Meeting" (Lev 15:29), who, in turn, went "before the Lord" on their behalf (Lev 15:29, 30). Out of this fundamental distinction emanated a number of exclusions and/or exemptions of women from most public cultic and religious practices in mishnaic culture such as the following:

1. being numbered in Israel's census,

2. slaughtering the paschal lamb,

3. performing priestly duties,

4. participating in the rite of the first fruits

5. giving the annual donation for the upkeep of the Sanctuary

6. circumcising and redeeming the firstborn

7. reciting the 'Shema,

8. wearing *tefillin* (phylacteries)

9. dwelling in *sukkah*,

10. reciting the required prayers

11. attending the three pilgrim feasts

12. reading from the Torah scroll before the assembly

It should be noted that an exemption (a matter that is not required) is not the same as an exclusion (a matter that is required). Exemptions can be waived, but for all practical purposes exemptions implied prohibitions; they therefore prevented women "from entering the public domain of religious practice."[35] This underlying presumption now is explored through four gender-specific realities and/or suppositions.

Public Census of the Israelite Community

Women along with slaves and/or minors were not numbered in the public census of Israel (*m. Sheq.* 1:3b). The counting of Israel (Num 1:2), the basis for defining the Israelite community authorized to come before the Lord, was reserved for only male Levites, Israelites, proselytes, and freed slaves (Exod 30:11–16; Num 1:2; *m. Sheq.* 1:3a). The language of the cen-

35. Wegner, *Chattel or Person?* 152.

sus is unmistakably gender and age specific. Based on the households of the fathers, "every male, head by head, from twenty years old and upward, any in Israel who is able to go forth to war" (Num 1:2–3) was counted. For example, in the census Israelite women, even though born in Israelite homes, lacked a social status comparable to male proselytes and freedmen whose public standing was achieved after birth.[36] Accordingly, women were exempted from making the half shekel donation to the Sanctuary prescribed in Exodus 30:13–14 because, the learned ones later reasoned, "these were not included in the census (Num 1:2)" (*m. Sheq.* 1:3b).

Heads of Israelite Households

Women did not legally qualify to occupy the position as leaders of Israelite households and thus could not perform religious rituals reserved for the household head. After all, it was reasoned, in all but two of the numerous scriptural references to Israelite parents in the Pentateuch, the "father precedes the mother everywhere [that Scripture mentions them]" (*m. Ker.* 6:9a). Of the two exceptions (Lev 19:3; 21:2) only one (19:3) was deemed significant because it accented the responsibility of children to honor mothers as well as fathers (*m. Ker.* 6:9a-e). Even though mothers were to be honored, they could not perform "religious duties that devolve upon the paterfamilias as head of household."[37]

This thinking manifested itself in two significant religious rites: the slaughtering of the paschal lamb (Exod 12:3) and the annual offering of the rite of the first fruits (Deut 26:1–11). The paschal lamb was to be slaughtered only by the male household head: "Every man a lamb according to their fathers' houses, a lamb for a household" (Exod 12:3; *m. Pesah.* 8:1a-b, 7a-d). Such was the case even if a woman was a widow, a divorcee, or an emancipated woman living alone.[38] Women ate the paschal sacrifice in the houses of either their husbands or their fathers (*m. Pesah* 8:1a-b) but could not constitute a fellowship group for the observance of the paschal sacrifice, since they were classified with slaves and/or minors (*m. Pesah.* 8:7d). Similarly, women could not make the annual donation of the rite of first fruits (Deut 26:1–11), because, the sages maintained, "they cannot [legally] declare (Deut 26:10), 'The first fruits of the soil which

36. Ibid., 149–50.

37. Ibid., 148.

38. Ibid.

you, O LORD, have given me'" (*m. Bikk.* 1:5b). Wegner explains, "God gave the Land of Canaan as a heritage to the Children of Israel (Deut 26:1). But women possessed no right of inheritance at the time [before the enactment of the rule in Num 27:8], so women landowners . . . could not claim that 'the soil' was originally given to them."[39]

Relegation to the Domestic Sphere

Although the principle is not explicitly stated—i.e., that domestic status and roles exempt women from public rites—women were in fact excused from most public cultic rites performed at specified times, such as reciting the *Shema'*, binding *tefillin*, hearing the *shofar*, or dwelling in the *sukkah*, probably because of their obligations and limitations within the domestic sphere.[40] Male supremacy is explicitly emphasized, especially in the case of dwelling in the *sukkah*. In this instance, mishnaic tradition held that minor boys no longer in need of constant maternal care and newborn sons were obligated (*m. Sukk.* 2:8b, c). Wegner, commenting on the newborn son, states:

> It would be hard to find a more graphic illustration of the superiority of the male than to insist that from the moment of birth he incurs more religious duties (hence more privileges) than his own mother, a grown woman. This rule reflects the boy's great potential; the passage of time will eventually turn him—but never his mother—into a full person in the mishnaic system.[41]

Other gender-specific exemptions include circumcision or redeeming the firstborn (*m. Qidd.* 1:7), cutting the hair or beard (Lev 19:27; *m. Qidd.* 1:7), contamination as the result of contact with the dead (priestly prohibition) (Lev 21:1; *m. Qidd.* 1:7d), most laws of sacrifice in the Priestly Code (*m. Qidd.* 1:8a), except the meal offering of the suspected adulteress and the female Nazirite (*m. Qidd.* 1:8b), attendance at the three pilgrim festivals to Jerusalem: Passover, Weeks, and Booths (Exod 23:14; Deut 16:16; *m. Hag.* 1:1a-b), and rites connected with a newborn son (*m. Sukk.* 2:8c). Finally, three time-contingent cultic duties incumbent on men but to be performed by women were (1) laws concerning the menstruant (*m. Shabb.* 2:6c; Lev 15:19–30; 18:19; 20:18), (2) the law of separating the

---

39. Ibid., 149.
40. Ibid., 150–53; *m. Qidd.* 1:7c.
41. Wegner, *Chattel or Person?*, 153.

dough offering (*m. Shabb.* 2:6c; Num 15:17–21), and (3) lighting of the Sabbath lamp (*m. Shabb.* 2:6d). Yet a wife's neglect of these duties made her husband a transgressor.[42]

It was not until the fourteenth century that the exemptions mentioned were given a domestic justification, but Wegner believes the state of affairs existed much earlier and grew out of the assumption of a woman's "value as an enabler (the 'fitting helper' of Gen 2:18)."[43] If so, the rationale not only defined a woman's primary social sphere, the home, but freed "her man from domestic chores that might impede his own performance of Scripture's precepts."[44] An economic incentive probably was involved because a woman's assigned tasks of spinning and weaving provided income for her husband (*m. Ketub.* 5:5). Wegner states: "If she drops her work three times a day to run to synagogue her output will surely suffer; and her husband has a personal stake in this because the law assigns to him the proceeds of her labor (*m. Ketub.* 6:1)."[45] In the end, the granting of exemptions restricted a woman's public participation in the cultus by entrenching her status and role(s) within the private domestic sphere.

Participation in Synagogue Worship

As noted,[46] women participated with men in community worship, prayed "along with men in the main room,"[47] on occasion served as "leaders," "elders," and "mothers of synagogues,"[48] and were qualified at least in principle (nothing is said for or against women's eligibility) to read publicly from the Torah scroll.[49] Conversely, a Tosefta reference states, "[But] one does not bring a woman to read [the Torah] in public" (*t. Meg.* 3:11b), and a Babylonian Talmud citation affirms, "But the sages ruled that a woman should not read from the Torah because of the dignity of the congregation (*mispenei kebod ha-sibbur*; *b. Meg.* 23a). Tomson interprets the statements, "In other words they are not accepted 'as deputy of the

42. Ibid., 155.

43. Ibid., 151.

44. Ibid.

45. Ibid.

46. Josephus, *Ant.*, 16:164; Loewe, *The Position of Women in Judaism*, 44; Tomson, *Paul and the Jewish Law*, 134.

47. Tomson, *Paul and the Jewish Law*, 134.

48. Brooten, *Women Leaders in the Ancient Synagogue*, 103–47.

49. Wegner, *Chattel or Person*, 158; *m. Meg.* 2:4.

community' (*shaliah tsibbur*) to pray or read in the name of the community."[50] Employing typical mishnaic reasoning, some commentaries indicate a woman did not have a biblical obligation to read and therefore was unable to fulfill the obligation of the community.[51] Apparently, a midrash on Deut 22:16 (*Sif. Deut.* 235, p. 269) states the rule: "Women have no authority to speak in the name of men," which to Tomson means "women could not officiate because of legal incompetence."[52] Understood in light of the disposition for the "general subordination of women" (*m. Abot* 15; *Ket.* 4:4; *Sota* 3:8) as a prevailing practice, women probably did not read the Torah.[53]

A similar ambiguity involved the study of Torah by women. Since Torah study was not time-contingent, women as Israelites were obligated in principle to its study. Rabbis differed, however, as to whether women should do so. Ben Azzai said, "A man is obligated to teach his daughter the law [Torah] so that if she has to drink, she may know that the merit [acquired by good deeds, etc.] holds her punishment in abeyance" (*m. Sota* 3:4a). Eliezer said, "If anyone teaches his daughter the law [Torah], it is as though he taught her lasciviousness" (ibid.). Both rabbis, however, probably used the term Torah in a more limited sense as referring to the law of ordeal.[54] When another term is used for Scripture (*miqra*), a father had no duty, according to the learned, to teach both his sons and daughters (*m. Ned.* 4:3a-c). But two factors should be kept in mind: (1) fathers taught their daughters (or sons) in the home, a private setting; and (2) a daughter might be married by the age of twelve, after which she came under the authority of her husband and consequently cared for her home and children.[55] Later, the Babylonian Talmud argued for the exclusion of women's study of sacred texts.[56] And even later, says Wegner, Maimonides treated "the exclusion of women from Torah study as an established rule."[57] Perhaps the exemption and/or exclusion of women from Torah study developed over time. The few, who studied, however, did not do so

---

50. Tomson, *Paul and the Jewish Law,* 134.

51. Albeck, *Introduction to the Mishnah;* see *m. Meg.*4:6 .

52. Tomson, *Paul and the Jewish Law,* 134, n. 214.

53. Ibid.

54. Wegner, *Chattel or Person?* 161.

55. Ibid., 150–53; Hopkins, "The Age of Roman Girls at Marriage," 309–27.

56. Biale, *Women and Jewish Law,* 33; *b. Qidd.* 29bff.

57. Wegner, *Chattel or Person?* 243, n. 249.

with men.[58] Wegner summarizes: "Certainly the sages evince a desire to restrain women from active participation in communal religious functions; and following the destruction of the Temple and the cessation of sacrifice, Torah reading at synagogue worship became the chief religious exercise in the public domain."[59] The *Encyclopedia Judaica* states, "There was general agreement that a woman was not obliged to study Torah."[60]

Women's participation alongside men in the public religious sphere of mishnaic culture was minimal. Through the utilization of Scripture the early rabbinical movement established a religious cultural tradition that exempted and/or excluded women. Even the most elite women, Wegner maintains, were "not allowed to participate in the public culture of the Israelite community."[61] Tomson concludes that women "attended synagogue but prayed silently and did not officiate."[62]

The absence of women in the public sphere of the mishnaic system parallels the basic status and behavior of women in an advanced agrarian society. But is this the case for the Gospel of Matthew? Even though Matthew's community is located in an advanced agrarian society and has its roots in the Israelite heritage, it brings from its cradle of tradition things "new and old" (13:52). There is no mention of circumcision. Food laws are abrogated. The moral teachings of Jesus are highlighted. In reference to the place of women in public settings, Matthew does seem to bring out that which is new and old, but the old apparently is fulfilled in what is new—the surrogate family of the kingdom of heaven stands over and against the household of an advanced agrarian society. As the writing is examined more closely, the first step is to determine the gender makeup of three groups: the disciples, the crowds, and the religious authorities.

GENDER ANALYSIS OF THE DISCIPLES, THE CROWDS, AND THE RELIGIOUS AUTHORITIES

Of the three groups present in public settings in Matthew (the disciples, the crowds, and the religious authorities), only one, the religious authori-

---

58. Ibid., 162.
59. Ibid., 159.
60. "Women," in *Encyclopedia Judaica*, 16:626.
61. Wegner, *Chattel or Person?* 146.
62. Tomson, *Paul and the Jewish Law*, 134.

ties, is clearly male. The gender identity of the disciples and the crowds is more problematic.

The Disciples

In Matthean studies the identity of the disciples is a debated issue that hinges on the use of the phrase "the disciples," "his disciples" (or the equivalent)[63] and the verbs *mathēteúein* ("to disciple" or "to train"), *ákoloutheîn* ("to follow"), and *diakoneîn* ("to serve"). A number of scholars[64] think that Matthew's usage of the phrase "the disciples" or "his disciples" refer only to the Twelve or their equivalent. Their argument is based principally on the use of the above phrases and the metaphorical use of the verb "to follow" to denote "coming or going after a person as his disciple."[65] Others think that the disciples encompass a larger, more inclusive group.[66] Their argument is based principally on a different understanding and usage of the verb "to follow," so as to encompass the women mentioned in Matthew 27:55–57 and their service as ministry. They also argue that although the above phrases may consistently refer to the Twelve, the matter is either unimportant to Matthew[67] or the disciples are a transparency for the later Matthean community which certainly included women.[68] The debate is significant because it raises the question of the status of women in Matthew.

Matthew, this study affirms, uses the phrases "the disciples" and "his disciples" in a restrictive sense to refer to the circle of male followers chosen by Jesus. His usage, however, does not denigrate other members of Matthew's community, that is, suggest that they are not followers, but underscores the authority and responsibility of the teaching ministry, which apparently belongs to those known in the Gospel as "the disciples." The argument is as follows:

---

63. Wilkins, *The Concept of Disciple in Matthew's Gospel.*

64. Anderson, "Matthew: Gender and Reading"; Wire, "Gender Roles in a Scribal Community"; Kingsbury, "The Title 'Son of David' in Matthew's Gospel," 599–600.

65. Arndt and Gingrich, *A Greek-English Lexicon of the New Testament*, 30.

66. Corley, *Private Women, Public Meals*; Ulrich Luz, "Die Junger im Matthäusevangelium," 141–71; Sheridan, "Disciples and Discipleship in Matthew and Luke," 235–55; Theimann, "The Unnamed Woman at Bethany," 179–88.

67. Luz, "Die Junger," 99.

68. Schweizer, "Matthew's Church," 136–37.

1. 1. The term *disciple(s)* almost always (exceptions are 8:21; 10:24, 42; 27:57) refers to the Twelve or a lesser number within that number. This is true whether the designation used is "the disciples," "his disciples," "his twelve disciples," or a smaller number within the immediate chosen circle.[69] The first exception (8:21) may refer to one who eventually became one of the Twelve.[70]

FIGURE 3.1: DISCIPLES IN MATTHEW

"His Disciples"	"The Disciples"	"His Twelve Disciples"
5:1; 8:23; 9:10, 11, 14 ("your"), 19, 37; 10:1; 11:1; 12:1, 49; 13:36; 15:23, 32; 16:13, 21, 24 19:23, 25; 23:1; 24:1; 26:1, 36; 27:64 (opinion of others); 28:7, 8, 13 (opinion of others), 16.	13:10; 14:15, 19, 22, 26; 15:12, 33, 36; 16:5; 17:6, 10, 19; 18:1; 19:10, 13, 25; 21:6, 20; 24:3; 26:8, 17, 19, 20, 26, 40, 45, 56.	10:1; 11:1; 26:20
		Smaller Number
		21:2 (two disciples)
		28:16 (eleven disciples)

The exceptions of 10:24, 42 are indefinite in nature, being translated "a disciple." Matthew's usage stands in contrast, for example, to that of Luke, who applies the designation to a wider, more inclusive group (Luke 6:13; see v. 17). The last Matthean reference is to Joseph from Arimathea (27:57), a male figure who appears and then disappears in Matthew's story.

2. Matthew's employment of the phrases is heightened by the manner in which Jesus calls his disciples. In contrast to the "Israelite Model" whereby a prospective disciple seeks a teacher (Matt 8:19),[71] Jesus deliberately calls "his disciples" (Matt 4:18–23; 9:9; 10:1–4) and consistently "depicts Jesus as the person who authoritatively issues the summons."[72] The perception of Jesus as the teacher of his chosen followers is so great (10:24; 23:8) that it is accepted by the disciples of John (9:14) and the Israelite leaders (8:19; 9; 11; 12:38; 17:24;

69. Kingsbury, "The Title 'Son of David' in Matthew's Gospel," 599–600.

70. Wire, "Gender Roles," 103, n. 57.

71. Bornkamm, et al., *Tradition and Interpretation in Matthew*, 37; Franzmann, *Follow Me*, 2; Hengel, *Nachfolge und Charisma*, 16–17.

72. Kingsbury, "The Verb ἀκολουθεῖν," 60.

19:16; 22:15–16, 23–24). This is true even though the disciples and others who approach Jesus in faith—Judas being the exception that strengthens the case (26:25, 49)—refer to him as "Lord" and not as "Teacher" or "Rabbi."[73] Matthew's only reference to "apostles" (10:2) seems to highlight the twelve disciples' commission to proclaim "the good news of the kingdom" (9:35), healing (9:27–31), raising the dead (9:18–26), cleansing lepers (8:1–4), casting out demons (9:22–24). They are literally the "sent ones."

3. The disciples' teaching responsibility is developed by Matthew in a manner not found in the other Synoptic Gospels. In common with Mark and Luke, Jesus sends the Twelve in the limited commission to preach and to heal (10:7, 8). But in the closing verses of the Parable Discourse, Matthew's special emphasis becomes clear. Only Matthew emphasizes that Jesus, having taught the crowds (13:1–35), "Left the crowds and went into the house. And his disciples came to him saying, 'Explain to us the parable of the weeds of the field'" (13:36). Following Jesus' explanation and the telling of three additional parables, he asks the disciples pointedly if they understand his teachings. When they answer "Yes" (13:51), Jesus makes the distinctive Matthean statement to them: "Therefore every scribe who has been trained for the kingdom of heaven is like a householder who brings out of his treasure what is new and what is old" (13:52; see 8:19–22). The phrase probably does not refer to Israelite scribes who became followers of the kingdom of God.[74] True, the term *grammateus* can have a nontechnical meaning and would in this sense identify teachers later in the Matthean community, perhaps not as a technical designation of a vocation, but still those nevertheless who would be trained as exegetes and teachers of Scripture. Further, Peter, as leader among the disciples, is given the power to "bind" and to "loose," that is, he has authority to "forbid" and "permit" some action about which a question has arisen (16:19). Later (18:18) the authority of binding and loosing is conferred upon the community. The disciples' teaching responsibility is climaxed in the scene of the Great Commission (28:16–20), when Jesus directs the eleven dis-

---

73. Bornkamm, *Tradition and Interpretation in Matthew*, 38; Kingsbury, "The Verb ἀκολουθεῖν," 60, n. 29.

74. See Luz, *Matthew 8–20*, 286, n. 18.

ciples (28:16) to meet him at the mountain in Galilee (perhaps an echo of the setting of the Sermon on the Mount) and commissions them to make disciples and to "teach them to observe all that I have commanded you" (28:20).

Although Matthew does not specify how later followers will carry on the role of the Eleven, a clue may be found in the verb *mathēteuein*, "to disciple" or "to train." This verb is used only in Matthew, three times (13:52; 27:57; 28:19). The first instance (13:52) may be a self-portrait of the Evangelist,[75] but may have also a wider application to one trained like the disciples. The second reference (27:57) is to Joseph of Arimathea, who "was a disciple of Jesus." Joseph's specified task, as noted above, is to bury Jesus. He appears and disappears in this sole pericope. Nothing indicates a teaching role for him. The third reference (28:19) is to those made disciples by the teaching of the disciples. Wire states: "Clearly others to come will be given training and expected to bear responsibility, but it is in some derived sense, as if as disciples of the disciples."[76]

4. Women are not called or named among Jesus' disciples (the Twelve), and there is no evidence they served as teachers (exegetical experts) in the Matthean community. Women were, as the four stories will demonstrate, full members of the kingdom or models for "the disciples." Therefore, their stories are essential to Jesus' critique of the disciples who are also male teachers within the community. The Canaanite woman (15:21–28) identifies Jesus as "Son of David," accepts his mission, asks for mercy, acknowledges him as Lord, is acknowledged as a woman of great faith, and is contrasted with the disciples who desire to send her away. The woman who suffers from a hemorrhage (9:20–22) is healed because of her faith. Wire states: "Women are prominent in the stories demonstrating faith, perhaps again because exemplary faith is considered most wonderful where least expected."[77] Peter's mother-in-law (8:14–15), the woman who anointed Jesus's body at the meal setting at Simon's house (26:6–13), and the women around Jesus (27:55–56) all minister to him. Harlots, Jesus says, "go into the kingdom of God" before the male religious

75. Harrington, *Gospel of Matthew*, 208.
76. Wire, "Gender Roles," 103.
77. Ibid., 104.

authorities (21:31). They belong to a catalog of faithful heroines like Tamar (1:3), Rahab (1:5), Ruth (1:5), and the wife of Uriah (1:6). In making this comparison we do not affirm that the four women of the genealogy and Mary are harlots. In contrast to these women of great faith, the disciples are characterized as "men of little faith" (6:30; 8:26; 16:8; 17:19–20); and Peter, their leader, is singled out as a man of "little faith" (14:31). In addition, Peter is rebuked by Jesus (16:22–23), and his denial of Jesus (26:33–35, 69–75) is never glossed over by Matthew. The disciples are bluntly criticized by Jesus for being indignant toward the woman who anointed Jesus with expensive perfume (26:6–13). The disciples, not the women, stop short of following Jesus to the cross (26:56; 27:55–57). The women, not the disciples (chap. 28), witness the empty tomb, convey the news of Jesus' resurrection to the disciples, and worship Jesus when they meet him (28:9). In contrast, some of the disciples doubt to the end (28:17). Women are part of Matthew's esteemed "little ones" and thus illustrate his great reversal. They are the ones who provide a model of greatness, faith and faithfulness in the kingdom of heaven. Never are the disciples "to despise one of these little ones" (18:10). When they stray, they are to be found (18:12). The disciples may be a transparency for Matthew's community,[78] but it may be the believers from among the crowds that are the better and most faithful example of lucidity for what the community should be like.[79] Besides Jesus, they are the standard by which the disciples are measured.

Wire probably is on track in distinguishing two narrative roles in Matthew—that of the disciples, and that of the people Jesus heals or helps.[80] She gives warning that the two roles should not be collapsed. Referring to the women, she states, "The sentences carried over from Mark that make women the witnesses to Jesus' death, burial, and empty tomb do not make them disciples, and even when this Gospel tells that Jesus appears first to the women, it is to send them to inform the disciples/his brethren (27:55–56, 61; 28:1–8)."[81] It should be noted that men as well as women

78. Luz, "Die Jünger," 109; Schweizer, "Matthew's Church," 136–37.

79. Care needs to be given. There are different kinds of crowds in Matthew. See Duling, "The Therapeutic Son of David."

80. Wire, "Gender Roles," 102–6.

81. Ibid., 103.

do not belong to the character group known as disciples in Matthew's gospel. Nevertheless, the gender makeup of those specifically designated as disciples is male. They are the ones who appear in the various public teaching settings of this Gospel.

The Crowds

The crowds, another major public character group,[82] follow Jesus in a literal sense and are repeatedly referred to as "great crowds."[83] Jesus speaks to and teaches the crowds in public settings,[84] but, as we might expect, little is said of their gender.

What, then, can be said of their identity? First, the woman who suffered from a continuous hemorrhage, Mark affirms, pursues Jesus among the throng (5:30).[85] Second, there are women and children present in the feeding of the five thousand and the four thousand (14:13–21; 15:29–39). Only Matthew tells his readers that those who ate were "five thousand men" and "four thousand men," adding in each case "besides women and children" (14:21; 15:38). Kathleen Corley[86] believes that in the ambiance of the two scenes, the singular references to women and children, and the similarity of vocabulary to the account of the Lord's Supper underscore "a large family celebration"[87] and a foreshadowing of the "Eucharists of the Matthean community."[88] The crowds do provide a major component in a demographic profile of Matthew's community. Corley believes they can be likened to the household of Joseph, Mary, and Jesus.[89] It should be remembered, however, that the story of the "holy household" is framed by an advanced agrarian social structure even though Mary's conception is extraordinary.[90] Also, the census language in the feeding scenes is androcentric. Apparently, it follows Israelite census practices to muster an army.

82. Ibid..; Minear, "The Disciples and the Crowds in the Gospel of Matthew," 28–44; Kingsbury, "The Title 'Son of David' in Matthew's Gospel," 599–600.

83. 4:25; 8:1, 10; 12:15; 14:13–14; 19:2; 20:29; 21:9.

84. 4:23, 25; 5:1; 7:28; 11:7; 12:46; 13:2, 10, 34; 15:10; 22:33; 23:1.

85. Matthew omits the reference to the crowds.

86. Corley, *Private Women, Public Meals,* 160–64.

87. Ibid., 160.

88. Ibid., 161.

89. Ibid.

90. Anderson, "Mary's Difference," 190.

Women were excluded from this service, probably because they might be unclean (menstruating) and could not be called up to participate in that religious exercise. Wars were a politico-religious ceremony. Matthew identifies two unequal groups, reflective of the dyadic relations in that social world. The superior group is men—mentioned first and numbered. The inferior group is women and children—not counted and mentioned last. Possible parallels are the census of the tribes (Num 1:1–54), the numbering of the first return (Neh 7:6–73; Ezra 2:1–70), and the mishnaic tradition (*m. Sheq.* 2a, b). In these examples only men are numbered except for the census of the first return, where at the end of the census and in a secondary position alongside other possessions—livestock, female slaves, and singers—women are counted but lumped together with their male counterparts (Neh 7:66–67; Ezra 2:64–65). Apparently, women and children reclined with men at the feeding scenes, and this is extraordinary (14:19)[91] but fails to demonstrate necessarily in itself that Matthew is the most egalitarian among the Synoptic Gospels. The writing still reflects its social world in which women and children hold an inferior status in comparison to men.

Third, and finally, the presence of prostitutes among the crowds may be safely assumed, apparently a matter dear to Matthew's heart.[92] "Matthew," Corley notes, "is the only Synoptic Gospel that states that 'prostitutes' (*pornai*), along with 'tax-collectors,' will enter the 'kingdom of God.'"[93] The two groups—tax collectors and prostitutes, are a rare gender-specific pair found only in Matthew. Both belong to the social group known as "sinners" (9:9–13) and as we shall see later they are part of a social profile of Matthew's community. Finally, prostitutes probably are a number of "homeless" among the crowds, persons cut off from the household, the basic social unit of the society, who have now found a new dwelling in Matthew's community. Probably there are no women from among the elite present among the crowds.

The gender of the three character groups is now identified: the Jewish religious leaders and Jesus' disciples are male, the crowds are mixed multitudes but predominantly male.

---

91. Corley, *Private Women, Public Meals*, 161.

92. Ibid., 147, 152–58.

93. Ibid., 152.

TEACHING DATA IN PUBLIC SETTINGS

But does teaching data in public settings—that is, locations where the disciples, the crowds, and/or Judean religious leaders are taught by Jesus and/or enter into confrontational dialogue with him—support the gender analysis to this point? Three public settings are now examined: the Sermon on the Mount (5:1—7:29, the Parables Discourse (13:1–52), and the final controversies in the temple (21:23—23:39) as representative samples. Appropriate questions include the following: Are the materials primarily directed to men or to women? Do topics and issues addressed say anything about the gender of the audience? Can anything be detected in the organization, language, images, and illustrations that indicates the gender to which the teachings are directed and the teaching role of the disciples? Are the issues for the most part gender-specific?

The Sermon on the Mount (5:1—7:29)

In the Sermon on the Mount Jesus appears as a teacher (5:2) who instructs his disciples and the crowds (5:1–2; 7:28). Much of the instruction is set against the teachings and practices of the scribes and Pharisees. The public character of the sermon is identified by its physical setting, the open area of the mountain (5:1), and the presence of the crowds (5:1; 7:28). The sermon's data is explored from four perspectives: (1) its organization, (2) issues, references, images, and illustrations used, (3) the presence of gender-specific terminology, and (4) the place of women in Jesus' teaching.

Organization

According to Jeremias,[94] the sermon's organization turns on the three groups mentioned in chapter 5: the scribes, the Pharisees, and the disciples (5:17–20). Accordingly, issues and examples of scribal righteousness are depicted in the six antitheses (5:21–48). Pharisaic righteousness is illustrated in the three acts of religious devotion: almsgiving, prayer, and fasting (6:1–18). The remainder of the discourse (6:19—7:27) is targeted to the disciples (and the crowds), since the scribes and the Pharisees no longer constitute a direct basis for comparison. The sermon's organization is oriented for males who are concerned for the law and its practice. Both the crowds and the disciples are Jesus' auditors, but the inner group in a

---

94. Jeremias, *The Sermon on the Mount*, 22–23.

concentric pattern is the disciples. It is as if Jesus teaches the crowds by teaching the disciples who are to serve as a counterpart to the scribes and the Pharisees.

References, Images, Issues, and Illustrations

Scribal issues in the six antitheses—murder, adultery, divorce, swearing, retaliation, and the love of enemies (5:21–48)—largely involve male concerns. The second and third examples (adultery and divorce) are male-centered. Concerning adultery, it is a man who looks after a woman lustfully (5:27–30) and it is a woman's husband who is offended (Deut 22:22–24). Jesus' teaching attacks core structures of gender-specific power in advanced agrarian societies by exposing rapacious male behaviors, reining in male supremacy, and authorizing a different basis for male-female relations. One key word is "heart" (5:28), the region of thought, intentions, and moral disposition, a leading concern for Matthew (5:8; 9:4; 11:29; 12:34; cf. Pss 24:3–4; 15:2). Another key word is "lust," a term that points to the more fundamental offense, idolatry (Job 31:1). Concerning divorce, it is a husband who initiates the divorce proceeding, gives his wife a certificate of divorce (5:31–32; Deut 24:1), and charges her with sexual irregularity ("ground of unchastity"). A divorce without justifiable reason causes a woman to commit adultery (5:32), and a man who marries a divorced woman commits adultery (5:32). These issues manifest a male perspective, and the language echoes the debates between the Schools of Shammai and Hillel and the teachings of Rabbi Aqiba.[95] Jesus' interpretation of the Deuteronomistic regulation (24:1–14) rejects the unlimited power of males to dismiss/divorce their wives capriciously. The repeated expression "but I say to you" (5:27–32) constitutes a direct and actual application to the audience at hand. As a result, these two prohibitions serve to protect women so vulnerable to male abuse.

Other examples involve issues and contain images and/or illustrations that best fit a male-centered audience. The question of murder (5:21–26) draws upon illustrations from the male dominated legal, cultic, and penal realms. The image of the court includes references to the "judgment" and "the council" (5:22), "the judge," and "the court" (5:25). Reconciliation to a "brother" precedes the cultic act of offering a gift at the altar (5:23–24). Penal images include the "guard" and being "put in prison" for a failure to

---

95. Manson, *The Teaching of Jesus*, 292–94; see Matt 19:3–9.

pay debts (5:25; see 18:34). The fifth antithesis, retaliation, includes five illustrations most applicable to males: (1) a violent act of striking the face (5:39), (2) a lawsuit (5:40), (3) forced bearing of burdens for the military (5:41), (4) giving to beggars, and (5) lending money (5:42). The sixth antithesis, love of friends and enemies (5:43–47), includes references to "toll collectors" (5:46) and "brethren" (5:47), and ends "so that you may be sons of your Father who is in heaven" (5:45; cf. v. 48). The antitheses best fit the religious social world of Israelite males responsible for the understanding and practice of the law.

Pharisaic concerns (6:1–18) turn on a reversal of public gender expectations. The disciples are not to practice their piety before men to be seen by them (6:1). The "hypocrites" do their almsgiving and prayer in public places, the synagogues, and the streets (6:2, 5). They disfigure their faces to be seen by men (6:16). The disciples, faced with a sensitive issue for public-oriented males, are taught to give alms and pray "in secret," that is, in private (6:4, 6), and to fast without public notice, that is, not to "be seen by men" (6:18).

Two explicit male references are located in the third division of the discourse (6:19—7:27). First, Jesus describes the disciples as "men of little faith" (6:30), a phrase used by Matthew only in reference to the disciples (8:26; 14:31; 16:8; 17:19–20). Second, Jesus questions fathers over their concerns for their sons/children. "Or what man of you, if his son asks him for bread, will give him a stone? Or if he asks for a fish, will give him a serpent? If you, then, who are evil, know how to give good gifts to your children, how much more will your Father who is in heaven give good things to those who ask him!" (7:9–11).

Some images and illustrations make better sense if directed to men, such as the analogies of laying up treasures (6:19–21) and serving two masters (6:24). Anxiety over economic survival (6:25–33) is a concern for all household members, but especially for men as providers and protectors of their families. A reference made to birds (6:26) draws upon an outdoor agricultural work image. Birds do not sow, reap, or gather into barns (6:26). Lilies are referred to in conjunction with spinning (6:28), the only reference to traditional women's activity.

The image of the speck and the log is combined with references to "your brother" (7:3–5). The final warning to hear and do the teaching of Jesus aptly compares two men who build their houses upon the rock or the sand (7:24–27). Although the data cited are representative and not exhaustive, they support the contention that the sermon is directed predominantly to males dedicated to the knowledge and practice of God's righteousness.

Gender-Specific Terminology

Although Matthew does use generic references (12:49; 25:40), the discourse abounds in apparent gender-specific vocabulary.[96] The disciples are to let their light shine before "men" (5:15). They are warned against practicing their piety before "men" (6:1) to be praised or seen by "men" (6:2, 5, 16, 17). They are to forgive "men" (6:14) and do to others what they wish "men" would do to them (7:12). Every person who is angry with a "brother" is liable to the council (5:22). Reconciliation with a "brother" takes precedence over making a gift at the altar (5:23). When the disciples salute only their own ("your brothers") they behave like non-Israelites (5:47). Judging others is illustrated by the speck in a "brother's" eye (7:3–5). Peacemakers are called "sons of God" (5:9), and disciples who love their enemies are "sons" of their "Father who is in heaven" (5:45). A "son" asks gifts from his father (7:9), and a man knows how to give good gifts to his son, his children (7:9, 11). Frequent references are made to God as the "heavenly father," "your father,"[97] and in one instance Jesus refers to God as "my father" (7:21).

The Place of Women in the Discourse

Only three references are made to women/wives (5:27, 31–32). The teaching on adultery and divorce underscores the esteem and dignity Jesus accords to women. His harsh criticisms of males assume the personhood of women. Women are not to be exploited or treated as chattel. Beyond the figure of spinning, no typical female image is found in the discourse.[98] Women probably are present among the crowds, but the teachings are directed to men.

96. We recognize that references to "men" can be gender inclusive. In this case the language appears gender-specific especially in light of our previous points.

97. 5:16, 45, 48; 6:1, 4, 6, 8, 9, 14, 15, 26, 32; 7:11.

98. Anderson, "Matthew: Gender and Reading," 27.

The Parables of the Kingdom (13:1–52)

Several matters about the Parables Discourse are noteworthy. First, as to the setting, Jesus is located both "outside the house" (13:1) and "in the house" (13:36), a public/private spatial distinction which divides the discourse. Outside the house Jesus is with "great crowds" (13:2) and has an exchange with the disciples (13:10–17), explaining to them why he speaks to the crowds in parables. The explanation seems to indicate that the disciples hear and accept the message about God's kingdom. According to their faith the disciples in this instance have access to deeper understanding. A deliberate break is made in verse thirty-six, at which time Jesus leaves the crowds and goes into the house where his disciples approach him. Outside the house Jesus sits in a boat as he teaches the multitudes standing on the beach (13:2). In the house, Jesus teaches the disciples privately. Only the disciples enter into dialogue with Jesus; the crowds listen in silence.

Second, the public teachings (13:2–9, 18–34) contain four parables appropriate for what might have been a mixed multitude, including women. The first three involve outdoor agricultural activities: the parables of the sower (13:3–9) and its interpretation (13:18–23), the weeds (13:24–30), and the mustard seed (13:31–32). The last parable, the leaven, compares the growth of the kingdom of heaven to a domestic procedure, a woman hiding leaven in flour (13:33). Twenty-nine verses are devoted to outdoor agricultural parables. Only one verse concerns an indoor domestic scene.

Third, the teachings of Jesus to the disciples in private are appropriate for a male audience. They include an explanation of the parable of the weeds (13:10–17, 36–43), followed by the parables of the hidden treasure (13:44), the pearl (13:45), and the net (13:47–50). The activities described (agriculture, business, and fishing) are typical of males. Finally, two appropriate images are used for the disciples in the closing words of the discourse (13:51–52), the first of a scribe who has been trained ("discipled") for the kingdom of heaven, and the second of a householder "who brings out of his treasure what is new and what is old" (13:52). The scribal image seems to join the disciples to Jesus' teaching ministry.

Similar results are obtained when the various parables are examined. In the public teachings principally to the crowds, the sower is a man (13:4). The work of plowing and a description of four types of soil, although understood by all, resonate with men. Major characters in the parable of the weeds (13:24–30) are a sower (13:24), a householder, and his servants (13:27). Illustrations of weeds and wheat growing together, reaping, binding, and gathering the weeds for burning and the wheat for storage particularize agricultural activities. In the parable of the mustard seed (13:31), the seed is sown by a man. A woman engaged in making bread (13:33), a singular feminine image, exemplifies a stereotypical feminine role.

In the private teachings to the disciples, the one who sows the seed is the "Son of man" (13:37), the good seed represents the "sons of the kingdom" (13:38), and the weeds signify "sons of the evil one" (13:38). The enemy is the devil (13:39), and the reapers are the angels (13:39). The righteous, Jesus affirms, "shine like the sun in the kingdom of their Father" (13:43). In the parables of the hidden treasure and the pearl of great price, a man finds treasure hidden in a field (13:44), and a merchant engages in commercial activity. Men draw up fish of every kind in the parable of the net (13:47, 48). The social data of the Parables Discourse point to a predominantly male-centered audience that distinguishes the disciples from the crowds as those who receive and understand Jesus' teachings.

Public Teaching in the Temple (21:12—23:39)

Our last teaching sample is located in a public setting, the temple, and involves at different points all three character groups. For the first time (among the samples) teachings are directed to the religious leaders. In the first section (21:12—22:46), various groups and one individual are mentioned, including "all who bought and sold" (21:12), the blind and the lame (21:14), the chief priests and scribes (21:15), children (21:15), the chief priests and the elders of the people (21:23), the Pharisees with the Herodians (22:15), and the Pharisees (22:41). Throughout the first section (21:23—22:46), the disciples and the crowds occupy a secondary position, almost as if they are not present. The second section (23:1–39) opens with teachings to "the crowds and his disciples," warning them about "the scribes and Pharisees" (23:1–12), and continues with a direct attack upon the scribes and Pharisees (23:13–36), identifying them as "blind guides' (23:16), "blind fools" (23:17), and "blind men" (23:19). Of all the individuals and/or groups mentioned, women may be found among the crowds and possibly among the blind and the lame (marginal persons) and the children (an inferior status group).

There are three types of teaching materials: confrontational dialogical exchanges, parables, and a series of polemical woes. A gender analysis reveals the following.

Confrontational Exchanges

Confrontational exchanges—the temple cleansing and its aftermath (21:12, 16, 23–27), paying taxes to Caesar (22:15–22), the question concerning the resurrection (22:23–33), the great commandment (22:34–40), and a question concerning David's son (22:41–46)—involve men. At least five indicators corroborate and/or enhance this assertion. First, since the temple is controlled by chief priests, the controversy over Jesus' authority to cleanse it is a male issue. Second, paying taxes to Caesar (22:15–22) primarily is the responsibility of men. Third, the controversy over a hypothetical Levirate marriage (22:23–33) centers on who is the husband, even though the story turns on a woman. Fourth, the summarization of the law (22:34–40) is a theological challenge for scribes and their followers. Finally, Jesus' question about David's son (22:41–46) calls into question matters about male linage and the lordship of the messiah.

Parables

Three parables are especially rich in male-oriented analogies and references. In the first (21:28–32), two sons are to work for their father in a vineyard, a story which revolves on the son who actually does the father's will (22:31). In the parable of the vineyard (21:33–41), a male householder plants a vineyard. Major characters in the story include tenants (21:33), servants (21:34), and the householder's son (21:37). A variety of violent images are used, including beating, stoning (21:35), and killing the son (21:38). A major issue is inheritance (21:38). In the third parable (22:1–14), a king gives a marriage feast for his son (22:1). The initial invitations are given to men, a fact revealed by the wording of the various rejections: "They made light of it and went off, one to his farm, another to his business, while the rest seized his servants, treated them shamefully, and killed them" (22:6). The king sends troops who destroy and burn the city of the murderers (22:7). Finally, at the wedding feast, a man is present who does not have a wedding garment (22:11). The attendants bind him and cast him out of the feast (22:13). The significant social reversal of inviting people from the streets (22:9–10) opens the way for the inclusion of marginal women. Even so, the three parables are stories about males told to a male audience.

Polemical Woes

The series of woes is introduced with warnings against emulating the practices of the scribes and Pharisees (23:1–11) and the passage con- cludes with Jesus' lament over the city of Jerusalem (23:37–39). The desire of the scribes and Pharisees to be seen by men in public places (23:5), that is, at feasts, in the synagogues, and in the market places (23:6) parallels material already noted from the Sermon on the Mount (6:1–18). Swearing (23:16–22), tithing (23:23), and the purification of cups and plates (23:25) are particular concerns of the scribes and Pharisees (23:23–26). They are described as being "sons of those who murdered the prophets" (23:31). The prophets, wise men, and scribes (23:34) may be leaders of the Matthean community. Women may be among the "prophets," but the "wise men" and "scribes" are probably male the latter possibly serving as a parallel to the disciples. Finally, male figures of the past, Abel and Zechariah the son of Barachiah, close the series of indictments (23:35).

A few women characters and female images appear. Harlots are mentioned in a positive light (21:31, 32), a woman is part of the story told by the Sadducees (22:23–33), and Jesus compares himself to a hen that gathers her brood under her wings as he weeps over the city of Jerusalem (23:37–39). No women are mentioned by name, but ten males are identi- fied: David, John, Caesar, Moses, Abraham, Isaac, Jacob, Abel, Zechariah, and Barachiah his father. The crowds and the disciples hear, observe, and receive Jesus' teachings, but only the disciples stand opposite to the scribes and the Pharisees. The disciples are to avoid the titles "rabbi," "father," and "master" so that Matthew's community can be a community of brothers.

The three public settings chosen for analysis do not exhaust such settings in Matthew. For example, synagogue scenes have been deliber- ately omitted because, out of nine references to the synagogue (4:23; 6:2, 5; 9:35; 10:17; 12:9; 13:54; 23:6, 34) only two (12:9 and 13:54) involve an actual incident. The controversies between Jesus and the authorities over the Beelzebul issue (12:22–50), the tradition of the elders (15:1–20), and the question of divorce (19:3–9), followed by the exchange between Jesus and the disciples over voluntary celibacy in the service of God's king- dom (19:10–12), seem to parallel our findings. Private discourses to the disciples (10:1—11:1; 18:1—19:1; 24:1—25:46) also have been omitted. With the possible exception of the parable of the virgins, the data of these teachings seems to confirm the assertion that the audiences are primarily male and the teachings are tailored for the audience.

EVALUATION

Matthew's portrayal of the religious authorities as a character group parallels advanced agrarian social realities. They are male, a social verity tied to their role identities (scribes, Pharisees, et al.) and reinforced by their orientation to the law and their manner of framing questions and religious issues. For example, the divorce question is stated from the perspective of males and is placed within the debate of the rabbinical schools of Shammai and Hillel and the teachings of Rabbi Aqiba. Although the public status and behavior of women as summarized in the mishnaic writings is never an issue in public settings like the synagogue and the temple, the writing's pervasive androcentrism indicates the authorities are at home in a public-centered, male-dominated religious social world.

The disciples are like and unlike the religious authorities. From the view point of the Evangelist, they are, like the religious authorities, males who in their role as teachers exercise the teaching task after Jesus' resurrection. In this respect the disciples as portrayed by Matthew seem to follow aspects of mishnaic practice for those who study and teach the law. Unlike the authorities, the disciples are not to exalt themselves by seeking places and titles of honor (23:1–10). Rather, their role is to be characterized by humility (23:11–12). Their model of greatness is found in children (19:13–15), and the paradigm for their faith and service is found among the women and other marginalized persons scattered throughout the writing. At this point Matthew's community runs counter to the crystallized social stratification of the synagogue, mishnaic culture, and advanced agrarian societies. But, following Wire's lead, there are two distinct roles in Matthew's community for those who follow Jesus in faith. If so, then the disciples as teachers depict a gender-specific task within the Matthean community, an undertaking, however, that is to eschew advanced agrarian domination.

What we have just affirmed may be difficult for modern readers to understand. We are attempting to describe an apparent struggle within an Israelite community deeply rooted in its social world. Therefore, we do not affirm that this example is normative for all early Jesus communities or for Christians today. Apparently we see a different model and social dynamic in the communities to which Luke writes. There, women teach as evidenced by the example of Priscilla (Acts 18:26). Matthew's community, as we will demonstrate in the women's stories, is challenged by the inclusion of marginal women both Israelite and non-Israelite in background. Questions of women participating in the teaching ministry apparently are not being challenged. However, as we will demonstrate, apparently marginal women in addition to being included are to be recognized as prophets, models of great faith, and possibly as wise persons within the community. Within Matthew's community all are to be sisters and brothers. But, in the end, it appears that the Evangelist's community is taught by male "scribes" of the "kingdom of heaven."

The crowds on the other hand open a real alternative for women. Both the women in the crowds and those who follow Jesus from Galilee (27:55) are "heroines of faith."[99] Jesus acknowledges their presence, considers them worthy, treats them as persons, and receives their hospitality and ministry. Their faith and faithfulness are juxtaposed to the disciples' little faith. As Wire states, "The disciples are called, understand, obey, and are given authority, but are continually challenged to learn what the first group already demonstrates."[100] As one example of Matthew's social reversal, the religious status of women stands counter to that of women in mishnaic culture. No longer are men the only ones who may come before the Lord. Circumcision has been set aside. No longer are women attached to males for their public religious identity. Jesus, as God's presence within the community (1:23; 18:20; 28:20), is the basis for this significant social change, which is manifest in a number of ways. Corley[101] has shown, for example, that women and children probably participated with men in the eucharistic meals of the Matthean community. Certainly, children are cast in roles as models of greatness (18:3, 4); the crowds are taught the greater righteousness of Jesus (5:2—7:28); harlots and toll collectors enter the kingdom before the religious authorities; and women evince indomitable faith in the face of extremity and criticism. All persons—men, women, children, and non-Israelites—are invited to the millennial marriage feast

99. Grassi, *Hidden Heroes of the Gospels.*.

100. Wire, "Gender Roles in a Scribal Community," 104.

101. Corley, *Private Women, Public Meals.*

and belong to God's new household. All are part of an inclusive community. No longer is ancestry, family role, religious patronage, or socio/economic status to be the basis for religious standing before God. Rather, for all members of the new family, what counts is obedience to the word of God.

The writing's treatment of women, therefore, draws upon the new as well as the old. The old is the androcentric framework that can be found on every page. The new, also to be found on every page, is the radical inclusion of all persons in the community. These two, equally real, social realities constitute a dynamic tension. To neglect either prevents one from understanding the social setting of the community as an alternative community and the possible struggle within it to uphold the millennial vision of the new surrogate family of the kingdom. Women in the public settings of Matthew's Gospel know the blessedness of being in the presence of God because of Jesus, and yet to some degree, at least from a contemporary perspective, still seem to watch from a distance and look on from afar within the Evangelist's community.

The larger gender-specific cultural backdrop now is established for the study of the four stories about women. However, before the accounts are examined it is necessary to construct three additional models that have bearing on a social-scientific reading of the stories. They are: (1) honor and shame, (2) healing in non-Western societies, and (3) a native taxonomy of illness involving degrees of impurity.

4

Models

Honor and shame:

> [24] But he answered and said, "I was sent only to the lost sheep of the house of Israel." [25] But she came and began to worship him, saying, "Lord, help me!" [26] But he answered and said: "It is not permitted to take the children's bread and to throw it to the dogs." [27] But she said: "Certainly, Lord, but even the dogs eat the crumbs that fall from the table of their masters." [28] Then Jesus answered her, "Woman, your faith is great! Let it be done to you as you want." And her daughter was healed instantly. (Matt 15:24–28, author's translation)

Jesus as Israelite healer:

> [30] And great crowds came to him, bringing with them the lame, the maimed, the blind, the mute, and many others. And they laid them at his feet, and he healed them, [31] so that the crowd was amazed when they saw the mute speaking, the maimed whole, the lame walking, and the blind seeing. And they praised the God of Israel. (Matt 15:30–31, author's translation)

Purity:

> [3] Then the chief priests and the elders of the people gathered together in the palace of the high priest, who was called Caiaphas, [4] and they conspired to arrest Jesus by stealth and kill him. [5] But they said, "Not during the feast, or there may be a riot among the people.
> [20] And behold, a woman who had suffered from a hemorrhage for twelve years came up behind him and touched the tassels of his garment, [21] for she was saying to herself, "If I only touch his cloak, I will be saved." (Matt 9:3–5, 20–21, author's translation)

The kinship domain:

> [6] Now when Jesus was at Bethany in the house of Simon the leper, [7] a woman came to him with an alabaster vessel of very costly ointment, and she poured it on his head as he reclined at the table. (Matt 26:6–7, author's translation)

INTRODUCTION

IN THE PREVIOUS TWO chapters one social-scientific model, an advanced agrarian model of the household, and one germane micro-index example of that model, the public place of women in the mishnaic writings, have been used to cast light on household data and the public place of women and men in the Gospel of Matthew. As a result we have established that the writing sets forth two household actualities that apparently stand in conflict—the one, a Christian household deeply embedded in advanced agrarian social norms, and the other, the same Christian household guided by alternative social criteria based on Jesus' theocratic mission that the kingdom of heaven is near. Nonetheless, this tension is significant because most of the women mentioned in the writing, whose number and images admittedly are not many, are paradigms of faith for the Evangelist's community. Jesus acknowledges their presence, considers them worthy, treats them with respect, and receives their hospitality and service. Their faith and faithfulness often is contrasted with that of the disciples. No longer is gender, ancestry, family status, ethnic background, religious patronage, or socio/economic circumstance the basis for their religious standing before Israel's God. The Evangelist's community is not an egalitarian group, but neither is it to correspond to the "agrarian mould"—and therein is the rub, the give-and-take between these two social actualities.

In addition, the use of the microsocial index of the public place of women in the mishnaic writings in chapter 2 deepens our findings that among three public teaching settings, the Sermon on the Mount (5:1—7:28), The Parables Discourse (13:1–52), and the clash between Jesus and the religious authorities in the temple (21:12—23:29), only among the crowds, not among the disciples or the religious authorities, is there a real but limited alternative for women in public settings, a matter we believe will prove important in the exploration of the four stories about women. Matthew's community, however, probably is taught by male "scribes" of the "kingdom of heaven." If so, there appears to be two distinct roles within the community for those who follow Jesus in faith.

The Gospel of Matthew draws upon, to use the writer's own terminology, the "new" as well as the "old" (13:52; 9:16–17; 5:17–20). The old is the androcentric framework that can be found on every page. The new is a universal inclusion within the community. These two, equally real, social realities, examples of "structural" and "cultural" marginality,[1] seem to defy one another in an unusual dynamic tension and the neglect of either perspective prevents us from understanding adequately the social setting of the Matthean community.

These findings establish a starting point for our study of the four stories of women. First, however, it is necessary to construct three additional models that are used more than once and have a more direct bearing upon a cultural anthropological reading of the accounts. They are: (1) honor and shame, (2) healing in non-Western societies, and (3) a native taxonomy of illness involving degrees of impurity. We begin, however, with a concise description of four social domains that are important in the study of ancient Mediterranean societies.

SOCIAL DOMAINS

Social scientists speak of four "social domains"—politics, economics, religion, and kinship.[2] These four spheres, K. C. Hanson states, "are never discrete entities that operate in isolation from one another."[3] Rather, they are embedded socially to the extent that one sphere's definition, structures, and authority may be dictated by another sphere. Yet two of the domains, politics and kinship, are so distinctively different that one may speak of political religion and domestic religion, but not simply of religion.[4] Or one may speak of political economy and domestic economy, but not simply of economy. The domains of religion and economics, accordingly, are embedded either in politics or in the family. For example, religious leaders such as Caiaphas, members of the Jerusalem Sanhedrin, and the Pharisees are political personages, and the Jerusalem temple is a political edifice

---

1. For definitions of "structural" and "cultural" marginality, see the Introduction.
2. Hanson, "BTB Readers Guide: Kinship," 183–94.
3. Ibid., 183.
4. Malina, "Criteria for Assessing the Authentic Words of Jesus," 30.

where sacrifices are made for the public good.[5] Conversely, domestic religion and economy are family-centered and focus on the kin group.[6]

Political Domain—Temple, Palace, Synagogue

The temple and palace, located in the central section of an ancient city,[7] form the commercial center and hub of wealth for the state. From this location rulers find both legitimization and the ideological means for controlling the population and the economic surplus.[8] The elite, which comprise no more than 2 percent of the population, live near the temple and palace. From these locations they control vital political, religious, and economic aspects of life for both city and countryside.[9] Outside the city are numerous villages and towns where peasants dwell comprising about ninety percent of the population. Consequently there is a fundamental divergence between the countryside and its villages and the city.[10] Jesus' ministry largely flourishes among the villages but experiences conflict in the city.[11] Matthew's community probably is an urban group.[12]

Jesus is portrayed by Matthew as teaching and preaching in "their synagogues" (4:23; 9:35; 10:17; 12:9; 13:54) and his authority as a teacher is compared to "their scribes" (7:29). In contrast, Matthew speaks of scribes within his community (13:52; 23:34), which suggests an alternative Israelite community that follows Jesus. Synagogues are public locations of the political domain, which means that the period of the Evangelist some forty to fifty years later is a time when Israelite synagogues and the Matthean community are at odds.

The economic structure of the political domain is fundamentally "a *redistributive* network."[13] This means that taxes and rents are levied on rural producers and redistributed in the cities, estates, and temples.

---

5. Ibid.

6. Ibid., 31.

7. Sjoberg, *Preindustrial City*.

8. Lenski and Lenski, *Human Societies*, (1987).

9. Rohrbaugh, "The Pre-Industrial City in Luke-Acts," 133; Malina, *New Testament World*, 82.

10. Oakman, "The Countryside in Luke-Acts," 152.

11. Ibid., 172.

12. Evidence for this assertion is provided in chapter 4.

13. Rohrbaugh, "The Pre-Industrial City in Luke-Acts," 156.

Instead of feeding extra mouths in villages, the surplus ends up being used for other purposes by "the ruling groups."[14] For example, when Jesus cleanses the Jerusalem Temple, he challenges its redistributive network (21:13). Hanson and Oakman state, "It is clear that when Jesus rejected the temple as a cave of bandits, he rejected it as a redistributive institution benefiting only the few."[15] The political involvement of the Israelite temple priesthood[16] explains why Herod and the Roman prefects appoint the Jerusalem high priests during the period of Jesus.[17] This Israelite religious and economic institution is firmly embedded in the political domain.[18]

In peasant societies all resources are thought to be in limited supply, a reality known to anthropologists as the "Limited Good." George Foster describes this pervasive economic reality.

> [A]ll of the desired things in life such as land, wealth, health, friendship and love, manliness and honor, respect and status, power and influence, security and safety, *exist in finite quantity* and *are always in short supply, . . .* There is *no way directly within peasant power to increase the available quantities.*[19]

Put another way, Malina states, "The good things constituting life, like land itself, are seen as inherent in nature, there to be divided and redivided, if possible and necessary, but never to be increased."[20] For example, if a person wins honor, someone else loses.[21]

Ideology for the political economy and political religion is embedded in what anthropologist Robert Redfield calls the culture's "Great Tradition." Malina defines Redfield's Great Tradition as an "embodiment of the norms and values which give continuity and substance to the society."[22] He then describes this phenomenon for Israelite society,

14. Ibid.

15. Hanson and Oakman, *Palestine in the Time of Jesus,* 144.

16. Ibid.; see Malina, "Patron and Client," 23; idem, *The Social World of Jesus in the Gospels,* 163.

17. Hanson and Oakman, *Palestine in the Time of Jesus,* 137.

18. Ibid.; Malina, "Patron and Client," 23; idem, *The Social World of Jesus in the Gospels,* 163.

19. Foster, "Peasant Society and the Image of Limited Good," 296. See also Foster, "The Image of Limited Good," 300–323.

20. Malina, *New Testament World,* 95.

21. Malina and Rohrbaugh, *Synoptic Gospel,* 369–70.

22. Malina, *New Testament World,* 89.

As bearers of the Great Tradition, the urban elite had political control, with two principal functions: exacting taxes (especially for the Temple, and its city, and the city elite) and maintaining order through a police force and a type of court system that supported order spelled out by the rules of sacred Scripture, the Torah, which was the law of the House of Israel.[23]

Significantly removed from the values of the city, peasants abide by what Redfield called the "Little Tradition" which Malina defines as a "simplified and often outdated expression of the norms and ideals embodied by the city elites."[24]

Jesus' behavior and words, including his healing activity and that of the Twelve, belong primarily to the public and political Israelite social domain. When Jesus proclaims a coming kingdom of heaven (4:17), he has an Israelite theocracy in mind (10:5; 15:24).[25] When Jesus heals the misfortunate, the crowds praise "the God of Israel" (15:31; see 8:11; 22:32). When Jesus recruits the Twelve to help in his theocratic task (4:18–22; 10:2–4), he commissions them as healers (10:1), and charges them not to go among non-Israelites and Samaritans. Their mission is to the "lost sheep of the house of Israel" (10:5, 6; see 15:24)—to "all the towns of Israel" (10:23; see also 7:6; 19:28–29). As we will see in our analysis of the story of the Canaanite woman (chap. 5), these particularistic words probably are authentic to the period of Jesus.[26] As Malina puts it, Jesus urges "Israelites to get their affairs in order and to heal those in need of healing (10:1–16)."[27] The political domain, accordingly, sets forth the following social-scientific criterion for authenticating the deeds and words of Jesus: *If an activity or statement attributed to Jesus in a healing story "makes direct and immediate political sense, then it is authentic."*[28] We will apply this criterion to the healing stories of the woman with hemorrhages (9:20–22) and the Canaanite woman (15:21–28).

23. Ibid., 87.

24. Ibid., 93.

25. Ibid., 36.

26. Ibid.

27. Ibid., 33.

28. Ibid., 43, italics original.

Kinship Domain

The opposite pole from the political domain is the kinship domain that entails the household and family. Elliott demonstrates in Luke-Acts that the household plays "no part in Palestine's power structure except as the supplier of its economic resources and the object of its devouring policies."[29] Quite opposite to the temple, the household is a social organization of reciprocity, not redistribution.[30] For example, in the end peasant families seek not how much is taken but what is left,[31] a different outlook of the Limited Good than what is observed among the political-religious elite. For peasants, food, drink, and clothing are subsistence issues of paramount concern. Peasants ask, after paying taxes and/or rents, will there be enough to survive?

There can be little doubt that Matthew's community belongs to the kinship domain. Matthew employs Jesus' physical household as a foil to advance the notion of the surrogate family of God. The only father is "my Father in heaven" (cf. 23:9). Members of this surrogate family— "my brother, and sister, and mother"—belong together because of their commitment to do "the will of my Father in heaven" (12:50). This new family, not based on physical lineage or blood line, is foundational to the identity and formation of the Evangelist's community. For example, the story of the woman at Simon's house in Bethany (23:6–13) belongs to the private, kinship domain. However, the surrounding context sets the account within the larger political domain of the Jerusalem temple and its religious officials (26:1–5, 14–15).

The kinship domain, however, as a plurisignificant social institution, also can have political significance. Embedded in the household, kinship is the most basic social organization in agrarian societies.[32] In ancient Israel, the household's core social identity flows out of an ethic of tribal solidarity that "shaped a network of understanding and care that moved beyond the immediate compound family to include . . . the totality of the children of Israel."[33] Ancient Israel as a household is a "cosmos for

---

29. Elliott, "Temple versus Household," 229.

30. Ibid., 235.

31. Moxnes, *The Economy of the Kingdom,* 81.

32. Elliott, "Temple versus Household."

33. Perdue, et al., *Families in Ancient Israel,* 167.

human dwelling."[34] Israel's head, Yahweh (Jer 3:4), creates and establishes (Deut 32:6; Mal 2:10) his beloved son (Exod 4:22; Isa 63:16; Jer 3:19; 31:9; Hos 11) or daughter (Lam 2:13). Household imagery warns Solomon's descendants that Israel will be cut off from the land if they fail to obey the Lord (1 Kgs 9:7–8; see Jer 12:7; 22:5). Jesus' lament over Jerusalem echoes this ancient theme: "See, your house is left to you, desolate" (Matt 23:38). Matthew labels the ancient Israelite tabernacle as the "house of God" (12:4) and recalls that God's house "shall be called a house of prayer" (21:13; see Isa 56:7; Jer 7:11). Phrases like "house of Israel" and "house of God," therefore, beyond their historical identity, are social metaphors that particularize Israel. Kinship as a plurisignificant social institution is important, especially when viewed in association with the public, political, social domain.

MODEL ONE—HONOR AND SHAME

In setting forth our three models we begin with a model of honor and shame because it is the "pivotal value" of Mediterranean society of the first century,[35] and essential to everything, including survival. Malina defines honor as "public reputation. It is name or place. It is one's status or standing in the community *together with the public recognition of it.*"[36]

Within Classical and Hellenistic Greek cultures, *honor* is closely related to the maintenance of public life within the *polis*.[37] Josephus provides an excellent example in an Athenian decree that honors the Israelite high priest Hyrcanus.

> it has therefore now been decreed . . . to honour this man with a golden crown as the reward of merit fixed by law, and to set up his statue in bronze in the precincts of the temple of Demos, and the Graces, and to announce the award of the crown in the theatre at the Dionysian festival when the new tragedies are performed, and at the Panathenean and Eleusinian festivals and at the gymnastic games; and that the magistrates shall take care that so long as he continues to maintain his goodwill toward us, everything which we can devise shall be done to show honour and gratitude to this man for his zeal and generosity. (*Ant.* 14.132–34; LCL)

34. Ibid., 178.

35. Malina and Rohrbaugh, *Synoptic Gospels*, 369.

36. Ibid., 370.

37. Danker, *Benefactor*.

Public honor and gratitude are extended to Hyrcanus for the goodwill he has acquired among the citizens. For the Romans honor underpins an official ideology largely for the emperor and the elite, which is achieved by war and the subjugation of other states to Rome's will (Cicero *Arch.* 12–32). P. A. Brunt identifies "the glory of imperial expansion" as a sanctioned philosophy.[38]

One pervasive facet of honor and shame within Mediterranean culture pertains to family, masculinity, and gender separation.[39] Honor and shame are vital in societies that emphasize families, clans, and lineages.[40] Halvor Moxnes states, "a collective honor, based on a system of patrilineal clans, is a common element in traditional communities all over the Mediterranean area, including Spain, Greece, Cyprus, Kayla in North Africa, and among Bedouin in Egypt."[41] Honor involves the separation of the sexes, men holding the dominant public position and women caring for the private or domestic sphere. (This generalization, however, is under critical refinement because it is difficult for male anthropologists to gain access to the women's world that female counterparts are now providing.)[42] Even so, honor and shame based on gender relate to the hierarchical power structure of the society.[43] Benjamin and Matthews point out that in the example of ancient Israel "Women were physical labels of honor or shame for a household, just like the arms, legs, eyes, feet, and testicles of its men."[44]

---

38. Brunt, *Roman Imperial Themes,* 288–323.

39. Moxnes, "Honor and Shame," 33; see Delaney, "Seeds of Honor, Fields of Shame"; Gilmore, "Introduction: The Shame of Dishonor."

40. See Abu-Zeid, "Honour and Shame," 243–59; Caro Baroja, "Honour and Shame," 79–137; Campbell, "Honour and the Devil," 139–70; Bourdieu, "The Sentiment of Honour in Kabyle Society," 191–241.

41. Moxnes, "Honor and Shame," 29.

42. For studies involving gender issues, see Caro Baroja, "Honour and Shame," 79–137; "Religion, World Views, Social Classes and Honor," 91–102; Abu-Lughod, *Veiled Sentiments.* Moxnes points out, "Especially important is Abu-Lughod's unraveling of the links between female sexuality, modesty, and the hierarchical social structure. Threats to established bonds of sexuality are threats to the loyalties of this hierarchical society. Modesty codes (e.g., veiling) are a way of denying sexuality and showing acceptance of the existing social structure." "Honor and Shame," 33.

43. Pitt-Rivers, "Honour and Social Status," 19–77.

44. Matthews and Benjamin, *Social World of Ancient Israel,* 148.

Honor is essential to social standing, the status of a person within a community. If it is *ascribed*, it is derived from birth. An example would be Israel's priests. If it is *acquired*, it is what a person has achieved in a social world of challenge and response, that is, when a person wins a verbal battle. An example is when Jesus answers his opponents' questions in the temple (21:1—22:45)—the temple cleansing (21:23–27), paying taxes (22:15–22), the resurrection (22:23–33), and the greatest commandment (22:34–40). All of life involves honor—who one marries, with whom one does business, where one lives, what religious role one plays. Conversely, to "be shamed" indicates that one has lost honor. Judas's betrayal of Jesus is an example (26:14–15; 27:3–10). But to "have shame" is "to be shameless" and "means to have proper concern about one's honor. This is positve shame. It can be understood as sensitivity to one's own reputation (honor) or the reputation of one's family."[45] An example is Joseph, identified in Matthew as a "righteous man" (1:19).

In Matthew issues of honor and shame appear frequently.[46] The writing opens with a genealogy of Jesus (1:1–17) in which a status claim is ascribed to Jesus; he is "Jesus the Messiah, the son of David, the son of Abraham" (1:1). Besides Mary, four women appear in the lineage, persons who have non-Israelite origins or connections, structurally marginal women who undermine typical agrarian marriage expectations. Their status is ascribed—they are non-Israelites included in the lineage of Jesus. Their status is also acquired—their stories of origin culturally marginalize them but they are, nonetheless, heroines within the greater Israelite story.

Challenge-and-riposte exchanges frequently appear in Matthew such as when Jesus heals the man with a withered hand on the Sabbath in "their synagogue" (12:9–14), or in the quarrel between Jesus and the Pharisees and scribes over the tradition of the elders (15:1–20), or in the testy exchange between the Canaanite woman and Jesus (15:21–28). In the unit on the tradition of the elders, explicit honor language is used over the care of parents (15:4)—"'Honor your father and your mother,' ...'Whoever speaks evil of father or mother must surely die.'" Jesus cites honor language from eighth-century Isaiah in his condemnation of the Pharisees and scribes, "This people honors me with their lips, but their

45. Malina and Rohrbaugh, *Synoptic Gospels*, 371.
46. For Matthew, see Neyrey, *Honor and Shame in the Gospel of Matthew*.

hearts are far from me;" (15:8; cf. Isa 29:13). Matthew portrays Judas' suicide as an exceptionally shameful act (27:3–10).

The term "glory," an explicit honor word, indicates the public acknowledgement of one's "worth and social value," especially in reference to God. For example, when the Son of Man comes with his angels, he does so "in the *glory* of his Father" (16:27). At the millennium, when Jesus triumphantly carries out God's purposes over all obstacles, the Son of Man will sit "on the throne of his *glory*." In the millennial discourse (chap. 24–25) the glory of the Son of Man will be accompanied by a heavenly sign, and all earthly inhabitants will lament when they see him "coming on the clouds of heaven with power and great *glory*" (24:30). At the time of judgment, the Son of Man will come "in his *glory*, and all the angels with him;" then he will sit on the "throne of his *glory*" (25:31).

Honor issues are critical in the two healing stories because Jesus's activity as an Israelite[47] healer renders honor to the God of Israel (4:23–25; 8:16–17; 9:35; 14:35–36; 15:29–31; 19:2). Further, honor issues involve all of the personages in the account of the woman at Simon's house (26:6–13) and its immediate context (26:1–5, 14–15)—the religious aristocracy who conspire to kill Jesus, the woman, the disciples who see her act as waste, and Judas who plays the fool as he betrays Jesus. Finally, the ultimate act of shame, Jesus' crucifixion at the hand of the Romans, is reversed in the triumph of his resurrection signifying God's victory over imperial tyrants (28:1–10; see Dan 12:1–3; 2 Macc 7), acts of shame and honor that are witnessed by the women at the cross and tomb.

MODEL TWO—HEALING IN NON-WESTERN SOCIETIES

Two of the women's stories involve Jesus as an Israelite healer, which raises the question as to how illness is experienced and treated in agrarian societies like the Roman Empire. Robert A. Hahn writes, "Anthropological observers in a variety of non-Western settings have noted that, in addition to roughly equivalent generic terms, sickness is connected to two broader phenomena: cosmological or religious forces, and social relationships and interpersonal conflicts."[48] In medical anthropology "illness" denotes a social-cultural perspective in which "many others besides the stricken

---

47. Reference to Jesus as an Israelite underscores that he was neither a Jew nor a Christian. See Elliott, "Jesus the Israelite," 119–55.

48. Hahn, *Sickness and Healing*, 24.

individual are involved."[49] Both patients and healers are "embedded in a cultural system," and it is the "whole system that heals." Attitudes and actions are embedded in the total fabric of life.[50] As Blum and Blum add, "Health beliefs and practices must be viewed within the context in which they occur, since focusing on them in isolation distorts or detracts from their meaning and function."[51] Jesus as an Israelite healer should not be viewed in isolation, but in association with the cultural *system*.[52]

Systems theory, accordingly, considers social relations and cultural expectations of societies in understanding sickness and healing. Sickness and healing belong to the organized patterns of thinking, judging, and behaving shared by members of a society.[53] This arrangement is different from the biomedical approach largely operative in advanced industrial societies like the United States and northern Europe, in which the focus too often is on a narrow hierarchy of molecules, cells, organs, and human bodies.[54] Persons in advanced industrial settings do not readily see Jesus' healing activity as essential to his task in a social-political sense.

In societies like ancient Rome, sickness and healing may be classified along the lines of witchcraft, sorcery, and spirit aggression.[55] "Without exception," Murdock states, "every society in the sample which depends primarily on animal husbandry for its economic livelihood regards spirit aggression as either the predominant or an important secondary cause of illness."[56] Spirit aggression assumes that sickness is a misfortune due to the effect of cosmic forces on human lives.[57] Sun and moon belong to the array of cosmic forces. The sun's power gives warmth and life; it also

49. Pilch, "The Health Care System in Matthew," 102.

50. Blum and Blum, *Health and Healing in Rural Greece,* 20.

51. Ibid.

52. Pilch, "Healing in Mark," 143.

53. Hahn, *Sickness and Healing,* 2; Blum and Blum, *Health and Healing,* chap. 2; Allbaugh, *Crete.*

54. Hahn, *Sickness and Healing,* 97.

55. Murdock, *Theories of Illness,* 73; Foster, "Disease Etiologies in Non-Western Societies," 773–82.

56. Murdock, *Theories of Illness,* 82; see Pilch, "Sickness and Healing in Luke-Acts," 200–209; idem, "A Spirit Named 'Fever.'"

57. Pilch, "The Health Care System in Matthew," 102, 104.

causes headaches. Seeds, women, and the moon wax and wane together, and ill people may be moonstruck.[58]

Evidence for spirit aggression abounds in Matthew. For example, the demon possessed son (17:14–20) is literally "moonstruck" (v. 15; often translated as "epileptic"); that is, he is under the moon's cosmic influence or power, a term found only in Matthew (4:24; 17:14–18).[59] Cosmic forces have made their habitation within him. Jesus rebukes the demon within the boy (17:18) as he rebukes the violent, life-threatening power of a storm on the sea (8:26). Other examples of demon possession (not being moonstruck) include the Gadarene demoniac (8:28–34); the Canaanite woman's daughter who "is tormented by a demon" (15:22); John the Baptist, whom Jesus' critics accuse of having a demon (12:18); and the identification of mutes and the blind as demon-possessed persons (9:32; 12:22).

Further, the religious and political implications of the Beelzebul controversy (12:22–32) hinge on whether Jesus "casts out demons by the prince of demons" (9:34; 12:24) or by the Spirit of God (12:26, 28). Matthew's language is unequivocal, forceful, uncompromising, and violent (12:22–30). The spiritual realms of God and Satan are like two kingdoms, cities, or houses that, if divided, cannot stand (12:25–26). The strong man (Satan) first needs to be tied before his house can be plundered (12:29). Blasphemy against the Spirit will not be forgiven (12:30–31). Accordingly, Matthew presents Jesus as a Spirit-led servant-prophet (see 12:18, based on Isa 42:1–4; Matt 12:28; 3:16; 4:1) who struggles with the religious and political powers of Jerusalem (see 21:14).

Magical practices flourish in pre-industrial settings among all social groups, but especially among lower class urbanites and villagers.[60] Sjoberg states, "Restorative magic has prevailed in feudal orders from the most ancient ones in the Near East to those in the Greek and Roman periods, in Central and Eastern Asia, in medieval Europe and pre-Columbian America, down to those that survive today."[61] Since evil spirits upset the order of life, causing illness or other social or physical disasters,[62] magical practices ward off evil and correct imbalances in the spiritual

---

58. Blum and Blum, *Health and Healing*, 31–32.

59. See Ross, "Epileptic or Moonstruck?" 126–28.

60. Sjoberg, *Preindustrial City*, 275; Blum and Blum, *Health and Healing*, 25, 31–35.

61. Sjoberg, *Preindustrial City*, 277–78.

62. Ibid.

order.[63] Magical rituals presume "the sympathy of word, deed, and concept: peasants believe that by naming their wish, what they wish shall be, with the proviso that the energies of the supernaturals will be enlisted toward this end."[64] Whether Jesus is a Hellenistic magician is a question that has sparked provocative discussion among scholars.[65] Even though Matthew appears to avoid "explicit magical-manipulative connotations,"[66] traces of magical influences possibly remain (9:20–21). Our purpose is not to decide whether Jesus is a magician or "charismatic healer,"[67] but to consider how persons like the hemorrhaging woman might perceive and respond to Jesus. Therefore, the employment of the term "magic" is used non-pejoratively "as the art of influencing the superhuman sphere of the spirits, demons, angels and gods."[68]

Finally, it is necessary to describe the social sectors in which illness is experienced. Based on Arthur Kleinman's cross-cultural materials on healing,[69] John Pilch has identified three overlapping social sectors.[70] First is the *popular sector*,[71] a family-centered environment of sickness and care that manages between 70 to 90 percent of sickness;[72] within this sector, "the lay, non-professional, non-specialist popular culture" provides treatment.[73] Since public-welfare services seldom exist,[74] the family (sometimes assisted by guilds) is the primary welfare-security agency. Persons outside this safety net frequently suffer social and religious isolation and ostracism. Second is the *folk sector,* a community context of care and healing. In this arena, villagers with recognized powers interpret for individu-

---

63. Blum and Blum, *Health and Healing*, 31–32.

64. Ibid.

65. Smith, *Jesus the Magician*; Hull, *Hellenistic Magic and the Synoptic Tradition*; Meier, *A Marginal Jew*, 535–75; Twelvetree, *Jesus the Exorcist*, 190–207.

66. Duling, "Matthew's Plurisignificant 'Son of David,'" 109; see Mark 7:31–37; 8.22–26.

67. Theissen and Merz, *The Historical Jesus*, 305–8.

68. Ibid., 305 n. 22.

69. Kleinman, "Concepts and a Model," 29–47; idem, *Patients and Healers*.

70. Pilch, "Sickness and Healing in Luke-Acts"; idem, "A Spirit Named 'Fever'"; idem, "Insights and Models."

71. Pilch, "Sickness and Healing in Luke-Acts," 194–97.

72. Kleinman, "Concepts and a Model," 33.

73. Pilch, "The Health Care System in Matthew," 103.

74. Sjoberg, *Preindustrial City,* 251.

als and their families the presence and absence of illness.[75] The deviant condition, illness, is "observed, defined and treated" by a "web of relations involving family, social network, village, etc."[76] Finally, the *professional sector* is composed of professionally "trained and credentialed healers,"[77] who serve mainly the urban upper classes.[78] Jesus is not a "professional" healer. Rural and urban lower-class populations—peasants, artisans, outcasts, and expendables—experience health care as mediated by the *popular* and *folk* sectors.[79] Jesus is a healer among those who experience and treat illness in the *folk* sectors.

MODEL THREE—A NATIVE TAXONOMY OF ILLNESS— DEGREES OF IMPURITY

Purity issues are involved in all of the women's stories, necessitating the creation of a purity/impurity model. A native taxonomy of illness based on "degrees of impurity"[80] follows certain insights of Mary Douglas.[81] For Douglas, purity is defined as normality and wholeness; pollution and taboo refer to matter "out of place"—dirt—and to a cultural system of order and disorder.[82] Purity rules are symbolic norms, a cultural language that expresses and reflects larger social concerns that work in concert with other structures of thought to deliver and support a common message. Douglas identifies four kinds of danger: (1) danger pressing on external boundaries (boundaries that demarcate the in-group from out-

---

75. Pilch, "Sickness and Healing Luke-Acts," 197–200; Sjoberg, *Preindustrial City*, 315–16.

76. Neyrey, "Miracles, In Other Words," 4.

77. Pilch, "Sickness and Healing in Luke-Acts," 192–94; Jackson, *Doctors and Diseases in the Roman Empire*, 9–31; Kee, *Medicine, Miracle, and Magic in New Testament Times*, 27–66.

78. Sjoberg, *Preindustrial City*, 315–16.

79. Sigerist, *A History of Medicine*, 306; Jackson, *Doctors and Diseases in the Roman Empire*, 138–69.

80. Neusner, *The Idea of Purity in Ancient Judaism*; idem, "History and Purity in First-Century Judaism," 1–17; Pilch, "Biblical Leprosy and Body Symbolism," 108–13; idem, "Sickness and Healing in Luke-Acts," 207; Malina, *New Testament World*, 161–97; Neyrey, "The Idea of Purity in Mark's Gospel," 91–128; idem, "The Symbolic Universe of Luke-Acts," 271–304.

81. Douglas, *Purity and Danger*; idem, *Implicit Meanings*.

82. Douglas, *Purity and Danger*; Isenberg, "Mary Douglas and Hellenistic Religions," 179–85; Isenberg and Owen, "Bodies, Natural and Contrived," 1–17.

groups); (2) danger from transgressing the internal lines of the system; (3) danger in the margins; and (4) danger from internal contradiction.[83] Douglas further indicates that when "rituals express anxiety about the body's orifices, the sociological counterpart is a care to protect the political and cultural unity" of a group.[84] Accordingly, Pilch locates so-called leprosy with the boundary of the human body, spirit-possession as an invasion against the boundary, and women's illnesses as a concern for domestic boundaries.[85] The two healing stories (a girl restored to life and the hemorrhaging woman, 9:18–26) and the Canaanite woman's daughter (15:21–28) relate not only to pollution boundaries concerning the human body but also to pollution boundaries of the public, Israelite, social domain. The story of the woman at Bethany (26:6–13) is not a healing story but involves purity boundary issues within the community set within the larger context of the public domain—the Jerusalem temple. The accounts of the women at the cross and the tomb (27:55–56, 61; 28:1–10) apparently involve boundary issues of both a public and private nature.

The human body is a center at which purity issues are manifest—a microcosm of the social body. Order and chaos at all cultural levels (the individual or the community) indicate social attitudes toward ill persons.[86] The Blums state, "Failure to observe the rites of purification, the sensitivities of the spirits, a disregard for the taboos that protect against pollution, are all dangerous omissions—omissions that will bring disaster to the offender."[87] In rural Greece, "one must avoid the menstrual woman for fear of the damage her own power can do the god, the crops, the first bread, or the fighting man."[88] If the hemorrhaging woman is a menstruant, according to Israelite law she is unclean and should not be touched (Lev 15:19–30). Ordinarily, such a woman remains at home. She may prepare meals and perform her household chores, but the family has to avoid lying in her bed, sitting in her chair, or touching her. For the woman's hemorrhage to last twelve years indicates the abnormality of the condi-

83. Douglas, *Purity and Danger,* 122.

84. Ibid., 124.

85. Pilch, "The Health Care System in Matthew," 104. As we will see, the stories of the woman with a hemorrhage (9:20–22) and the Canaanite woman (15:21–28) involve domestic issues healed in open, outdoor, nondomestic, public space.

86. Neyrey, "Clean/Unclean," 93.

87. Blum and Blum, *Health and Healing,* 21.

88. Ibid., 33–34.

tion and the seriousness of the social restriction and/or exclusion. That she is located in open space also suggests a danger of pressing against external boundaries.

Great concern for Israel's external boundary—that is the opposite pole, the social body—may be identified in the political religion of Second Temple Israelite culture. Accordingly, Jesus' healing activity done in public settings has political consequences evidenced explicitly when he heals the blind and the lame in the temple (21:14–17) at the time that he cleans it (21:12–17). During the period of the Evangelist, the political pole has shifted from the Jerusalem temple to the synagogue.

Purity issues are articulated and measured against biblical stipulations in Leviticus 21:16–20. Priests with body blemishes, even though not technically impure or unclean, are not to draw near to the temple altar to offer the bread of God (21:17). This Leviticus tradition is known and stressed by Philo (*Leg.* 1.80; also 1.117), Josephus (*J.W.* 1.269–70; *Ap.* 1.15; see also *Ant.* 14.366; and *t. Parah* 3:8), and the Qumran community. References from Qumran (4QD^d; lQSa 2:5–10; lQM 7:3–6) are noteworthy for the lists they supply not only for priests but also for those who participate in military action and those who would enter the sacred city and temple. Two passages relate physical impairment and social impurity to sacred locations. The first text (4QMMT^b 49–54) excludes the blind and the deaf from the community. The second text (11QTemple 45:12–14) excludes any blind man from entering the holy city where the holy temple is located. Strictures like these possibly illumine as well the conflict over healing between Jesus and the religious authorities in the Temple (Matt 21:14).

Accordingly, acts of touching in a number of the healing stories (the microcosmic level) are implicitly cultural issues for leaders of political religion (the macrocosmic level). Guardians of the social order label Jesus a social deviant after he touches and is touched by the impure.[89] Purity issues cut across Second Temple Israelite society—from the social body to the individual body. Cases in public settings have potential political ramifications for Jesus as an Israelite healer, even though a given example might not describe an actual controversy with representatives of the Second Temple's power structure. Matthew's story of the hemorrhaging woman seems to fit this categorization. As Neyrey states, there is a

---

89. Neyrey, "Clean/Unclean," 91–95.

"thorough correlation between socio-political strategy and bodily concerns."[90] This correlation may become clearer in figure 4.1.[91]

FIGURE 4.1: PURITY/POLITICAL MAP

	Social-Religious Political Elite	Jesus
Political Locus— Temple/Jerusalem/ Rome	*Network of control:* from the Jerusalem Temple to Galilee	*Social network but not a network of control:* mostly rural villages and peasants of Galilee
God of Israel	*Core value:* God's holiness *Mission:* maintain political control	*Core value:* God's mercy *Mission:* inaugurate Israel's theocracy
Structural Implications	*Strong boundaries* Exclusivistic strategy	*Weaker boundaries* Inclusivistic strategy among Israelites
Legitimation in Scripture	Law, except Genesis	Genesis and prophets
Strong Purity Concerns	Strong bodily control Avoid public bodily contact with sick, demon-possessed, bodily deformed	Weaker bodily control Public, bodily contact with sick, demon-possessed, bodily deformed

CONCLUSION

All of the models used more than once have been described. Three other models, however, are used one time, and their construction is reserved for the story in which they appear. They are (1) prostitutes in advanced agrarian societies, employed in the Canaanite woman's story (15:21–28); (2) a patronage and clientage model utilized in the account of the woman at Bethany (26:6–13); and (3) a rite-of-passage or altered-status-ritual model developed for the reading of passages pertaining to the women at the cross and tomb (27:55–56, 61; 28:1–10). In the next chapter we apply the models presented in this chapter to the account of the girl restored to life and the woman with a continuous blood flow (9:18–26).

90. Ibid., 93; against Levine, "Discharging Responsibility," 379–97.
91. For the use of maps, see Neyrey, "Clean/Unclean," 91–95.

5

Jesus Heals the Hemorrhaging Woman
and Restores a Girl to Life

[9] As Jesus was walking, he saw a man called Matthew sitting at the tax booth; and he said to him, "Follow me." And he got up and followed him.

[10] And it happened that he was reclining at the table in the house, and look, many tax collectors and sinners came and reclined at table with Jesus and his disciples. [11] When the Pharisees saw this, they said to the disciples, "Why does your teacher eat with tax collectors and sinners?" [12] But he heard it and said, "It is not those who are well who need a physician, but those who are sick. [13] Go and learn what this means, 'Mercy is what I want, and not sacrifice!'—for I came not to call the righteous, but sinners!"

[14] Then the disciples of John came to him, saying, "Why do we and the Pharisees fast often, but your disciples do not fast?" [15] And Jesus said to them, "Can the wedding guests mourn as long as the bridegroom is with them? But the days will come, when the bridegroom is taken away from them, and then they will fast. [16] And no one puts a piece of unshrunk cloth on an old garment, for then the patch tears away from the garment, and the tear becomes worse. [17] Neither do people put new wine into old wineskins; if they do, the skins tear, and the wine is spilled, and the skins are destroyed. Instead, they put new wine into new wineskins, and so both are preserved.

[18] While he was saying these things to them, behold a civic ruler came in and bowed down before him, saying, "My daughter has just died; but come and lay your hand on her, and she will live." [19] And Jesus stood up and with his disciples followed him.

[20] And behold, a woman who had suffered from a hemorrhage for twelve years came up behind him and touched the tassels of his garment, [21] for she was saying to herself, "If I only touch his cloak, I will be saved." [22] But Jesus turned, and seeing her said, "Take

courage, daughter; your faith has saved you." And instantly the woman was saved.

[23] When Jesus came to the leader's house and saw the flute players and the crowd wailing, [24] he said, "Go away; the girl has not died; she is only sleeping." And they laughed at him. [25] But when the crowd was driven outside, he went inside and took her hand, and the girl arose. [26] And the report of this spread throughout the land. (Matt 9:9–26, author's translation)

INTRODUCTION

THE STORY OF THE girl restored to life and the hemorrhaging woman constitutes a double pericope, that is, one that consists of two interwoven healing stories within the same literary unit that features a male household leader, two females, Jesus' powerful touch, and faith.[1] The account is part of a sequence of nine miracle stories (8:1—9:38) divided into three series with three stories in each series (8:1–17; 8:23—9:7; 9:18–31). There are units concerning discipleship, controversy with the religious authorities, and an emphasis on theological themes such as faith and mercy between each series and at the end of the entire sequence of miracle stories (8:18–22; 9:9–17; 9:35–38).[2] The pericope at hand (9:18–26) opens the third group.[3]

The above translation begins with the call of Matthew (9:9) and is followed by a private banquet of social outcasts with Jesus and his disciples (9:10–13) because unlike Mark (5:21) and Luke (8:40) Matthew connects this private event of the meal and the question about fasting (9:14–17) with the opening of the healing stories of the two women (9:18–26). According to Matthew, the civic leader whose daughter "has just died" (9:18) suddenly breaks into the banquet scene to announce the death of his daughter and to entreat Jesus to come to his home to lay his hands on her so that she might live. Matthew opens and closes this entire section in the private space of the "house." These private settings depict scenes of the surrogate community of the kingdom of heaven. In between and outside these household settings we find the story of the woman "who had suffered from a hemorrhage for twelve years."

1. Hagner, *Matthew 1–13*, 247.
2. Meier, *Matthew*, 79–81.
3. Duling, "The Therapeutic Son of David," 392–410.

Her story, following Matthew's redaction, has no essential connection to the larger narrative and is couched in open public space (9:20–22). This movement of the larger narrative illustrates Jesus' activity in both private and public settings.

From a social-scientific perspective we advance the hypothesis that both of these settings, private and public, have significance for Matthew's community. In addition, we believe that Matthew's treatment of the healing of the woman originates in the activity of the historical Jesus. In view of this assertion a twofold purpose is pursued in this chapter: (1) to provide an assessment of the historicity of Matthew's account of the woman's healing and (2) to explore how her story and the account of the ruler's daughter might have functioned within the Christian community to which the Evangelist is writing. Both stories remained noteworthy to a community in transition particularly in its clash with a Pharisaic party following the destruction of the temple in 70 CE. We affirm the uncharted map of this transition also includes the community's social struggle to work out Jesus' millennial vision concerning structurally and culturally marginal persons.

We will demonstrate that Matthew's redaction of the woman's story,[4] because it is located entirely in public open space, originated in the time of Jesus' activity. In other words, for that portion of the pericope Matthew's rendition points the contemporary interpreter in two directions: to the historical period of Jesus as an Israelite healer and to the *Sitz im Leben* of the Evangelist's day. It is also asserted that the portion of Matthew's redaction featuring the girl's restoration to life belongs principally to the private kinship domain. This does not preclude that the story is devoid of data related to the activity of the historical Jesus, but that its location in kinship that is private space, best fits the Evangelist's *Sitz im Leben*. Both events are significant for the time of Matthew's community. Measured by social-scientific criteria, the account of the hemorrhaging woman bridges both the period of Jesus and the time of the Evangelist, while the story of the restoration of the girl is more appropriate for the Evangelist's time.

Our first step is to set forth in an abbreviated form the cross-cultural models utilized in reading the stories.

---

4. Hagner notes that the "major structural feature of this pericope ..." is "... the insertion of the story of the hemorrhaging woman" (*Matthew 1–13*, 247).

MODELS

Two models are employed that were set forth in chapter 3: (1) healing in non-Western societies characterized especially by spirit involvement and aggression and (2) a native taxonomy of illness involving degrees of impurity. (As applicable, data is drawn from the larger descriptions and applied to the story. The model of honor and shame serves as a cultural backdrop for what transpires as do the social realities of the political and kinship domains.)

The first model, healing in non-Western societies, broad in scope, is designed to better understand illness, healing, and healers in a social-cultural perspective different from the biomedical approach largely operative in advanced industrialized societies like the United States and northern Europe.[5] The notion of spirit aggression assumes that illness is a misfortune caused by attacks by maligning spirits and cosmic forces. The model of a native taxonomy of illness involving degrees of impurity more specifically assists us in interpreting the accounts. The purity/impurity model casts light as to how the human body, in which purity issues are manifest, is a microcosm of the social body. Knowledge of the political and kinship social domains helps us answer the question, what does it mean for the woman and the girl to be healed in open space and private space, respectively? What possible implications might this have for the woman's kinship ties? The woman's story it will be shown belongs to the greater fabric of social, religious, and political issues related to Matthew's portrayal of Jesus as a healer. A brief summary now is given of each model.

Model One—A Model Summary of Healing in Non-Western Societies

The following salient features are emphasized:

1. Because both patients and healers are "embedded in a cultural system" Jesus as an Israelite healer should be viewed not in isolation but in association with the cultural system.

2. In societies like the Roman Empire, sickness and healing may be classified along the lines of witchcraft, sorcery, and spirit aggression.[6] Evidence for spirit aggression abounds in Matthew.

5. Hahn, *Sickness and Healing*, 97.
6. Murdock, *Theories of Illness*, 73; Foster, "Disease Etiologies," 773–82.

3. Magical practices flourish in preindustrial settings among all social groups but especially among lower-class urbanites and peasants.[7] Our analysis does not decide whether Jesus is a magician or a charismatic healer,[8] but suggests how persons like the hemorrhaging woman might perceive Jesus and act accordingly. Therefore, the term "magic" is used non-pejoratively "as the art of influencing the superhuman sphere of the spirits, demons, angels and gods."[9]

4. Jesus is not a "professional" healer, but a recognized healer in the community context of the *folk sector*[10] of care and healing.

5. Rural and urban lower-class populations—peasants, artisans, outcasts, and expendables—experience health care mediated not by the professional sector but by the popular and folk sectors.[11] Jesus heals those who experience and treat illness in those two arenas. "Folk" networks can be detected in Matthew (see 4:24; 9:2; 14:35).

6. Jesus' behavior and words, including his healing activity and that of the Twelve often take place in the public, political, Israelite, social domain—a matter that leads us to the second model.

Model Two—A Summary of a Native Taxonomy of Illness, Degrees of Impurity

The purity/impurity model features the following elements:[12]

1. Purity is defined as normality and wholeness and pollution or taboo is defined as matter "out of place"—dirt in the house—a cultural system of order and disorder.[13]

---

7. Sjoberg, *Preindustrial City,* 275; Blum and Blum, *Health and Healing,* 25, 31–35.

8. See chapter 3.

9. Sjoberg, *Preindustrial City,* 305, n. 22.

10. See chapter 3.

11. Sigerist, *A History of Medicine,* 2:306; Jackson, *Doctors and Diseases in the Roman Empire,* 138–69.

12. Neusner, "History and Purity in First-Century Judaism," 1–17; Pilch, "Biblical Leprosy and Body Symbolism"; "Sickness and Healing in Luke-Acts," 207; Malina, *New Testament World*; Neyrey, "The Idea of Purity in Mark's Gospel," 91–128; and idem, "The Symbolic Universe of Luke-Acts," 271–304.

13. Douglas, *Purity and Danger*; Isenberg, "Mary Douglas and Hellenistic Religions," 179–85; Isenberg and Owen, "Bodies, Natural and Contrived," 1–17.

2. Purity rules are a cultural language that expresses and reflects larger social concerns that work in concert with other structures of thought to deliver and support a common message.

3. Purity boundaries are fourfold: external, internal, at the margins, and marginal lines of internal contradiction. Crossing boundaries constitutes dangerous individual and social purity infractions.

4. The human body is a center where purity issues are manifest—a microcosm of the social body. There is a correlation between socio-political strategy and bodily concerns.[14] This correlation is clarified through the use of purity "maps." In the case of the hemorrhaging woman the following "map" is used.[15]

FIGURE 5.1: PURITY/POLITICAL MAP

	Social-Religious Political Elite	Jesus
Political Locus—Temple/Jerusalem/Rome	*Network of control:* From the Jerusalem Temple to Galilee	*No network of control:* A social network mostly of rural villages and peasants of Galilee
God of Israel	*Core value:* God's holiness *Mission:* Maintain political control	*Core value:* God's mercy *Mission:* Inaugurate Israel's theocracy
Structural Implications	*Strong boundaries* Exclusionary strategy	*Weaker boundaries* Inclusionary strategy among Israelites
Legitimation in Scripture	Law, except Genesis Strong bodily control	Genesis and prophets Weaker bodily control
Strong Purity Concerns	Avoid public bodily contact with sick, demon-possessed, bodily deformed	Public, bodily contact with sick, demon-possessed bodily deformed

14. Neyrey, "Clean/Unclean," 93.

15. For the use of maps see Neyrey, "Clean/Unclean," 91–95.

A Summary of the Political and Kinship Social Domains

The following salient features of these two social domains are stressed:

1. In the ancient Mediterranean social world there are four "foundational social domains" which social science scholars analyze—politics, economics, religion, and kinship (family/household).[16]

2. These four spheres are socially related to the extent that one sphere's definition, structures, and authority may be dictated by another sphere.

3. However, two of the domains, politics and kinship, are opposites. This means that the domains of religion and economics, accordingly, are embedded either in politics or the family. Jesus' behavior and words including his healing activity and that of the Twelve belong primarily to the public, political, Israelite social domain. Accordingly, the following social-scientific criterion for authenticating the deeds and words of Jesus is, *If an activity or statement attributed to Jesus in the healing story "makes direct and immediate political sense, then it is authentic."*[17]

4. Related to the household, the kinship domain is the most basic unit of social organization in advanced agrarian societies,[18] embracing families, villages, cities, and empire.[19]

5. The community of the Evangelist belongs to the kinship domain referenced by an emphasis upon the surrogate, millennial family of God.

6. The kinship domain, however, as a plurisignificant social metaphor, may also have political significance especially when viewed in association with the public, political social domain.

---

16. Hanson, "BTB Readers Guide; Kinship," 183–94.

17. Malina, "Criteria for Assessing the Authentic Words of Jesus," 43.

18. Elliott, "Temple versus Household in Luke-Acts."

19. McIver, "The Family as Government in Miniature," 7–11; Meeks, *First Urban Christians,* 30; Tidball, *Social Context of the New Testament,* 70; Elliott, *A Home for the Homeless,* 175–80; Crosby, *House of Disciples,* 23–32.

JESUS HEALS THE HEMORRHAGING WOMAN

Having summarized the models, we will apply them first to the hemorrhaging woman and then to the girl restored to life. First, though, three other matters need to be addressed: (1) the difficulty of doing an historical assessment of healing stories, (2) the need to develop a social profile of those healed in Matthew, and (3) a notation of certain aspects of the author's redaction.

Level One—Historicity of the Woman's Story

Difficulty of Historical Assessment

First, as Meier points out, the woman's story lacks multiple attestations—there is no other incident of its type, that is, of a woman apparently with a private gynecological problem, perhaps a chronic uterine hemorrhage.[20] This was according to the Levitical law a constant source of ritual impurity.[21] Meier therefore treats the account's historicity as unclear *(non liquet)*.[22] Second, the account having passed through at least the initial compilation and the time of Jesus' activity no doubt describes the Evangelist's setting in life. Accordingly, the final form of the narrative is heavily edited (in comparison to Mark) and tends to suppress certain features for ideological reasons.[23]

Historical assessment of the healing stories is most problematic. As Malina points out, all persons "seeking to evaluate the historical authenticity of Jesus' deeds must necessarily assume and apply some theory of reading, of language and of social meaning, whether they are aware of it or not."[24] Also, for many scholars, the healing deeds of Jesus, a major component of the "miracles" of Jesus, are "problem-ridden behaviors," largely "because there is no room for them among the patterns of conduct and perception available in contemporary U.S. and northern European social systems."[25] A final difficulty is that since the Enlightenment the deeds of Jesus as a healer have been variously interpreted out of conceptions

---

20. Whether the woman's hemorrhages were a gynecological problem is debated.

21. Meier, *A Marginal Jew*, 709.

22. Ibid., 707–10.

23. Held, "Matthew as Interpreter of the Miracle Stories."

24. Malina, "Assessing the Historicity of Jesus' Walking on the Sea," 351–52.

25. Ibid., 352.

"available from the contemporary social system" to which scholars have been enculturated.[26] As Pilch states, "The advent of modern science in about the seventeenth century disrupted the bio-psycho-spiritual unity of human consciousness that had existed until then."[27] Required is an assessment of the "constructs of readers and/or hearers of the Gospel documents."[28]

To this end, cross-cultural anthropological models are useful, because the social conceptions of reality described therein are more analogous and indigenous to first-century Mediterranean, Palestinian society. A social-scientific systems analysis provides a thick description based on the cognitive maps of how people in Palestine believed their universe worked. A difficulty, but not an insurmountable problem, is that the models utilized can be analogous both to the periods of Jesus and the Evangelist. Even so, it will be shown that a social-scientific reading of Matthew's account of the woman's healing favors the position that the story originated in the activity of Jesus.

A Social Profile of Healing Accounts in Matthew

Most of Jesus' healing activity occurs among the "poor"—peasants, artisans, outcasts, and expendables (Matt 11:2–6[Q])—and Jesus' fame as a healer draws large crowds, mostly from rural environs throughout and beyond Palestine (4:23–25; 9:35; 14:35–36; 15:29–31). Figure 5.2, below, identifies locations in which healing activities are reported and the means by which Jesus heals.

FIGURE 5.2: TYPOLOGY OF HEALING STORIES IN MATTHEW

Passage	Illness/Bodily Affliction	Location	Means
8:2–4	leper	open space	"touched him"
8:5–13	paralytic	open/house	word of Jesus
8:14–17	Peter's mother-in-law	house	"touched her hand"

26. Ibid., 353.
27. Pilch, "Visions in Revelation and Alternate Consciousness," 233.
28. Malina, "Assessing the Historicity of Jesus' Walking on the Sea," 351.

8:23–27	the storm	open space	command
8:28–34	two demoniacs	open space, tombs	command
9:2–8	paralytic	uncertain in Matthew	command
9:18–19, 23–26	ruler's dead daughter	house	"took her" (v. 25)
9:20–22	hemorrhaging woman	open space	woman touches Jesus
9:27–31	two blind men	open space, house	"touched their eyes"
9:32–34	demon-possessed mute	open space	command (implied)
12:9–14	man with withered hand	synagogue	command
12:22	demoniac	open space (implied)	command (implied)
15:21–28	Canaanite woman	open space	word of Jesus
17:14–20	moonstruck boy	open space	command (rebuked demon)
20:29–34	two blind men	open space	touch
21:14	blind and lame	temple	not stated

The stilling of the storm (8:23–27) presupposes that the wind operates like spirit aggression—the wind is exorcised like casting out of a demon (compare 8:26 with 17:18). It draws together cosmological forces and social relationships. To classify the story as a "nature miracle" fails to understand both the incident's social implications and its literary relationship with the succeeding stories of the two demoniacs (8:28–34) and the paralyzed man (9:2–8). Jesus' healing power circumscribes "all misfortune."[29]

A summary of the locations indicates the following:

1. Nine take place in open space (outdoors) (8:2–4, 23–27, 28–34; 9:20–22, 32–34; 12:22; 15:21–28; 17:14–20; 20:29–34).

2. Two are in public locations (synagogue/temple) (12:9–14; 21:14).

3. Two are in private settings (houses) (8:14–17; 9:18–19, 23–26).

29. Pilch, "The Health Care System in Matthew," 105.

4. One is located both outdoors and in a house (9:27–31).

5. One location is uncertain (9:2–8) even though Mark locates it in a house (Mark 2:1–12).

6. Men usually are healed in open space, a procedure having possible political implications.[30] The hemorrhaging woman and the Canaanite woman also encounter Jesus outside the private household domain.

A summary of the means of healing indicates the following:

1. Six accounts entail touching, nine involve the word and/or command of Jesus, and in one instance the means of healing is unknown. Duling suggests that Matthew is less exorcistic and tones down earlier, traditional magical elements.[31]

2. Incidents of touching probably involve purity issues (the second model). The word or command of Jesus relates to the healing of paralytics, those suffering from demons, a demon-possessed mute, the man with a withered hand, and the "moonstruck" boy (the first model).

3. Even though the healing of the hemorrhaging woman lacks multiple independent attestation, it belongs to the larger social profile of those Jesus heals. Deviant elements include both the woman's illness and that she is healed outside the private, kinship domain.

Aspects of Matthew's Redaction

In all three Synoptic accounts, the story of the hemorrhaging woman is associated with the raising of a dead girl (Matt 9:18–19, 23–26; Mark 5:22–23, 37–43; Luke 8:40–42, 49–56). Matthew's redaction, however, indicates that the woman's healing has no essential connection to the larger narrative. For example, unlike Mark and Luke, Matthew reports at the outset that the girl is dead (9:9); in Mark she is "at the point of death" (5:23), and in Luke the girl is dying (8:42). Often overlooked is that Matthew omits that the girl is "twelve years of age" (Mark 5:42; Luke 8:42), thus restricting the number twelve to the older woman. Finally, even though Jesus and the disciples follow the father to his home, all "intermediaries" in the woman's story are omitted. Only Jesus and the distressed person

30. Pilch, "Healing in Mark," 147.
31. Duling, "The Therapeutic Son of David," 392–410.

("the two poles")[32] are featured; there are no representatives, embassies, or opponents. The woman is alone with Jesus in open space. This may indicate her lack of a family network and/or community support (4:35). The social irony is that an intensely private and apparently gender-specific misfortune is healed outside a domestic setting. At any rate, Matthew's account can be analyzed separately.

Further, even though Matthew's tradition most probably is drawn from Mark, his redacted version is much briefer and ignores the rudeness of the disciples as it depicts Jesus in absolute control. Matthew omits the negative opinion about physicians (Mark 5:26), that the woman has spent all that she had (Mark 5:26), that she has heard reports about Jesus (Mark 5:27), and that she experiences healing within her body (Mark 5:29). Matthew also omits that Jesus perceives that power has gone forth from him and that, in the press of the crowd, he asks who touched his garments (Mark 5:30).[33] He also omits the disciples' incredulous reaction to Jesus' question (Mark 5:31), that the woman comes to Jesus in fear and trembling (Mark 5:33), and that Jesus tells her to go in peace (Mark 5:34). For some, it appears that Matthew's "meltdown" is done solely for ideological reasons[34] and is, therefore, further removed from the healing activity of Jesus than Mark's account. Matthew's redaction features Jesus' distinctive mission to Israel (Matt 10:5; 15:24) and that Jesus' healing activity results in praise to "the God of Israel" (Matt 15:31; see 8:11; 22:32).[35]

Finally, does the woman perceive Jesus as a healer with magical powers? The woman comes up behind Jesus, touches "the fringe of his garment," and thinks, "if I only touch his garment, I shall be made well" (9:21; see 14:36; cf. Mark 6:56; Acts 19:12). As indicated in the first model, Matthew probably suppresses hints of magic. He omits Mark's stories of the healing of the deaf-mute (7:31–37) and the healing of the blind man at Bethsaida (8:22–26)—accounts with possible magical implications. Matthew also omits Mark's emphasis that healing power leaves Jesus' body, as Meier puts it, "almost as though it were an electric current."[36]

32. Theissen and Merz, *The Historical Jesus*, 284–85.

33. This is possibly an example of Matthew's omission of magic; see, Duling, "The Therapeutic Son of David," 392–410.

34. Held, "Matthew as Interpreter of the Miracle Stories," 165–99.

35. Therefore, Matthew's toning down of magic does not necessarily remove us further from the period of Jesus' healing activity.

36. Meier, *A Marginal Jew*, 709.

Yet the woman's behavior parallels popular beliefs about magic in agrarian societies; that is, she believes the healer's clothing has healing power, a notion repeated in 14:36 (see Acts 5:15; 19:12). If an aura of magic remains, it could fit either the period of the Evangelist or the time of Jesus—or both.

Applying Social Domains and the Model of Degrees of Purity

What is the basis for asserting that Matthew's story originates with an event in the life of Jesus? It is demonstrated in a combination of the woman's faith, her identity as an Israelite outcast, the location of the healing in open space, and the violation of the Second Temple's purity boundaries. These factors coalesce to validate the woman's identity as a structurally marginal Israelite in need of healing (Matt 10:1–16)[37]—the heart of Jesus' theocratic mission to Israel. How does the evidence support these assertions?

First, in a "purity system" the physical body manifests concerns of the social body.[38] In the case of Matthew's story, the social body is the Second Temple and its far-reaching, hierarchical religious system that replicates purity expectations in the symbolic world of culture.[39] In other words, the "symbolic universe" of the woman and her social world includes an ideological geography extending from Jerusalem to Galilee.[40] According to the Pharisees' world order, the hemorrhaging woman is "dirt out of place," not whole, imperfect.[41] Her body is a bounded system. Her continuous flow of blood is proof to all who know her that she has crossed a forbidden "frontier."[42] Accordingly, she is "unclean" and dangerous to the guardians of the purity system centered in the Jerusalem Temple. This is true even though the text does not label her "unclean" since this would have been a common perception of the bystanders anyway.[43] This is true even though she is not the direct object of ideological confrontation. And this is true because the location of the healing in open space makes it potentially

37. Malina, "Criteria for Assessing the Authentic Words of Jesus," 33.

38. Wright, "Holiness (OT)," 729–41.

39. Pilch, "Biblical Leprosy and Body Symbolism," 108–13.

40. Neusner, "Map without Territory," 105.

41. Douglas, *Purity and Danger,* 5; idem, *Implicit Meanings,* 50–51.

42. Douglas, *Purity and Danger,* 115; Neyrey, "The Idea of Purity in Mark's Gospel," 101.

43. Neyrey, "The Idea of Purity in Mark's Gospel," 101.

a political issue. The Pharisees' core value of maintaining holiness (Lev 11:44) has been violated, their exclusionary strategy bypassed.[44] The woman's story fits the Purity/Political Map of the third model.

Second, the story corresponds to political expectations of the spheres of social domains, primarily because Matthew uses the number twelve in association with Jesus' mission to Israel. "Twelve" identifies the disciples/apostles (10:1, 2, 5; 11:1; 19:28; 20:17; 26:14, 47; 26:20), whose limited mission is only to the "lost sheep of the house of Israel" (10:5) and whose destiny is to sit on twelve thrones judging the twelve tribes of Israel (19:28). "Twelve" designates the full baskets collected after the feeding of the five thousand (14:20)—probably a symbolic reference to Israel (see 19:28). Jesus could appeal to his Father, who would at once send more than twelve legions of angels (26:53). Matthew consistently uses the number twelve to reinforce Jesus' mission. His omission that the ruler's daughter is twelve years old (Mark 5:42) indicates that the number has significance only in reference to the woman. It identifies the time of her suffering (twelve years), but it also reinforces Matthew's message that the woman is an example and paradigm of the lost sheep of the house of Israel (10:6; 15:24). She is "helpless" and without a shepherd (9:36). The combination of her sickness, faith, and healing serves as a paradigm of Israel's sick condition and need of salvation before Israel's God—the basis of Jesus' historical proclamation of the kingdom of heaven (Matt 10:1–16).[45] The woman's healing underscores Jesus' Israelite mission. Her paradigmatic significance as a symbol of Israel also fits the time of the Evangelist.

Social realities related to the political and kinship domains demonstrate that the kinship sphere as a plurisignificant social institution has political significance. In Matthew's version of the woman's story, this is indicated when Jesus addresses her as "daughter" (9:22). This endearing word, a tender form of recognition, is also a social metaphor that particularizes Israel (Lam 2:13; Matt 21:5). Only two times in Matthew does Jesus address women by gender—here and in the case of the Canaanite woman (15:28). The first instance designates an Israelite; the second identifies a non-Israelite.

---

44. Neyrey, "Unclean, Common, Polluted, and Taboo," 72–82.
45. Malina, "Criteria for Assessing the Authentic Words of Jesus," 33.

By stripping away numerous Markan allusions, Matthew highlights the healing as a distinctive Israelite event that parallels the model of social domains. The woman probably is a rural Israelite expendable whose courageous initiative—her faith—makes her a symbol of Israel. If so, she represents the "house of Israel" in the new theocratic kingdom, in contrast to the house of Israel that will be left desolate (23:38).

Conclusion—Differences that Matter

But what difference does the healing make for the woman? The woman's blood flow may have cut her off from blood ties. The healing would bring two possibilities: a return to her household or becoming one of the many women at the cross, who follow Jesus from Galilee and behold Jesus' death from a distance (27:55). At any rate, it is unrealistic, let alone anachronistic, to view her now as an autonomous woman. She belongs either to her family or to the women at the cross—possibly both. Returning to her household would remove family shame and open the extended household to Jesus as their healer because the kin group itself would be made whole by her healing. Family renewal would mean provision and protection for the woman and increased productivity for the family—essential for the subsistence of agrarian households. No longer would she be avoided for fear of the damage her own power could do before God, the crops, and family well-being.[46] The woman's good fortune would spread to her family and to other members of her community. Family and community boundaries would be restored—no longer would she be "dirt out of place." The one boundary still violated would be the political boundary of the temple and its far-reaching establishment.

The fallout for the healer would be mixed. Among peasants, Jesus' reputation and status would be magnified. The God of Israel would be praised for his mercy (15:31). Increased authority would bind the healer's actions, teachings, and preaching. Conversely, the relationship between Jesus and the center of Judean political, economic, and religious power—the Jerusalem Temple—would deteriorate.[47] The core value of God's holiness once more would have been violated, the temple-based network of control weakened, scriptural authority sullied, and strong purity concerns

---

46. Blum and Blum, *Health and Healing*, 33–34.
47. See Hollenbach, "Jesus, Demoniacs, and Public Authorities," 567–88.

ignored. Jesus would have crossed forbidden boundaries, and his standing with the Second Temple's power structure would be "dirt out of place."

Level Two—The Period of Matthew's Community

What is the basis that Matthew's account poses a social/theological challenge to Matthew's community some forty or fifty years later? First, following the social realities of the political and kinship spheres and a taxonomy of purity/impurity the woman's faith possibly stands over/against the disciples' "little faith." "Little faith" is Matthew's stereotypical expression for the twelve disciples (6:30; 8:26; 14:31; 16:8; 17:20), the character group whose mission is a "prototype of the continuing mission of the church,"[48] especially in its teaching task (13:52; 23:8–10, 34; 28:18–20). For example, when the disciples cry out for deliverance in the story of the storm Jesus associates their fear with their little faith (8:26). Little faith possibly is juxtaposed not only to the woman's faith, but also to the faith of the centurion (8:10), those who bore the paralytic to Jesus (9:2), and the two blind men (9:28–29), who were outsiders and/or outcast persons when measured against the purity standards of the synagogue. Matthew's community would hear these stories not in isolation but one after another producing a cumulative warning to the community as a kinship community to be socially inclusive of outcasts and expendables cutoff from household ties. In fact, only two of the nine stories in chapters 8 and 9 are firmly fixed in the private, kinship domain, the healing of Peter's mother-in-law (8:14–15) and the ruler's daughter (9:18–21, 23–26). All of the other incidents take place in public, open space. Matthew's community, accordingly, must receive without social reservation persons like those Jesus heals whose life scripts originally locate them in marginal, open, public space.

Second, following the purity/impurity model the woman's standing as a rural, outcast Israelite may present a social problem for an urban and reasonably well-to-do Christian community. As indicated, most of Jesus' healing activity occurs in rural environs, whether within or beyond Palestine (4:23–25; 9:35; 14:35–36; 15:29–31). This is true even though there are instances of healings in a village/town like Capernaum (8:5–13, 14–16) and the Jerusalem Temple (21:14). Following Kingsbury, Matthew's

---

48. Luz, *Matthew 8–20*, 67.

community probably is located in an "urban" locale,[49] made obvious primarily by Matthew's use of the terms for "city," *polis,* and "village," *kōmē.* References to *polis* are found no fewer than twenty-six times. Matthew uses the term *kōmē* only four times (9:35; 10:11; 14:15; 21:2), whereas Mark uses the term seven times. The ratio for Matthew is twenty-six to four, almost seven to one, *polis* over *kōmē.* This data, Kingsbury believes, "is all the more striking when it is observed that several occurrences of the word 'city' seem to relate to circumstances in Matthew's own time."[50] Following an advanced agrarian model, persons from rural areas often migrate to cities for subsistence if they lose their lands or suffer from the ravages of famine, sickness or war. Also, it is not known how Jesus' itinerant followers might have fared after Jesus' death. At any rate, as Elliott points out, in a "system of economic and social stratification legitimated by purity classifications," urban dwellers would see themselves as being above the rural peasantry.[51]

Further, as previously shown, Jesus' healing activity occurs predominantly among the "poor"—peasants, artisans, outcasts, and expendables (Matt 11:2–6[Q]). Conversely, Matthew's community is composed at least in part by the well-to-do.[52] Evidence supporting this assertion includes the number of references to coins and precious metals throughout the writing. In the mission of the Twelve, Mark's Jesus instructs the disciples not to take a relatively valueless "copper coin" (*chalkós*) (6:8), but Matthew directs the disciples not to take "gold, or silver, or copper" in their belts (10:9), all relatively valuable. Further, Matthew refers to a wide range of money:

1. *kodrántēs* (5:26)
2. *ássárion* (10:29)
3. *dēvárion* (18:28; 20:2, 9, 10; 22:19)
4. *dídrachmon* (17:24)
5. *statēr* (17:27)
6. *tálanton* (18:24; 25:15, 16, 20, 22, 24, 25, 28)
7. *chalkós* (10:9)

49. Kingsbury, *Matthew,* 99.

50. Ibid., see 10:11, 14, 15, 23; 23:34; and 5:14.

51. Elliott, "Temple versus Household," 221–22.

52. Kingsbury, *Matthew,* 99; Kilpatrick, *The Origins of the Gospel according St. Matthew,* 135–37.

8. *árgúrion* (25:18, 27; 26:15; 27:3; 28:12) and *árguros* (10:9)
9. *chrusos* ("gold") (2:11; 10:9; 23:16, 17)

In addition, there are striking differences concerning the treatment of money and belongings among Matthew, Luke, and Mark. Luke includes the parable of the ten *pounds,* or "minas," equivalent to about three months' wages for a laborer. Matthew includes the parable of the talents (25:14–30), a far costlier measurement. One talent was worth approximately fifty times more than one "mina." But there is other evidence. Both Mark (15:43) and Luke (23:50–51) identify Joseph of Arimathea as a member of the council who was looking for the kingdom of God, but Matthew identifies Joseph as a "rich man from Arimathea" (27:57). Luke in the parable of the great dinner speaks of bringing in "the poor, the crippled, the blind, and the lame" (14:21). Matthew states instead, "Go therefore into the main streets, and invite everyone you find to the wedding banquet" (22:9). Finally, the Sermon on the Mount begins with the beatitude of the "poor in spirit" (5:3) whereas the beatitude that opens Luke's Sermon on the Plain is addressed to the "poor" (6:20).

This is not to say that Matthew is unconcerned about the disciples' outlook toward wealth. Quite the opposite is the case. The sayings in 6:19–34 contrast an orientation to property and Rome's values as opposed to an orientation to God—"you cannot serve God and mammon" (6:24). Anxiety over life's necessities (6:25) is the first Matthean pericope in which the disciples are referred to as "you of little faith" (6:30). In Jesus' explanation of the parable of the sower (13:18–23), the word of the kingdom warns against those who hear the word, but the *cares of the world* and the *lure of wealth* choke the word, and it yields nothing (13:22). Further, Matthew's Jesus teaches the rich young man that if he would be "perfect" he must "go, sell" his possessions then come and follow Jesus (19:21), a passage that ends with the warning that "many who are first will be last, and the last will be first" (19:30). Jesus drives out of the temple those who sell and buy, and he overturns the tables of the money changers and the seats of those who merchandise doves (21:12). The scribes and Pharisees, Jesus warns his disciples, are "full of greed and self-indulgence" (23:25). In Jesus' parable of the judgment of non-Israelites (25:31–46), "the righteous" are those who feed the hungry, give drink to the thirsty, welcome strangers, visit those in prison, and clothe the naked. Finally, Judas suffers great remorse and commits suicide for betraying Jesus for thirty pieces of silver (27:3).

The cumulative weight of this evidence strongly suggests that Matthew's community is urban, relatively prosperous, and is being warned about the dangers of wealth. In this light the community needs to welcome without reservation persons like the hemorrhaging woman. Her story combined with other incidents like the leper, the demoniacs, the paralytic, and the two blind men are witnesses to that possibility. Matthew is concerned about social status within the community. Members are to be like children (18:3)—those who have the lowest standing in the family. The expression *little ones* (18:6, 10) possibly refers to such persons. Nothing should be done to cause these lowly believers to "stumble." When they go astray, community leaders should leave the "ninety-nine" in search of them (18:12). If so, the community possibly faces boundary dangers involving internal contradiction over inclusion issues. An urban and wealthy community possibly opposes the addition of those who are rural and poor. Following Elliott, in a "system of economic and social stratification legitimated by purity classifications" the rich would view themselves as superior to the poor.[53] But in Jesus' surrogate, kinship group, whoever does the will of God is "brother and sister and mother" (12:50).

Finally, the woman's story poses a social/theological challenge because her example, as well as other healing accounts in chapters 8 and 9, is informed by *logia* on discipleship. In the first instance (8:18–22), a scribe and a disciple, an outsider and an insider, seek to follow Jesus but are sternly warned that such commitments involve radical domestic, kinship decisions. In the case of the scribe, leaving the synagogue illustrates the danger of crossing a boundary, a forbidden frontier.[54] His example also illustrates how the kinship domain can have political significance as a *plurisignificant* social institution. In the case of the "true" disciple, Jesus' instruction to let "the dead bury their own dead" (8.22) is one of the sharpest *logia* in Matthew. Donald Hagner maintains that it runs counter to "law, piety, and custom"[55] concerning the care of one's family based on Torah observance. In contrast to these two examples is the call of Matthew who immediately leaves his toll booth to follow Jesus (9:9).

53. Elliott, "Temple versus Household," 221–22.

54. Douglas, *Purity and Danger*, 115.

55. Hagner, *Matthew 1–13*, 217; Hengel, "On the Exegesis of Mt 8.21–22," 14.

The ensuing banquet pericope (9:10–13) depicts Jesus and his disciples as dining with tax collectors and sinners, social and moral outcasts. Following the purity map the scene describes the exercise of God's mercy (mercy is greater than sacrifice [9:13]), the implementation of weaker social boundaries (outcasts are honored guests) that embrace an inclusive strategy among Israelites (Jesus is a "physician" whose mission is to heal and to call not the "righteous" but sinners [9:12–13]). The scene illustrates at a cultural level the pouring of new wine into new wineskins, so that both new and old "are preserved" (9:17). In contrast, the Pharisees, Jesus' critics, representatives of the synagogue kinship group, are motivated by God's holiness (social contact with sinners is forbidden) and the need for political control as an exclusionary strategy (Jesus' social behavior is out of step with the synagogue's expectations for social separation). Matthew's community does not follow the synagogue; rather it emulates Jesus' example of widespread inclusion.

Conclusion—Differences That Matter

As demonstrated, the hemorrhaging woman is both an example and paradigm of the lost sheep of the house of Israel (10:6; 15:24), those within Israel who are "helpless" and without a shepherd (9:36). Her significance as a symbol of Israel also fits the time of the Evangelist, that is, her example and others within the ten healing stories of chapters 8 and 9 coalesce to instruct the Matthean community about the composition, nature, and interrelationships of the community as a surrogate kinship community, one that is to welcome the lost sheep of the house of Israel because their stories, based on the deeds and words of Jesus, are examples of faith for the community.

JESUS RESTORES THE GIRL TO LIFE

Matthew's story of Jesus restoring the ruler's daughter to life (9:18–19, 23–26) also has great importance for the time of the Matthean community.

Level Two—The Girl's Story and Matthew's Community

As indicated, Matthew's account of the girl belongs to the private kinship/household domain, level two, the time of the Evangelist. But before the models are applied, it is necessary to note some of the ways Matthew redacts the story.

Matthew's Redaction

Redactional changes that have a bearing on a social-scientific reading of the account include the following: First, Matthew ties the story to an earlier banquet scene (9:9–17) and not to Jesus' return to Galilee after the healing of the Gerasene demoniac as found in Mark and Luke (Mark 5:21; Luke 8:40). In other words, Matthew opens and closes—brackets—the material from 9:10 through 9:26 with household scenes; the house of the banquet and the house of the ruler. Second, from the very outset the father reports to Jesus that the girl is dead (9:18) and not on the verge of death as in Mark (5:23) and Luke (8:42). Third, Matthew's readers know the father only as a "ruler" and not as a "leader of the synagogue," whose name is Jairus (Mark 5:22; Luke 8:41). Fourth, Matthew addresses the girl simply as "daughter" (9:18) and not as "little daughter" as found in Mark (5:23). In so doing, Matthew establishes one of the few parallels between the girl and the hemorrhaging woman who also is addressed by Jesus as simply "daughter" (9:22). Fifth, Matthew refers to those present at the house as the "crowd" (9:23, 25). And finally, only Jesus, not the father and mother or any of Jesus' disciples, enters the house, the death chamber, after the crowd has been driven outside (9:25; cf. Mark 5:40).

Illuminating the Story

Following the social realities of the political and kinship domains the ruler has high community status, not because he is a synagogue ruler (Mark 5:23; see Luke 8:41) but because, as Luz indicates, he is "some aristocratic person, perhaps a high official."[56] Probably, the hostility between the community and synagogue at this juncture precludes that Matthew's auditors honor a synagogue ruler. The girl's father, therefore, is not like the Pharisees who criticize Jesus during the tax collector's banquet (9:10–13); nor is he like the "crowd" who derisively laughs at Jesus' statement that "the girl is not dead but sleeping" (9:24). Rather, he represents for Matthew a person whose need for the exercise of mercy far outweighs issues concerning eating with sinners and fasting. His unmentioned but apparent faith is so great that even though his daughter is dead, he believes Jesus is able to restore her life (9:18). Accordingly, the ruler's behavior parallels the trust of the hemorrhaging woman. Otherwise, the ruler and the woman are polar opposites: he is a respected household leader; she is an outcast

---

56. Luz, *Matthew 8–20*, 41.

woman subsisting in public space. The community is reminded that both stories frame an acceptable social paradigm for those included in Jesus' mission to Israel.

The ruler's daughter is like and unlike the hemorrhaging woman. Both are female in a society dominated by adult males. Both are designated "daughter" and, therefore, should have inclusive standing within the Matthean community. However, there is a significant difference. The girl's status is not socially problematic because she belongs to an honorable household in which her father, a person of privilege and power, is able to act on her behalf. In other words, her father is an example of a respected male within the "agrarian mould," who enjoys both authority and communal status.[57] Conversely, the woman is an example of a person whose marginal standing identifies her as one of the many "helpless" persons who are without male agency and the protection and provision of an established household. Therefore, the combination of these two women, two "daughters" within one story, reminds the Matthean community that the gospel of the kingdom requires a significant social leveling. All persons belonging to Jesus' surrogate household have parallel standing because all are recipients of the God of Israel's mercy.

Following the purity model, danger from a gaggle of boundary issues is evident. On the one hand, the ruler crosses a frontier by entering a problematic household scene (9:10–13)—a banquet gathering of tax collectors, sinners, Jesus, and his disciples. His need for mercy far outweighs the Pharisees' concern for maintaining political control and God's holiness through an exclusionary strategy (see figure 5.1, the Purity/Political Map). Instead, he finds himself in a location marked by weak boundaries, an inclusionary strategy, and weaker bodily control where he is received by Jesus and becomes the recipient of the core value of God's mercy (9:18).

Then again, boundary issues of another sort, taboos concerning death, are violated by Jesus when he arrives at the ruler's house. In a reversal of social expectations, Jesus throws *outside* the hired mourners who typically are expected to be present, and then he alone enters *inside* the

---

57. Gundry, *Matthew*, 175, notes that "Even the poorest families hired at least two flute players and one female wailer for funerals"—see *b. Ketub.* 46b; cf. Josephus *J.W.* 3.437; Str-B 1:521–23. Among the Greeks the tradition is the same. See Marquardt, *Das Privatleben der Römer*, 351–52; Lucian *De luctu* 12.19. Matthew reports that those present include multiple flute players and a crowd of mourners, an indication of the ruler's economic and social status.

private location where the dead girl reposes. He then touches her impurity by taking her hand (see Table: Typology of Healing Stories in Matthew).[58] In so doing, Jesus fulfills the ruler's request precisely.

> Vs 18—"My daughter has just died; but *come and lay your hand on her, and she will live.*"

> Vs 25—"But when the crowd was driven outside, *he went inside and took her hand, and the girl arose.*"

The community would see in Jesus' behavior its own experience. As Luz describes it, the community is protected by Jesus' outstretched hand.[59] Beyond the community's protection, however, the reader is reminded that touching happens in both stories—the woman touches Jesus and Jesus takes the girl's hand. In both instances the healing power and authority of Jesus is effective. They both owe their well-being to Jesus' merciful action. The community should behave similarly—that is, the kinship community should break down traditional purity taboos and treat as whole what previously has been thought of as "dirt out of place." God's household is not a bounded system. Therefore, it matters not what social disparities prevail—illness, death, gender, age, male agency or lack of it. The community, like Jesus, should be committed to healing, the restoration of life, and the inclusion of all in that process.

CONCLUSION

Our models demonstrate that during the period of Jesus' activity as an Israelite healer a hemorrhaging woman with courageous faith healed by Jesus is also a rural Israelite, an expendable whom Jesus encounters in public space. Her healing underscores Jesus' Israelite mission and symbolizes Israel's need of salvation—the basis of Jesus' historical proclamation of the kingdom of heaven (10:1–16). She is representative of those helpless Israelites without a shepherd (9:36). Her good fortune makes possible her return to her household or her becoming one of the women who followed Jesus from Galilee (27:55), or both. Her healing also magnifies Jesus' reputation among Israelite peasants but complicates his relationship with the

---

58. Five other healing accounts in Matthew involve touching: the leper (8:2–4), Peter's mother-in-law (8:14–17), the hemorrhaging woman (9:20–22), two blind men (9:27–31), and two other blind men (20:29–34). In each case, touching involves some form of purity issue.

59. See Luz, *Matthew 8–20*, 41.

center of Judean political, economic, and religious power—the Jerusalem temple. The healing in open space shows how Jesus violates the political boundary of the temple and its far-reaching establishment.

Her paradigmatic significance as a symbol of Israel also pertains to the time of the Evangelist; that is, her status as a rural, outcast Israelite probably presents a social problem for an urban, reasonably well-to-do Christian community. Her story thus would be heard as a warning to the community about the treatment of Israelite outsiders within the Christian community. The community needs to welcome without reservation such persons because the woman's story is for them an example of great faith and discipleship and illustrates Jesus' millennial vision.

The dead girl's story located in a private kinship/household setting demonstrates how a person socially opposite to the hemorrhaging woman, the daughter of a respected household leader, also is a recipient of Jesus' mercy. The combination of these two stories, two "daughters" of Israel, would remind the Evangelist's community that the gospel of the kingdom requires a significant social leveling. All persons belonging to Jesus' surrogate family have parallel standing because all are recipients of the God of Israel's mercy. As Jesus "saved" both women, the community should behave accordingly, that is, like Jesus himself, be committed to healing, the restoration of life, and the inclusion of all Israelites.

In the next chapter the healing story of the Canaanite woman's daughter (15:21–28) is considered. It will be shown that her story parallels and/or is analogous in several ways to the healing account of the hemorrhaging woman (9:20–22). Our approach will be to investigate the account at two levels: the activity of Jesus and the time of the Evangelist. Once again, it will be affirmed that Matthew's redaction of Mark does not take his readers farther away from the historical Jesus; quite the contrary, the Canaanite woman's story underscores the period of Jesus' activity even while it features social and theological concerns of the Christian community. It is, as Luz says, "transparent," and operates on two levels. A major difference between the two women, however, is that the hemorrhaging woman is an Israelite and the Canaanite woman is a non-Israelite. Finally, the Canaanite woman, it will be shown, is a wise woman who becomes Jesus' teacher.

6

Jesus Heals the Canaanite Woman's Daughter

[21] And when Jesus left that place he went away into the regions of Tyre and Sidon. [22] And behold, a Canaanite woman from that locality came out and started shouting, "Have mercy on me, Lord, Son of David, my daughter is tormented from being possessed by a demon." [23] But he did not answer her even a word.

And his disciples came and pressed him and said, "Send her away, for she keeps hounding us." [24] But he answered and said, "I was sent only to the lost sheep of the house of Israel."

[25] But she came and began to worship him, saying, "Lord, help me!"

[26] But he answered and said: "It is not permitted to take the children's bread and to throw it to the dogs."

[27] But she said: "Certainly, Lord, but even the dogs eat the crumbs that fall from the table of their masters." [28] Then Jesus answered her, "Woman, your faith is great! Let it be done to you as you want." And her daughter was healed instantly. (Matt 15:21–28, author's translation)

INTRODUCTION

The healing story of the Canaanite woman's daughter (15:21–28) parallels and/or has points of comparison with the healing of the hemorrhaging woman (9:20–22). Both are structurally marginal persons but for different reasons. The hemorrhaging woman is an Israelite pariah probably due to her continuous physical impurity (Lev 15:25–30). The Canaanite woman's outsider status is due to her being a non-Israelite, possibly a prostitute, and her daughter's demon possession (15:22). Jesus commends both women for their faith (9:22; 15:28), and Matthew locates both stories in open, outdoor space. Jesus heals the woman who suffers from hemorrhages while making his way to the house of a civic leader. Unlike Mark (7:24), Matthew identifies the confrontation among the disciples, the Canaanite woman, and Jesus as taking place outside the house (15:22).[1]

The woman's story, as was the case with the hemorrhaging woman, is examined at two levels. The first is concerned with its historicity. That is, to what extent is this story rooted in the activity of Jesus?[2] Does the author's redaction of Mark take his audience farther away from, or closer to, the historical Jesus? Meier articulates well the former position when he states, "Weighing all the pros and cons, it seems to me that the story …is so shot through with Christian missionary theology and concerns that creation by first-generation Christians is the more likely conclusion."[3]

The second level is concerned with the time of the Matthean community. Does the story provide a social window into the period of the First Evangelist, that is, depict a community struggling over the radical inclusion of non-Israelite outcast women as a part of Jesus' new surrogate family? Does this woman's story add to the list of internal transitions, challenges, and changes needed within the Matthean community?

Concerning these two levels, we shall argue that Matthew's redaction of Mark does not take us farther away from the historical Jesus; quite the contrary, Matthew's version of the story underscores the historical period of Jesus' ministry even while it features theological concerns of the *Sitz im Leben* of the later Christian community.

SOCIAL-SCIENTIFIC MODELS

As in the hemorrhaging woman's story two social scientific models are utilized: (1) a model of healing in non-Western societies especially characterized by spirit possession/aggression, and (2) a model of a native taxonomy of illness—that includes degrees of impurity. The reader is reminded that the model on healing, broad in scope, is designed to better understand illness, healing, and healers in a social cultural perspective quite different from the biomedical approach largely operative in advanced industrialized societies like the United States. The notion of spirit

---

1. This open spatial setting is antipodal to the domestic environs of the healing stories of Peter's mother-in-law (8:14) and the civic leader's daughter (9:23–25).

2. For the difficulties of doing a historical analysis of Jesus as a healer in a post-Enlightenment period see the discussion in chapter 3.

3. Meier, *A Marginal Jew,* 660–61.

aggression assumes that illness/sickness is a misfortune due to malignant spirits and cosmic forces. Further, as was the case of the hemorrhaging woman's account, the model of purity/impurity assists in interpreting the actual reading of the story. As noted in chapter 3, a purity model helps clarify how the human body, where purity issues are manifest, is a microcosm of the social body. How might the woman and her daughter's impurity interface with the fabric of social, religious, and political issues of Jesus as a healer and the community's call for a radical inclusion of non-Israelites who seek out the God of Israel?

A third and new model of prostitution in advanced agrarian societies will be created to provide additional insight. Is it possible that the Canaanite woman is a prostitute? If so, what social implications would this example of gender-specific marginalization have for the Matthean community?[4]

Finally, as in our previous chapters, these three models are informed by previous thoughts on honor and shame and cultural realities associated with the social domains of politics and kinship.[5] For example, what does it mean for a non-Israelite woman to persistently and aggressively petition Jesus, an Israelite healer, to heal her daughter in open and ambiguous space in the district of Tyre and Sidon, that is, Phoenicia, which is part of the Roman province of Syria (15:21)? This question is political in nature and especially pertinent in light of Jesus' particularistic statement to the contrary, that he was sent only to "the lost sheep of the house of Israel" (15:24; cf. 10:5, 6). However, at the time of the Evangelist, a period concerned with internal (and outside) issues for the Christian community, emphasis shifts to the kinship domain, the social sphere of the community rather than to the political domain, its polar opposite. At that level, how is the woman's story to be interpreted in light of the challenges facing Jesus' surrogate family? Drawing upon our earlier and fuller notions about the political and kinship domains, the following salient features are emphasized:

1. In the ancient Mediterranean social world there are four "foundational social domains" that scholars who use socialscientific methods analyze—politics, economics, religion, and kinship (family).[6]

---

4. It will be shown that this model is closely aligned with the purity model.

5. A fuller description of the models is provided in chapter 3.

6. Hanson, "BTB Reader's Guide: Kinship," 183–94.

2. These four spheres are socially embedded to the extent that activity characteristic of one sphere may be dictated by or overlap with another sphere.

3. However, two of the domains, politics and kinship, are opposites. This means that the other two domains, religion and economics, are embedded either in politics or the family. Jesus' behavior and words including his healing activity and that of the Twelve belong primarily to the public, political, Israelite social domain.

4. Our understanding of social domains sets forth the following social-scientific criterion for authenticating the deeds and words of Jesus. *If an activity or statement attributed to Jesus in the healing story "makes direct and immediate political sense, then it is authentic."*[7] In that light the statement of Jesus to the disciples, "I was sent only to the lost sheep of the house of Israel" (15:24), has historical probability. The political issues of the period of Jesus are past but the Canaanite woman's story, still remembered by the community, has possible public, political significance in the period of the Evangelist due to its social setting in open space.[8] However, the gravitational point of tension for the Evangelist's community has shifted from the temple to the synagogue.

5. Embedded in the household, kinship is the most basic unit of social organization in agrarian societies,[9] consisting of families, villages, cities, and the empire.[10]

6. The community of the Evangelist belongs to the kinship domain referenced by the writing's emphasis upon the surrogate family of God.

7. When viewed as a plurisignificant social metaphor in literature, however, the kinship domain (household/family) may also have political significance especially when viewed in association with the political social domain. Jesus is said to belong to the particularistic societal entity of "the household of Israel," a domestic metaphor for a political collectivity. The Canaanite woman is outside Israel's

7. Malina, "Criteria for Authenticating the Authentic Words of Jesus," 43.

8. Pilch, "Healing in Mark," 147.

9. Elliott, "Temple versus Household in Luke-Acts," 221–38.

10. Elliott, *A Home for the Homeless*, 165–266.

political/kinship domain and belongs to a particularistic societal entity labeled as "Canaanite," which is also political. With these thoughts let us now turn to the three models.

Model One—Healing in Non-Western Societies

The following salient features about healing are emphasized and particularized in light of the Canaanite woman's story:[11]

1. Because both patients and healers are "embedded in a cultural system," Jesus as an Israelite healer should be viewed not in isolation but in association with the cultural system.

2. In societies like the ancient Mediterranean sickness and healing may be classified along the lines of witchcraft, sorcery, and spirit aggression.[12] Evidence for spirit aggression abounds in Matthew.

3. Magical practices flourish in preindustrial settings among all social groups but especially among lower-class urbanites and peasants.[13] As indicated previously, we do not decide whether Jesus is a magician or a charismatic healer, but how persons like the Canaanite woman might perceive Jesus and act accordingly. Therefore, the term "magic" is used non-pejoratively "as the art of influencing the superhuman sphere of the spirits, demons, angels and gods."[14]

4. Jesus is not a "professional" healer but a "folk" healer. Neither is there evidence that the Canaanite woman has economic resources to procure professional care (see the contrasting example of the hemorrhaging woman in Mark [7:26]).

5. Rural and urban lower-class populations—peasants, artisans, outcasts, and expendables—experience health care mediated not by the professional sector but by the popular and folk sectors.[15] Jesus is a healer among those who experience and treat illness in the popular and folk sectors. The woman also belongs to these sectors.

11. See chapter 3 for a more-developed model description.

12. Murdock, *Theories of Illness,* 73; Foster, "Disease Etiologies," 773–82.

13. Sjoberg, *Preindustrial City,* 275; Blum and Blum, *Health and Healing,* 25, 31–35.

14. Theissen and Merz, *The Historical Jesus,* 305, n. 22.

15. Sigerist, *A History of Medicine,* 2:306; Jackson, *Doctors and Diseases in the Roman Empire,* 138–69.

6. Nothing in the story indicates that the woman is part of a "web" of "folk" relations to which she could turn, even though such "folk" networks can be detected in Matthew (see 4:24; 9:2; 14:35). Instead, without male agency or help from others she aggressively appeals to a healer belonging to an outside social group about which she would have had ethnocentric attitudes.

7. Jesus' behavior and words, including his healing activity and that of the Twelve belong primarily to the public, political, Israelite, social domain—a matter that leads to the second model.

Model Two—A Native Taxonomy of Illness, Degrees of Impurity

A summary of a native taxonomy of illness based on "degrees of impurity" features the following components, all of which have points of contact with the Canaanite woman's story:[16]

1. Purity is defined as normality and wholeness; impurity is pollution and taboo, that is, matter "out of place"—dirt in the house—a cultural system of order and disorder.[17]

2. Purity rules are also symbols, a cultural language that expresses and reflects larger social concerns that work in concert with other structures of thought to deliver and support a common message.

3. Purity dangers are fourfold: external, internal, at the margins, and internal contradiction. The encounter between Jesus and the Canaanite woman involves principally the danger of pressing against external boundaries. However, the woman's outcast status also threatens the other three types of marginal dangers. Accordingly, boundary making, crossing, and breaking both externally and internally constitute an ongoing process. The social reality of pollution/taboo/ continues to threaten the social fabric of a community in transition.

---

16. Neusner, *The Idea of Purity in Ancient Judaism*; idem, "History and Purity in First-Century Judaism," 1–17; Pilch, "Biblical Leprosy and Body Symbolism," 119–33; idem, "Sickness and Healing in Luke-Acts," 207; Malina, *New Testament World*, 164–80; Neyrey, "The Idea of Purity in Mark's Gospel," 91–128; idem, "The Symbolic Universe of Luke-Acts," 271–304. For a full development of the model, see chapter 3.

17. Douglas, *Purity and Danger;* Isenberg, "Mary Douglas and Hellenistic Religions," 179–85; Isenberg and Owen, "Bodies, Natural and Contrived," 1–17.

4. Finally, the human body is a center where purity issues are manifest—a microcosm of the social body. There is a correlation between
socio-political strategy and bodily concerns.[18] This correlation may
be clarified through the use of the following purity/political "map"
that highlights a social/purity tension for this particular story—the
Canaanite woman is not Israelite.

FIGURE 6.1: PURITY/POLITICAL MAPS

Purity/Political Map for Jesus	Purity/Political Map for the Canaanite Woman
Political locus—Kingdom of Heaven No network of control Mostly rural Israelite villages/peasants located in Galilee	*Political locus—Unknown, Non-Israelite, Ancient Canaanite Identity* No known network of control Marginal locus, typically non-Israelite location, "district of Tyre and Sidon" A liminal person outside the house of Israel
God of Israel Core value: God's mercy	*Not the God of Israel* Core value: unknown, but faith in Jesus as the God of Israel's healer
Mission Inaugurate Israel's Theocracy	*Mission* Healing for her daughter
Structural Implications Weak boundaries Inclusive strategy among Israelites	*Structural Implications* Weak boundaries/No known family structural ties No political strategy/ "strategy" for healing includes Israelites
Legitimation in Israelite Scripture Genesis and Prophets	*Legitimation in Israelite Scripture* None
Weaker Purity Concern Weak bodily control Public, bodily contact with sick, demon-possessed, bodily deformed	*Purity Concerns Unknown* Weak bodily control Public contact with Israelite healer and his disciples

Jesus is constrained by the political limitations of his mission to Israel.
But he is prompted also by the core value of God's mercy that follows

18. Neyrey, "Clean/Unclean," 93.

weak structural boundaries and weak bodily control. As a result he faces a dilemma. Can he heal the Canaanite woman's daughter as he did the Israelite hemorrhaging woman?[19]

Model Three—Prostitutes and Prostitution in Advanced Agrarian Societies

Most prostitutes are among those designated as expendables in advanced agrarian societies. Gideon Sjoberg classifies prostitutes as those who perform *defiling* tasks such as "night-soil carriers, leather workers, butchers, many barbers, midwives, dancers and lepers."[20] Accordingly, most prostitutes are outcasts and economically unable to maintain large households. Their isolation from any family unit often results in a struggle for subsistence; most prostitutes suffer a slow death due to starvation and disease.[21]

In agrarian societies, women isolated from the kinship system are readily reduced to prostitution.[22] In ancient Israel, such persons are liminal. Benjamin and Matthews state:

> But there were women in the villages of Israel who did not belong to any social class. These women were liminal. They had no status. The orphan, the prostitute, and the widow without children were all liminal women. . . . Liminal women were not just out of the house but were without a household. They were legally homeless, without any social, political, or economic status in the village. But because they had nothing, they also had nothing to lose."[23]

Benjamin and Matthews present the following diagram of the household and liminal women.[24]

---

19. For the purity/political map of Jesus as healer of Israelites see chapter 3. (The purity map in this chapter is for non-Israelites (the Canaanite Woman).

20. Sjoberg, *Preindustrial City,* 134.

21. Ibid., 160.

22. Ibid.

23. Matthews and Benjamin, *Social World of Ancient Israel,* 133.

24. Ibid., 134.

FIGURE 6.2: HOUSEHOLDS AND LIMINAL WOMEN

Women of a Household	Liminal Women
The Daughter with a Father	The Female Orphan without a Father
The Wife with a husband	The Prostitute without a husband
The Widow with a son	The Widow without a son

We cannot affirm that the Israelite example is paralleled among Canaanite communities, but both groups belonged to the same geographical and cultural environ documented by Israelite and Ugaritic evidence.

In urban examples, children more often girls, orphaned or from poor families, frequently were sold to buyers who made them into servants, entertainers, or prostitutes.[25] The Lenskis state, "Many of the sisters of the men who made up the urban lower classes earned their livelihood as prostitutes."[26] They also observe that

> Moralists have often condemned these women as though they elected this career in preference to a more honorable one. The record indicates, however, that most of them had little choice: their only alternative was a life of unrelieved drudgery and poverty. . . . The men they might have married were too poor to afford wives, and the system of prostitution was often, in effect, a substitute for marriage that was forced on people by society.[27]

It is true that others besides the poor availed themselves of the services of prostitutes. It is also true that not all prostitutes were poor, but "economic factors were clearly the chief cause of its high incidence in advanced agrarian societies."[28] Conversely, the "elite" insulated themselves from all "outcasts" including prostitutes by a distinctive lifestyle reflected in idiosyncratic speech forms, personal mannerisms, and clothing.[29]

In terms of social mobility, advanced agrarian evidence suggests that few prostitutes were able to move upward socially and that most fell readily into the ranks of the outcast and/or expendables.[30] For example, a

25. Ibid.

26. Lenski and Lenski, *Human Societies* (1987), 192.

27. Ibid.

28. Ibid.

29. Sjoberg, *Preindustrial City*, 134–35.

30. Ibid., 141; Lenski and Lenski, *Human Societies* (1987), 290.

lower-class woman without family ties "may enter prostitution in order to eke out a livelihood, thereupon assuming a status from which there is little hope of escape."[31] The Lenskis include prostitutes among social groups who had only their bodies and animal energies to sell which quickly destroyed them, for example, rickshaw pullers, porters who took the place of pack animals, and miners who did heavy work under dangerous conditions.[32] The Lenskis state, "For such persons, this type of work was often a transitional step, leading to the ranks of the expendables."[33] Cities and towns in agrarian societies "often swarmed with beggars of both sexes, comprising from a tenth to as high as a third of the total population of urban communities."[34] In Matthew, the Canaanite woman is located alone in open, male space with alien Israelite men. She has no male "intermediary" to represent her to Jesus.

Having set forth the models, we now apply them to the story of the Canaanite woman and her daughter according to the period of the historical Jesus and the period of the Evangelist. First, though, thoughts on Matthew's vision of a non-Israelite mission and a redaction of Mark's account of the "Syrophoenician" woman are noted.

LEVEL ONE—JESUS HEALS THE CANAANITE WOMAN'S DAUGHTER

Does the First Evangelist Have a Vision for a Non-Israelite Mission?

Our first problem is whether the First Evangelist envisions a non-Israelite mission.[35] A traditional view holds that Matthew has a mission vision that includes non-Israelites. Evidence for this perspective begins as early as the genealogy (1:1, 2–6a) and as late as the instructions given to the Eleven to spread the good news of the kingdom of heaven to *pánta tá éthnē*, "all the peoples" (28:19).[36] Other supportive evidence includes not only the Canaanite woman's story but Matthew's distinctive rendition of the wise

31. Sjoberg, *Preindustrial City*, 141.

32. Lenski and Lenski, *Human Societies* (1987), 281.

33. Ibid.

34. Ibid., 192.

35. For a description of earlier interpretive options see Luz, *Matthew 8–20*, 70–72.

36. See Senior, "Between Two Worlds," 1–23. As pointed out in the introduction to this book, *éthnē* has a number of meanings in Matthew but always refers to a group of people. It can identify a group of non-Israelites, but apparently that is not always the case.

men (2:1–12), the assertion that God can raise up children to Abraham from stones (3:9), the Isaiah fulfillment quotation concerning "Galilee of the Gentiles" (4: 15), the centurion's faith (8: 10–11), and a non-Israelite inclusion that precedes the end (24:14; see 25:32 and 26:13). From this perspective the Canaanite woman's story supports Matthew's non-Israelite mission because Matthew emphasizes the woman's submissive demeanor through the use of *prosekúnei* (imperfect tense; see 8:2; 9:18; 14:33; and 20:20)—"she began to worship" him (15:25) and by Jesus' commendation of the woman's faith, "Woman, great is your faith!" (15:28).

A more recent perspective, however, argues that in Matthew's final edict (28:18–20) Jesus sends his disciples only to all Israelites living among non-Israelites.[37] The First Evangelist's "universalism" is limited to Israelites except for non-Israelites who look for the God of Israel like the magi who seek for the "child who has been born king of the Jews" (2:2) or the Canaanite woman who comes out to Jesus, an Israelite healer, in her distress. In this scenario the centurion (8:5–13) is not a non-Israelite. Rather, he is an Israelite, one of the auxiliary troops that populate the Roman army in Palestine during the first century. In contrast to the Pharisees, who are noted for excluding fellow Israelites, the community of the First Evangelist is to uphold an Israelite in-group inclusion, a matter made clear in the distinctive Matthean emphasis that the mission of the Twelve is to "Go nowhere among the Gentiles, and enter no town of the Samaritans, but go rather to the lost sheep of the house of Israel" (10:5; 15:24).[38] In other words, in contrast to the Pharisees, the Matthean community is to seek out the entire people of God, including the "black sheep" in Israel.

Redactional Considerations

In addition, certain redactional features of Matthew's account of the Canaanite woman's story seem to support the second position. Matthew omits Mark's statement by Jesus to the woman, "'Let the children first be fed . . .'" (Mark 7:27) and inserts in its place, "It is not permitted to take the children's bread and to throw it to the dogs" (15:26).

---

37. See Sim, *The Gospel of Matthew and Christian Judaism,* 188–211; idem, "Matthew's Anti-Paulinism," 767–83; "Matthew 7:21–23," 325–43.

38. Matthew's Jesus uses the word "only" emphatically in the Canaanite woman's story. "'I was sent *only* to the lost sheep of the house of Israel.'"

Nowhere else does Matthew attribute such negative and particularistic language by Jesus toward a non-Israelite, let alone a woman.[39] Accordingly, the Canaanite woman illustrates another kind of marginality identified by social-scientific research as "cultural marginality."[40] She is a woman who is faced with living between two competing cultures, historic traditions, and religions; she is a person with status incongruence. In contrast, Jesus readily accepts the centurion who comes and makes his appeal that his servant is made whole. Unambiguously he affirms, "I will come and heal him" (8:6). Is this because the centurion is an Israelite? Or, can this be understood in another manner? Further, Matthew's account accentuates a number of refusals by Jesus. The healer ignores the woman's repeated cries for mercy (15:23a, 22) and refuses to send her away even though the disciples press him to do so (15:23). Apparently, she is not this Israelite's concern. In addition, by modifying Mark's statement from "and he said to her" (Mark 7:27a) to "and he answered" (the disciples, Matt 15:26a) Matthew underscores Jesus' refusal to deal with the woman until the actual challenge and response (15:26–28). Matthew makes abundantly clear that Jesus' behavior and language are grounded in his exclusive mission to "the lost sheep of the house of Israel" (15:24; 9:24; 10:5–6; see also 9:36; 18:12; Jer 50:6). Perhaps this is why Luke omits the story—its Israelite ethnocentric perspective is out of step with a universal vision.[41]

We acknowledge the strengths (and weaknesses) of both positions. However, we believe the evidence still tips in favor of a non-Israelite mission in Matthew's final declaration to the Eleven disciples (28:18–20). Ultimately, both perspectives fit our reading of the story because our pivotal concern is whether Jesus and/or the Matthean community are willing to receive and minister to those who are culturally marginalized.

39. On the tension between Matthew's particularism and universalistic vision, see Levine, *The Social and Ethnic Dimensions of Matthean Salvation History*, 193–221; Brown, "The Matthean Community and the Gentile Mission," 193–221; "The Mission to Israel in Matthew's Central Section (Mt. 9:35—11.1)," 73–90; "Universalism and Particularism," 388–99.

40. I am indebted to Dennis Duling for this observation.

41. Burkill, "The Historical Development of the Story of the Syrophoenician Woman," 25.

Further Thoughts on Matthew's Redaction of Mark

Another difficulty rightly observed is that Matthew's account, like Mark's, follows and fits the context of the dispute initiated by Pharisees sent from Jerusalem to examine Jesus over purity matters (15:1–20; cf. Mark 7:1–23). But a number of issues once more emerge over Matthew's alterations of Mark's account. To begin with, Matthew's usual practice of shortening sayings, dialogues, and stories from Mark is not followed in this instance. Instead, Matthew lengthens the narrative that in turn alerts us more especially to what is omitted, altered, substituted, or added. At the outset Matthew singles out the woman as a "Canaanite" (15:22), a disparaging reference apparently conjuring up the ancient enmity between Israelites and Canaanites.[42] By doing so, Matthew deletes Mark's more neutral identification, a "Greek, a Syrophenician by birth" (Mark 7:26)—an identity shift that may alter as well any assumption that the woman has a relatively high social/economic status.[43] Further, Matthew changes the scene's venue to outdoor, open space (15:21)—male turf, whereas Mark begins the story by telling his readers that Jesus "entered a house" (15:21//Mark 7:24) and ends it with the woman returning home to her daughter healed and lying on the bed (15:21//Mark 7:29). Nothing in Matthew's rendition points to a domestic environment—it is not known even if the woman has a home. In addition, Matthew omits Mark's secrecy motif (7:24) and tells his readers that the woman "came out" to Jesus (15:22). By doing so she seizes the initiative and speaks frequently and persistently (15:22, 25, 27)—an abridgement not only of Mark's development but a reversal of gender expectations. Mark further softens a potential gender embarrassment by reserving the woman's words to the end of the story and envisaging them as a response to what Jesus says (7:27, 28). A final addition is the woman's address to Jesus, "Lord, Son of David" (15:22, 25, 27),[44] interpreted typically as a messianic christological title (1:1; 9:27; 12:23; 20:30, 31; 22:42). But would a Canaanite woman have understood the address in this way?

---

42. Davies and Allison, *Matthew*, 2:547.

43. *Contra* Theissen, *The Miracle Stories of the Early Christian Tradition*, 210–11.

44. Duling, "Matthew's Plurisignificant 'Son of David,'" 99–116.

Political/Purity Issues for the Historical Jesus

How then does a social-scientific reading demonstrate that the foundation of the account originated with Jesus? First, and perhaps foremost in light of the political domain, Jesus' statement to the disciples, "I was sent only to the lost sheep of the house of Israel" (15:24), has authentic historical probability in that it "makes direct and immediate political sense"[45] for Jesus' mission to establish an Israelite theocracy (10:5; 15:24).[46] This includes as well the assignment of the disciples to go nowhere among the Gentiles and Samaritans. Following Jesus' example and instructions, their mission is only to the "lost sheep of the house of Israel" (10:5, 6)—to "all the towns of Israel" (10:23; see 7:6 and 19:28–29). They, too, should ignore this unexpected, aggressive, invasive behavior of the woman.

Following the purity/political map of Jesus, the political locus of the kingdom of heaven is centered in the God of Israel and his healing activity is predominantly among Israelite peasants in Galilee. Jesus' mission is to inaugurate Israel's theocracy, an inclusive strategy among Israelites.

Linked as well to this criterion is the political plurisignificance of the phrase "house of Israel" (15:24; 10:6), a household metaphor that captures the ethnocentric particularism of Israel. When Matthew identifies the woman as a "Canaanite" rather than Mark's "Syrophoenician," he reinforces the historic enmity separating two ancient particularistic political households—Israel and Canaan. The woman's ancient heritage also entails its own particularism, a historic political enmity that is probably reinforced by Jesus' statement, "It is not permitted to take the children's food and throw it to the dogs" (15:26). Only in Matthew does Jesus teach, "Do not give dogs what is holy; and do not throw your pearls before swine, lest they trample them under foot and turn to attack you" (7:6). The term "children" identifies the "house of Israel." The term "dogs" probably identifies in this case Canaanites, that is, outsiders who are also called

---

45. Malina, "Criteria for Assessing the Authentic Words of Jesus," 43.
46. Ibid., 36.

"swine," implying that they are unclean.[47] The term "holy" probably refers to arm bands, a type of jewelry.[48]

The proverb communicates a powerful, ethnocentric social symbol that is challenged by the woman's response, "Yes, Lord, yet even the dogs eat the crumbs that fall from their masters' table" (15:27). Her riposte is not only a clever rebuttal but also a continued appeal for mercy.[49] She seeks one "crumb" from this Israelite folk healer. She wants him to heal her daughter whose suffering outweighs the social kinship boundaries that separate her and Jesus. Now, Jesus is faced with a dilemma: a non-Israelite makes her appeal based on the core value of God's mercy. By doing so, she also challenges the stronger boundaries of Jesus' inclusive strategy only to Israel. This forthright tension is enlarged by Matthew's consistent appeal that Jesus' mission is legitimated out of the prophetic tradition of Hosea, "'Go and learn what this means, 'I desire mercy not sacrifice'" (9:13, repeated in 12:7 from Hos 6:6 [LXX]). It is also amplified by the way Matthew links the verbs "to have compassion," "to have mercy," and the titles, "Lord" and "Son of David." The theme of mercy is found in 9:27; 15:22; 17:15; 20:30, 31; the theme of compassion is found in 9:36; 14:14; 15:32; 17:20; 20:34; and the title "Son of David" is located in 9:36; 12:23; 15:32; 17:20; 20:34. These instances should be compared also with 5:7; 15:25; 18:26, 27, 33. As Dennis Duling notes, "Four of the five instances of the verb 'to have compassion' (*splangchnízomai*) and five of the eight instances of the verb 'to have mercy' (*élleō*) occur in connection with healing and in almost every case the poly-significant titles Lord and/or Son of David appear as part of the semantic field."[50] All of this adds to the scriptural appeal of the purity/political map of Jesus and heightens the impediment of extending mercy to a non-Israelite woman.

---

47. The notion that "dogs" are house pets (Luz, *Matthew 8–20*, 340–41) is probably wrong. Malina and Rohrbaugh state, "Dogs were unclean animals in ancient Palestine and were not kept as pets. Dogs attached themselves to villages and patrolled the perimeters expecting handouts, belonging to the group rather than to individuals" (Malina and Rohrbaugh, *Synoptic Gospels*, 50–51).

48. Ibid.

49. "Mercy," Malina and Rohrbaugh state, "means the willingness to pay back and the actual paying back of one's debts of interpersonal obligation to God and fellow humans," ibid., 84–104. The reason Jesus owes mercy is because he is the Son of David. See also Malina, "Eleoj y la ayuda social."

50. Duling, "Matthew's Plurisignificant 'Son of David,'" 112.

This anomaly does not fit the central Matthean trajectory of Jesus' confrontation with the temple establishment. What one might expect, given Jesus' mission to Israel, is a clash of the prophetic call for mercy in the social/political context of the Jerusalem Temple. This, indeed, is the case when in Jerusalem two Israelite political/religious "systems" collide as Jesus heals the blind and lame in the temple (21:14). Duling states,

> like David, but unlike the Sadducees and Pharisees, Jesus need not maintain temple purity; indeed, as the great healer/exorcist, the great patron or benefactor of the peasants, the impure, and the expendables, he heals in the very center of Jewish political, economic, and religious life, the seat of religious purity, the Jerusalem Temple. The response of the children signifies that he stands against the Temple establishment, as well as the High Priestly aristocracy and the scribal retainers [Matt 21:1–17].[51]

Nevertheless, Matthew preserves an instance of a clash between Jesus' theocratic mission to Israel and his commitment to the core value of mercy.

Applying the Model of Prostitutes in Advanced Agrarian Societies— Is the Woman a Prostitute?

Returning to the narrative, the woman's single-handed persistence may be due as well to her social status; there is a reasonable possibility that the woman is an outcast prostitute. Most probably she is not an urban prostitute under the control of a pimp.[52] However, being alone in open space without male representation suggests a woman isolated from the security of a family or household. Anderson describes the woman as being "alone with no indication of an embedded status in a patriarchal family."[53] Under such conditions she most probably faces subsistence issues as she contends with the illness of her daughter (15:22). Following the model, a woman in such circumstances often pursues a life of prostitution.[54]

Hypothetically, she could be a destitute widow, but Matthew refers to widows only once, ("Woe to you, Scribes and Pharisees, hypocrites! For you devour widows' houses . . ." [23:14])—a verse that has sufficient

51. Ibid., 113.

52. This we cannot prove. However, her location appears not to be urban.

53. Anderson, "Matthew: Gender and Reading," 11.

54. Sjoberg, *Preindustrial City,* 160. Against Theissen's view that the woman has relatively high status, see *The Miracle Stories of the Early Christian Tradition,* 210–11.

textual difficulties to be placed as a footnote in the NRSV. Matthew also omits the unit of the widow's offering, a significant story to Mark and Luke (Mark 12:41–44; Luke 21:1–4). Thus, if we exclude 23:14 on textual grounds, there are no references to widows in Matthew.[55]

Hypothetically, she could be divorced or a person never married, but, if so, it still must be remembered that she is alone in male space. Also, according to the model, many of the sisters of the men who comprised the urban lower classes earned their livelihood as prostitutes and since the men they might have married were too poor to afford wives, the system of prostitution was, in effect, a substitute for marriage "that was forced on people by society."[56] Following the model, if the Canaanite woman is an orphan or from a poor family, she probably would have been sold to buyers who would have in turn sold her as a slave, entertainer, or prostitute. Ringe points out, "she appears to be totally isolated from family support, for if there had been any male relative in her family (or among her in-laws if she had been married), he would have had the responsibility of caring for her and her daughter and of interceding on their behalf."[57] In other words, the woman should have been invisible. "No Jewish man, especially one with a religious task or vocation," would have been "approached by a woman (Jew or Gentile), except perhaps by one of the many lone women reduced to prostitution to support themselves."[58] In the end, it matters not whether she is a single person, divorced, or a widow because prostitution would have been a major means of survival for most women in similar social circumstances in agrarian societies.

As indicated, for Matthew widows apparently are of little consequence, but prostitutes are noteworthy. At least two of the women mentioned in the genealogy, Tamar and Rahab, behave as prostitutes and/or are identified as prostitutes in the Israelite Scriptures (1:3, 5; see Gen 38; Josh 2:1, 12, 14, 15–21).[59] Perhaps this is the reason Matthew chooses to call her a "Canaanite woman" rather than a "Syro-Phoenician"

---

55. In contrast, widows are an important social group in Luke-Acts (2:37; 4:25, 26; 7:12; 18:3; 20:47; 21:2, 3; Acts 6:1; 9:39, 41).

56. Lenski and Lenski, *Human Societies* (1987), 192.

57. Ringe, "A Gentile Woman's Story," 70.

58. Ibid.

59. Tamar poses as a prostitute and plays the whore (Gen 38:15–26) but proves to be more in the right than Judah (38:26). Rahab devises the means of saving the Israelite spies and thereby spares herself and her family (Josh 6:22–25).

(Mark 7:26). Corley asserts that both Tamar and Rahab were Canaanites[60] and argues that "given Israel's struggle with temple prostitution assimilated from Canaanite religious ritual, Canaanite women" had "a strong connection with prostitution and sexual sin in Jewish biblical tradition."[61] Corley concludes, "Thus, even more clearly in Matthew than in Mark Jesus is portrayed as ministering to a woman associated with harlotry, a 'sinner.'"[62]

Prostitutes also are significant to the Evangelist because twice in the parable of the two sons (21:28–32), distinctive to Matthew, Jesus refers to them alongside tax collectors (21:31, 32), a phenomenon otherwise unknown among canonical gospel traditions. To affirm that Jesus' statement, "Truly I tell you, the tax collectors and the prostitutes are going into the kingdom of God ahead of you" (21:31), is simply an oral, idiomatic slur with no substance in the social reality of his ministry, fails to take into account that a second reference one verse later is linked specifically to the ministry and preaching of John. "For John came to you in the way of righteousness and you did not believe him, but the tax collectors and the prostitutes believed him" (21:32). Further, if the reference to "prostitutes" is merely a denigrating colloquialism the same would have to be said of tax collectors since Matthew says, "the tax collectors and the prostitutes are going into the kingdom of God ahead of you" (21:31). And yet, tax collectors, as in the call story of Matthew (9:10, 11), play an important social role in Matthew's narrative and message (5:46; 10:3; 11:19; 18:17; 21:31, 32). Prostitutes apparently do the same.

Put another way, most probably the Canaanite woman is not a matron or wealthy widow with an urban household at her disposal. Her lack of male agency best explains her venturing into male space alone. As a "single parent" she would find subsistence a daily issue. The model of healing in non-Western societies reinforces this reading. She must seek help for an illness of spirit aggression without social systemic relief. She belongs to the popular and folk social sectors, but as an outcast and/or expendable she cannot depend on a network of healing. Her need outweighs the social-historical ethno-centric barriers between Canaanites and Israelites. She knows only that a famous itinerant Israelite healer has come her way this

60. Corley, *Private Women, Public Meals*, 150–51, 166.

61. Ibid., 166.

62. Ibid.; see Thompson, *Matthew's Advice to a Divided Community*, 282; and Burkhill, "The Historical Development of the Story of the Syrophoenician Woman," 177.

one time. She believes that he alone can heal her daughter. Perhaps that is why the woman bests the healer in the challenge/response, prompting Jesus to state, "Woman, great is your faith! Let it be done for you as you want" (15:28). Ethnocentric issues have been challenged—overcome and/or suspended—by the distinctive nature of the encounter and exchange. The uniqueness of these factors also points to the activity of Jesus, a social embarrassment that is preserved in the Matthean account.

The Woman's Address, "Lord, Son of David" (15:22)

Finally, there is an issue over the meaning of the woman's address, "Lord, Son of David" (15:22). At the level of the Evangelist, the term "Lord" probably connotes Jesus' divinity because it is used of God in scripture and in Matthew it is linked with terms of worship: the woman addresses Jesus as "Lord" three times (15:22, 25, 27) and kneels before him (15:25). However, the term may be an address of respect by an inferior to a superior (7:21; 9:24).

Similarly, the expression "Son of David" is used as a title in requests in a number of Matthew's healing stories (9:27; 12:33; 15:22; 17:15; 20:31) signifying a messianic meaning at the time of the Evangelist (1:1; 12:23; 21:9; 22:42). Jesus as the "Son of David" is the expected messianic healer-king.[63] Nonetheless, it seems unlikely that a Canaanite woman would address Jesus in this manner unless she understood the words in another way. We propose that this is possibly the case and that she identifies Jesus out of a social setting of magic and healing set forth in the model of healing in non-Western societies. Since evil spirits upset the order of life, causing illness,[64] magical practice corrects imbalances in the spiritual order.[65] As a "peasant" she believes that she could enlist divine help for this end.[66] Seizing the initiative, the woman names her wish and names her healer. She sees Jesus as a holy man with magical powers.

But why would she specifically address Jesus as "Lord, Son of David"? She might do so out of a widespread Solomonic/Son of David-healer/

---

63. Healing is never associated with the Son of David in pre-Christian texts.
64. Sjoberg, *Preindustrial City*, 277.
65. Blum and Blum, *Health and Healing*, 31–32.
66. Ibid., 32.

exorcist tradition. Here, I draw on research by Duling,[67] Fisher,[68] Lövestam,[69] and Berger,[70] who have identified a pre-Christian "Solomon-as-exorcist" (Son of David-exorcist) trajectory in both literary and popular Jewish culture in Egypt, Palestine, Mesopotamia, the DSS (11 QpsApa), Pseudo-Philo, Josephus (*Ant.* 8.2, 5), and from a later period probably influenced by the Second Testament in the *Testament of Solomon* and perhaps elsewhere (the magical papyri; *Testament of Solomon*).[71] This tradition may have been available to non-Israelites in such regions as Tyre and Sidon, the region of the Canaanite woman. Interestingly, Matthew compares Jesus to Solomon in a context of casting out unclean spirits/demons and declares that something greater than Solomon is here (12:42). Not to be forgotten is that Matthew uses the title "Son of David" for Jesus as a healer (9:27; 12:23; 15:22; 20:30; 20:31; 21:15). Thus, the woman possibly uses the address, "Lord, Son of David," out of a social background of magic and healing. She perceives Jesus to be a "Solomon-as-exorcist" healer and persistently pursues her wish, believing the gods could supply her need. Indefatigably but deferentially she appeals for mercy and addresses Jesus as "Lord, Son of David." By the use of "Lord" she shows respect to Jesus' authority as a healer. By the use of "Son of David" she identifies Jesus out of the "Solomon-as-exorcist" tradition. This interpretation parallels the pervasive place of magic in societies like Roman Palestine and lends credence to the assertion that the central part of Matthew's story belongs to the most primitive layer of gospel tradition—the activity of Jesus. How the title might have been understood by Israelites in the time of Jesus' activity could have been different. Certainly, by the time of the Evangelist the address is understood christologically within the Christian community.

---

67. Duling, "Matthew's Plurisignificant 'Son of David,'" 99–116; idem, "Solomon, Exorcism, and the Son of David," 235–52; idem, "The Therapeutic Son of David in Matthew's Gospel," 392–410; idem, "The Eleazar Miracle and Solomon's Magical Wisdom in Flavius Josephus' *Antiquitates Judaicae*," 1–25; idem, "The Testament of Solomon: Retrospect and Prospect," 87–112; idem, "Solomon, Testament of," 117–19; cf. *Testament of Solomon, A New Translation and Introduction*, 935–87.

68. Fisher, "Can This Be the Son of David?" 82–97.

69. Lövestam, "Jésus Fils de David chez les Synoptiques," 97–109.

70. Berger, "Die königlichen messiastradition des Neuen Testaments," 1–44.

71. Duling, "Solomon, Exorcism, and the Son of David," 249.

Differences That Matter

But what difference does this social-scientific reading of the story make for the woman, her daughter, and Jesus? The woman's status, if she is a prostitute, probably is not altered. She still lacks the systemic support of the kinship domain, the resources of the folk sector. She cannot "go home"—return to a family or count on male agency in a male dominated society. She still must go it alone in a social world characterized by household and/or community solidarity. But her life is made less burdensome. The woman and her daughter no longer are dominated by the oppression, both social and personal, that the weight of misfortune produces due to cosmic affliction—spirit aggression. Now she can devote her energies more vigorously to issues of subsistence. She also has learned that she can penetrate dangerous social-political boundaries—external boundaries of open space, male territoriality, and the ethnocentric walls that separate Canaanite and Israelite heritages—even though at great risk. Perhaps she follows the famous peasant principle: "Nothing ventured, nothing gained." Peasants hope for the best, bet their last shekel in lotteries, and if nothing happens, the response is, "Never mind." The woman's daring venture into the Israelite circle of Jesus and his disciples is such a willingness propelled by "nothing ventured, nothing gained." And if no healing is forthcoming, then "never mind."[72] But in the Canaanite woman's case her daughter is healed. Therefore, she, too, can give praise to the "God of Israel" whose healing power has been mediated through an Israelite healer.

For Jesus, the heart of his theocratic mission has been complicated in that he has extended the core value of mercy and crossed over his own defined limit to "go nowhere among the Gentiles" (10:5). This relatively isolated incident will not impair his final confrontation aimed at the heart of the political, economic, and religious Israelite system, the Jerusalem temple. But, he must now take into account that as an Israelite healer he has become a patron or benefactor of an outcast non-Israelite woman. The scope of his task among Israelite peasants, the impure, and expendables (the "lost sheep of the house of Israel") now embraces a non-Israelite. By acknowledging the woman's "great faith" he has placed her alongside such Israelites as the woman who suffers from hemorrhages.

---

72. I am indebted to Bruce J. Malina for this observation.

A story deemed laden with "Christian missionary theology and concerns," and therefore the "creation by first generation Christians,"[73] can, through social-scientific inquiry, be seen in another light. In doing so there is probability that the story is rooted in the activity of Jesus. Matthew's redaction of Mark does not necessarily take us farther away from the historical Jesus; quite the contrary, in this instance it underscores essential characteristics of Jesus' mission and activity.

LEVEL TWO—AT THE TIME OF THE FIRST EVANGELIST AND THE MATTHEAN COMMUNITY

The Canaanite woman's story remains a significant memory for the Matthean community. Old external/internal boundaries have been crossed or are being challenged due to the Christian community's separation from the synagogue and Pharisaic-led Judaism (21:28—23:39), rejection of the dietary laws of the Pentateuch (15:11), and a mission that calls for baptism without circumcision (28:19–20). Internally, the community confronts problems such as "false prophets" (7:15–23), the faith of the "little ones" (18:6–7, 10–14), the "little faith" of the disciples (6:30; 8:26; 14:31; 16:8; 17:20), community dispute resolution (18:6–20), succession and leadership (16:18–20), the future (24–25), and a community composed of good and bad followers of Jesus (13:24–30, 47–50; 22:1–14).

But what can be said about marginal, non-Israelite women in this contentious, polemical, fluid, and uncertain period? Does the Canaanite woman's story provide a social transparency of a gender issue being faced by Matthew's community?

What follows demonstrates the probability that the woman's story poses an ongoing social/theological challenge for the time of the Evangelist to the extent that the memory of Jesus' cutting encounter with her holds up a new authoritative social norm that not only discloses pollution within the community but also renders pastoral instruction to Matthew's surrogate kinship group. The models are now applied a second time. As they are applied, however, it should be recalled from chapter 4 that a social profile of Matthew's community identifies it as an urban and relatively prosperous Christian community.

---

73. Meier, *A Marginal Jew*, 660–61.

Application of the Models

The purity model helps identify the woman as an outcast non-Israelite. As such, her example probably depicts a social/theological challenge to the community. What is the evidence? First, the woman's location warns against what Douglas identifies as a danger of boundaries in the margins.[74] She is from the "the district of Tyre and Sidon" (15:21) or, at least within the rural border region between Israel and Tyre, a non-Israelite area despised by Judeans (see Ezek 26:1—28:19; Joel 3:4–8) but inhabited by a number of Israelites. An ethnocentered, urban, well-to-do predominantly Israelite community could be threatened by persons from such a socially mixed region.

As the First Evangelist's community hears the woman's story it is confronted with a non-Israelite woman without male agency in public space who has a sick daughter in a society that devalues both women and daughters. She is as Ringe puts it "the poorest of the poor and most despised of the outcasts—a Gentile woman on her own before God and humankind."[75] A society organized along purity lines would carefully avoid contact with persons "judged impure or unholy."[76]

Further, the woman's story apparently advances the social irregularity of the four non-Israelite women (Tamar, Rahab, Ruth, and the "wife of Uriah") of Matthew's genealogy (1:3–6). As we've observed, Meier describes these women as "a very strange sorority."[77] Luz maintains that they provide "a universalistic overtone" to the genealogy.[78] Although scholars differ over their social identity and function, as well as a definition of Matthew's universalism, Brown believes the first three Tamar, Rahab, and Ruth, are not Israelites,[79] and the fourth (the "wife of Uriah") is not married to an Israelite.[80] All four, Hagner asserts, represent "surprise and

---

74. Douglas, *Purity and Danger,* 122. Meier believes the woman has crossed over to Jesus into Israel (*Matthew,* 171), and that Jesus does not enter the territories of Tyre and Sidon. The area can refer to the communities along the Syrophoenecian coast (see 11:21–22) or to the territories identified as Tyre and Sidon, where the population could have been largely Israelite (Hagner, *Matthew 14–28,* 440–41).

75. Ringe, "A Gentile Woman's Story," 72.

76. Elliott, "Temple versus Household," 221.

77. Meier, *Matthew,* 4.

78. Luz, *Matthew 1–7,* 110.

79. Tamar is an Aramaean, Rahab an inhabitant of Canaan, and Ruth a Moabite.

80. Brown, *Introduction to the New Testament,* 175.

scandal,"[81] or as Meier puts it, "holy irregularities" in God's orderly plan and discontinuities within the continuity of salvation history.[82] We believe the inclusion of these women in the genealogy anticipates the "surprise and scandal" of the Canaanite woman's story.[83] But as in the time of Jesus who as an Israelite healer had difficulty negotiating his own defined boundary limits (only to Israel), so now, the Matthean community must pass through its own boundary taboos by accepting outcast non-Israelite women. Following the model, her example upsets the "order of the social system."[84]

In light of the women of the genealogy who acted wisely in their social circumstance, a question may be asked, "Does the woman's behavior and speech indicate that she is a woman of wisdom?" In Israelite tradition a number of women are known as wise persons such as Abigail, wife of Nabel, as well as David (1 Sam 25:3). The woman from Tekoa (2 Sam 14:2) and another unnamed woman (2 Sam 20:16) are described as "wise," probably indicating that they were skilled in rhetoric. Perhaps women prophets like Deborah (Judges 4–5) and Huldah (2 Kings 22) should be included in such a catalog.

But are there examples that possibly connect the Canaanite woman to Israel's wisdom tradition? We suggest that there are two unexpected cases, the ideal woman of Proverbs 31 and Ruth. At first glance these two women are unlikely candidates—an elite woman of a wealthy household and a Moabite peasant widow seeking subsistence in an Israelite environ. But when their accounts are more closely examined their correlation comes to light as well as their possible connection to Matthew's story. The capable or worthy woman (Prov 31:10) is honored as a person who serves as a fitting conclusion to a writing that begins with Woman Wisdom (1:1—9:18). Among several commendations, she is described as one who "girds herself with strength and makes her arms strong" (31:17), language that probably connotes both physical and moral strength (see 8:14; 31:25). Even as she provides for her household she is able to care for the poor (31:20). And when her mouth opens, "wisdom and the teaching of kindness" are on her lips (31:26). The "ways of her house are wisdom"

81. Hagner, *Matthew 1–13*, 10.

82. Meier, *Matthew*, 5.

83. The four women seem to have more in common with the Canaanite woman than with Mary, the mother of Jesus.

84. Neyrey, "The Symbolic Universe of Luke-Acts," 274.

(see Proverbs 9:1–6) and the fruit of her hands, "her works," elicit praise to her in the city gates. Thus far we have described a person hardly like Ruth or the Canaanite woman.

So, then, what is the basis of the connection? First, in the Hebrew Bible, the book of Ruth follows the book of Proverbs among the Writings, possibly suggesting that Ruth, too, is an example of Israel's wisdom literature.[85] Second, both women, Ruth and the woman of Proverbs 31, are described the same (*'ēshet' ḥayil*); they are capable or worthy women (Prov 31:10; Ruth 3:11). Ruth's honor language, however, is placed on the lips of an elite Israelite male, Boaz, "And now, my daughter, do not be afraid, I will do for you all that you ask, for all the assembly of my people know that you are a worthy woman" (3:11). This is significant because a similar phrase is used of Boaz earlier in the book; he is an *'ish' gibbor ḥayil*, translated in the NRSV as "a prominent rich man" (Ruth 2:1). The term "rich," however, has as its basic meaning "powerful" or "strong." Thus, Boaz seems to relate Ruth's new status to his own social standing. She is no longer to be perceived as a servant or a foreigner (cf. 2:10, 13), but as a strong, capable, worthy and appropriate wife for Boaz. Finally, the writing ends by connecting Ruth to David's genealogy (cf. Matt 1:5) and in so doing turns a family story into the account of the royal house and hence the nation. Further, the genealogy (4:18–22) looks back to Perez, which demonstrates that neither of Obed's parents had a flawless line of descent. Ruth's ancestry can be traced to an incestuous union between Lot and one of his daughters (Gen 19); Boaz is descended from an illicit union between Judah and his Canaanite daughter-in-law (Gen 38); and David is a fourth-generation descendant of a Moabite woman.

Matthew's genealogy of Jesus, "the messiah," adds to the list of David's infamous female ancestors by naming Rahab (the harlot from Jericho in Josh 2:1–21; 6:22–25) as the mother of Boaz. As "foreigners who join themselves to the Lord" (Isa 56:6), Ruth, Tamar, and Rahab are given "an everlasting name" (Isa 56:6) as mothers of the messianic line of kings. Similarly, the desperate behavior and words of the Canaanite woman in the end, denominate her as one who has received God's mercy at the hands of Israel's messiah. She, too, should be given "an everlasting name" as a foreigner who honors the God of Israel even if her status is that of a liminal person. She, like the women of the genealogy, wise women in

---

85. My colleague, Rick Marrs, first brought this to my attention.

their life settings, courageously speaks and behaves as a capable, worthy woman whose strength is manifest in her persistence with Jesus. Wisdom is seen in her behavior. She openly confronts Jesus and the disciples with her need and in Jesus' presence she kneels, as did the wise men (Matt 2:2), as she makes her verbal appeal (15:25) and responds to Jesus' challenge. Her convincing riposte, "Yes, Lord, yet even the dogs eat the crumbs that fall from their masters' table" (15:27) suggests a wise reply to Jesus' expression of folk wisdom, "It is not fair to take the children's food and throw it to the dogs." Wisdom is revealed in her language. There is no other such example in Matthew. There are examples of women who speak. Prompted by her mother, Herodias' daughter asks for the head of John the Baptist (14:8), a clever power move made at a public, political banquet among Galilee's elite. We hear the request of the mother of James and John that Jesus declare for her sons hierarchical positions of power in his kingdom (20:21). Matthew's Jesus, however, does not give the mother an answer. His reply instead is directed to her sons (20:22). Pilate's wife, prompted by her dream, sends a note to Pilate as he sat in judgment over Jesus requesting that he not have anything to do with Jesus because she believed he was an innocent man (27:19), a wise request that went unheeded. In regard to other women in Jesus' presence, Matthew's auditors hear only that Peter's mother-in-law serves Jesus (8:15), that the woman with hemorrhages talks to herself (9:21), but not to Jesus, that the woman who anoints Jesus never speaks as is the case of the women at the cross and tomb (27:55, 56, 61; 28:1–10). Only from the lips of this non-Israelite woman do we hear words consistent with Matthew's view of the values of the kingdom of heaven. She is a capable, worthy, and wise person who teaches Jesus.

But it may be asked, how does her story differ from that of the centurion (8.5–13) assuming as well that he is a non-Israelite?[86] First, the spatial locations of the two accounts are decidedly different. The centurion's home is Capernaum, the Galilean home of Jesus (4:13), the heartland of the Galilean ministry. The Canaanite woman's locality is in a border district despised by Judeans, "Tyre and Sidon" (15:21). Second, when the centurion approaches and describes his servant's condition, Jesus immediately and positively responds, "I will come and heal him" (8:7). But Jesus has no concern for the woman's request. Third, as previously observed, at the outset Matthew identifies the woman as a "Canaanite" (15:22)—

---

86. As indicated earlier, the centurion is possibly an Israelite auxiliary in an Israelite auxiliary legion.

a social slur that connotes longstanding hatred and prejudice between Israelites and the Canaanites.[87] No such disparaging reference is made of the centurion. Fourth, Matthew carefully depicts the centurion as a person sensitive to spatial purity boundaries that separate Israelites and non Israelites. Jesus is willing to enter the centurion's home, but the centurion protects Jesus from crossing that frontier, "Lord, I am not worthy to have you come under my roof" (8:8). Nothing in the woman's account hints of private household spatial boundary issues. Fifth, in the centurion's story Matthew inserts from Q that many from east and west will sit at table with Abraham, Isaac, and Jacob in the kingdom of heaven (8:11–12; see Luke 13:28–29). It appears that Matthew uses the story of a male, respected household leader to carry the freight of an anticipated non-Israelite mission (28:19). Nothing of that mission is even hinted at in the Canaanite woman's story. In fact, just the opposite occurs when Jesus asserts, "I was sent only to the lost sheep of the house of Israel" (15:24). If Matthew's community is a prosperous, mixed congregation of Israelites and non-Israelites[88] still struggling over non-Israelite inclusion, it would be one thing to socially embrace an established, respected householder like the centurion, but quite another matter to welcome a non-Israelite woman with dubious, polluted social credentials even though her demeanor and speech in Jesus' presence depict a person who is prudent—a wise woman. The woman's example upsets purity classifications that rank the rich over the poor.[89] Following Douglas, there is the possible danger that the internal lines of the community are being polluted and/or that there is an internal contradiction concerning those boundaries marked by a refusal to accept marginal, wise non-Israelite women.

Finally, within the larger literary context, the Canaanite woman's story illustrates an ongoing purity challenge because it follows the pericope over Israelite dietary laws (15:1–20). In that politically based controversy, Jesus tears down boundaries concerning food traditions that keep Israelites and non-Israelites separate.[90] One could argue that Jesus now "acts out" his previous teaching in the woman's story.[91] But in each instance

---

87. Davies and Allison, *Matthew,* 2:547.

88. Brown, *Introduction to the New Testament,* 175.

89. Elliott, "Temple versus Household," 221–22.

90. Meier, *Matthew,* 168–69.

91. Ibid., 169.

the disciples have problems. Over food issues they lack understanding (15:15–16). And over the problems posed by the woman's presence, they want nothing to do with her and urge Jesus to send her away (15:23). Do the disciples provide a transparency of the Matthean community?

We should not overlook, however, that the two pericope are different. In the defilement account Jesus unequivocally maintains his position— what goes into the mouth (food) does not defile. But in the woman's story, Jesus seems to reverse himself—he seeks no contact with an outsider. If so, this may indicate that the community has worked through issues concerning the binding character of dietary laws but continues to struggle over the inclusion of outcast non-Israelite women.

Finally, how does the kinship domain cast light on the woman's story? For Matthew, radical inclusion within the kinship domain is a matter of faith—"great faith" as opposed to "little faith." On the one hand, the disciples' insistence that Jesus send the woman away (15:23) illustrates "little faith," an attribution mentioned three times in the larger context of 13:54—17:27 (see 14:31; 16:8; 17:20). On the other hand, Jesus' new surrogate community is called to extend mercy to such women. Internally, the kin group of the Evangelist needs to practice the God of Israel's core value of mercy as Jesus did, that is, to maintain weak structural boundaries and to follow an inclusive strategy that welcomes non-Israelite women of "great faith" (15:28). By doing so, Matthew's community would demonstrate that it acts as the surrogate family of God as it relates to its fellow members simply as "brother, and sister, and mother,"—a community committed to doing only "the will of my Father in heaven" (12:50). To so act, however, would not enhance the community's socio-political standing with the synagogue because a Pharisaic party after 70 CE would most likely view the social inclusion of prostitutes as additional evidence of "dirt out of order" within the Christian community. From the synagogue's perspective, Matthew's kin group has not only rejected traditional food laws and circumcision, it has demonstrated in its acceptance of the *éthnē* an inclusion of impure and unholy non-Israelite women. Thus, the woman's story modeled within Matthew's kin group adds one more nail to the coffin: the two groups, Matthew's community and the synagogue, have parted company or are deeply in the midst of that transition.

CONCLUSION—DIFFERENCES THAT MATTER

A cultural anthropological analysis demonstrates that to the list of transitions, challenges, and changes within the Matthean community, there is also the problematic social status of non-Israelite outcast women. The woman's story provides a social window of a community struggling over the radical inclusion demanded by Jesus' new surrogate family. The models cast light on another aspect of a community in transition—a well-to-do, ethnic-centered community is challenged to break out of its cultural insulation in order that it may remain righteous according to the norms of the kingdom of heaven. To do this, social mobility and status issues involving non-Israelite women must be met head-on.

Based on the activity of Jesus' ministry the First Evangelist's community cannot devalue women and others attached to them who are ill, no matter how difficult this may be. The Canaanite woman's story of "great faith" is a paradigm for the community. Following the purity norms of the kingdom of heaven, what fits is appropriate and in place; non-Israelite outcast women should be received without discrimination. Based on the core value of the God of Israel's mercy, Jesus, in the historical period of his mission, was not only a patron or benefactor to the Canaanite woman but one who acknowledged her great faith.

In our next chapter we turn to the story of the woman who anoints Jesus for his burial (26:6–13). As the Canaanite woman exemplifies a wise woman, we will learn that the woman who anoints Jesus behaves as a prophet.

7

The Woman Who Anoints Jesus

[1] When Jesus had finished all these words, he said to his disciples, [2] "You know that after two days the Passover will come, and the Son of Man will be delivered up to be crucified."

[3] Then the chief priests and the elders of the people gathered together in the palace of the high priest, who was called Caiaphas, [4] and they conspired to arrest Jesus by stealth and kill him. [5] But they said, "Not during the feast, or there may be a riot among the people."

[6] Now when Jesus was at Bethany in the house of Simon the leper, [7] a woman came to him with an alabaster vessel of very costly ointment, and she poured it on his head as he reclined at the table.

[8] But when the disciples saw this, they were angry and said, "Why this waste? [9] This ointment could have been sold for a large sum and the money given to the poor."

[10] But Jesus, aware of this, said to them, "Why do you trouble the woman? She has performed a good work for me. [11] For you always have the poor among you, but you will not always have me. [12] For in pouring this ointment on my body she prepared me for burial. [13] Truly I tell you, wherever this good news is proclaimed in the whole world, what she has done will be told in remembrance of her."

[14] Then one of the twelve, who was called Judas Iscariot, went to the chief priests [15] and said, "What will you give me if I deliver him to you?" They paid him thirty pieces of silver. [16] And from that moment he sought an opportunity to betray him. (Matt 26:1–16, author's translation)

INTRODUCTION

So FAR, WE HAVE examined healing stories of two Israelite women in Matthew 9:18–26, and a non-Israelite woman's daughter in Matthew 15:21–28. In the first passage, the hemorrhaging woman depicts a person from among the crowds—a marginal person located in open space whose healing has socio/political implications for the political domain of the temple. Her healing is sandwiched into the story of a girl restored to life, which portrays a respected Israelite household and demonstrates Jesus' healing activity within the private kinship domain. Quite different from either of these two examples, the Canaanite woman's set of social circumstances represents a culturally marginal non-Israelite woman situated alone in public border space (the district of Tyre and Sidon) where she actively and successfully seeks out and challenges Jesus as an Israelite healer by means of her wise behavior and words. She and the hemorrhaging woman are commended for their faith by Jesus and their examples depict, at the time of the Evangelist, a transparency of the Matthean community's struggle to include such marginal persons within its fellowship.

Now our attention is drawn to an unnamed woman who unwittingly anoints Jesus for burial. Her story is not a healing account. Rather, it is Jesus who is the unexpected recipient of honor (favor) from a grateful client. By anointing Jesus at Simon's house she crosses a frontier from public to private space. Her subsequent behavior portrays a difficult and controversial navigation among several forbidden and/or marginal boundaries. We begin the woman's story by introducing the setting of the meal within its larger social context.

The Social Context of the Story of the Woman Who Anointed Jesus

Matthew's account takes place in a private setting, the *house* of Simon the leper (26:6–13). The story is situated, however, between two accounts that occur in public, political settings: (1) the plot to kill Jesus by the "chief priests and the elders of the people gathered in the *palace* of the high priest" (26:3–5); and (2) the agreement between Judas and the religious authorities in the *temple* to betray Jesus (26:14–16). The sequence is public space—private space—public space.

Viewed from another perspective, the woman's story positioned as it is involves four points of view concerning Jesus' death: conspiracy and murder, pre-death anointing, misunderstanding and correction, and betrayal. The chief priests and the elders conspire to arrest Jesus by "stealth and kill him." The woman, who out of devotion to Jesus honors him by pouring an alabaster jar of costly ointment on his head, unwittingly performs his pre-death anointing. The disciples, angered by the woman's act, misunderstand and correct her because they believe the ointment should be sold and its considerable proceeds given to the poor. Judas, in contrast to the woman and her bountiful gift, allies himself with the chief priests and bargains to hand over Jesus for thirty pieces of silver. Clearly, the woman's story does not stand alone. It is situated in a larger and most vital political, religious context—the death of Jesus.

Further, even though the anointing account has multiple attestations in the canonical gospels (Matt 26:6–13; Mark 14:3–9; Luke 7:36–50; John 12:1–8), from a social-scientific perspective it is in all cases located in the private kinship domain and not in the public, political sphere, even though it is placed between two highly redacted public, political incidents—the plot to kill Jesus (26:3–5) and Judas' betrayal (26:14–16). We do not affirm that the story is devoid of data related to the activity of the historical Jesus, but its stress on hospitable behavior in the kinship domain best fits the Evangelist's *Sitz im Leben*. That time, as noted previously, is a contentious, polemical, fluid, and uncertain period. Certainly, her narrative remains significant in the community's social memory if for no other reason than the final words of Matthew's Jesus: "'Truly, I tell you, wherever this good news is proclaimed in the whole world, what she has done will be told in remembrance of her'" (26:13).[1]

---

1. The story begs interpretation through the lens of social memory. Social memory studies, following Jeffrey Olick and Joyce Robbins ("Genre Memories and Memory Genres," 112), are "a general rubric for inquiry into the varieties of forms through which we are shaped by the past, conscious and unconscious, public and private, material and communicative, consensual and challenged." Social memory advances the awareness of a group's unity and peculiarity. For example, a given text, Matthew 26:5–13, supplies a "fixed point"—a record that shapes the basis for the Matthean community's identity. Matthew's account can be compared and contrasted with social memory records of other groups in early Christianity, e.g., Mark (14:3–9), Luke (7:36–50), and John (12:1–8). Thus, the First Evangelist's rendition gives insight to the life situation of his group "by refracting the texts through the lens of its own perspective and experience." See Hearon, "The Story of 'the Woman Who Anointed Jesus' as Social Memory," 99; and Olick and Robbins, "Genre Memories and Memory Genres," 122. We do not utilize this method in our treatment of the story. The reader, however, is encouraged to consider its possibilities as a sociological tool.

MODELS OF INTERPRETATION

To interpret the story we utilize two social-scientific models: (1) patronage and (2) a taxonomy of degrees of impurity understood within the social realities of the political and the kinship domains as well as the "pivotal value of Mediterranean society of the first century,"[2] honor and shame.

Honor, as previously modeled, is essential to everything, including survival.[3] It is essential to social standing, the status of a person within a community. If it is *ascribed* it is derived from birth. If it is *acquired* it is what a person has achieved in a social world of challenge and response. All of life involves honor—who one marries, with whom one does business, where one lives, what religious role one plays. To "be shamed" indicates that one has lost honor. Conversely, to "have shame" appropriately "means to have concern about one's own reputation (honor) or the reputation of one's family."[4] Honor is critical for all of the personages of our passage: the religious authorities who conspire to kill Jesus, the woman who anoints Jesus, Jesus who is about to die a shameful death, the disciples who see her act as waste, and Judas who plays the fool as he betrays Jesus.

Further, our two models need to be understood within our earlier development in chapter 3 of the political and kinship domains. The following features of these two social domains relate to the woman's story:

1. In the ancient Mediterranean social world there are four "foundational social domains" that social science scholars analyze—politics, economics, religion, and kinship (family).[5]

2. These four spheres are socially embedded to the extent that one sphere's definition, structures, and authority may be dictated by another sphere.

3. However, two of the domains, politics and kinship, are vastly different. This means that the domains of religion and economics are embedded either in politics or the family. For example, the disciples' interpretation of the woman's extravagant economic waste takes place in the kinship domain, but the political bargain of Judas with the religious authorities to betray Jesus transpires within the politi-

2. Malina and Rohrbaugh, *Synoptic Gospels,* 369.

3. Ibid., 369–72.

4. Ibid., 371.

5. Hanson, "BTB Readers Guide: Kinship."

cal location of the temple.[6] The Jerusalem temple and the house of Simon in Bethany are geographically opposite locations representing two distinct social domains.

4. The temple and palace, located at Jerusalem's geographical heart,[7] form the commercial center and hub of wealth for Roman Palestine. Out of these locations the elite control vital political, religious, and economic aspects of life for both city and country.[8] Outside the city are numerous villages and towns where peasants dwell.

5. Consequently there is a fundamental divergence between the countryside and its villages and the city.[9] Jesus' ministry largely flourishes among the villages of the countryside but experiences conflict in the city.[10]

6. The economic structure of the political domain is fundamentally "a *redistributive* network."[11] Taxes and rents move away from the rural producers to the cities, estates, and temples. The Israelite temple, embedded in political relationships, is an Israelite citadel of religious and economic relations firmly embedded in the political domain.[12]

7. In peasant societies all resources are in limited supply, a reality known to anthropologists as the limited good.

8. Ideology for the political economy and political religion is embedded in the culture's Great Tradition, an "embodiment of the norms and values which give continuity and substance to the society."[13] However, peasants abide by a society's "Little Tradition," a "simplified and often outdated expression of the norms and ideals embodied by the city elites."[14]

---

6. Ibid.

7. Sjoberg, *The Preindustrial City*.

8. Rohrbaugh, "The Pre-Industrial City in Luke-Acts," 133; Malina, *New Testament World*, 87.

9. Oakman, "The Countryside in Luke-Acts," 152.

10. Ibid., 172.

11. Rohrbaugh, "The Pre-Industrial City in Luke-Acts," 156.

12. Ibid., 146; Malina, "Patron and Client," 23; idem, *The Social World of Jesus in the Gospels*, 163.

13. Malina, *New Testament World*, 87.

14. Ibid., 88.

9. The kinship domain, the opposite pole from the political domain, entails the household and family. The family is a social organization of reciprocity, not redistribution. Peasant families seek not how much is taken but what is left,[15] a different outlook of the Limited Good than that of the political-religious elite. Peasants ask, after paying taxes and/or rents, will there be enough to survive?

10. There can be little doubt that Matthew's community belongs to the kinship domain. Members of this surrogate family—"my brother, and sister, and mother"—belong together because of their commitment to do "the will of my Father in heaven" (12:50). This new family, not based on physical lineage or blood line, is foundational to the identity and formation of the Evangelist's Christian community. The story of this unnamed woman takes place in the kinship domain and reflects religious and economic issues of that sphere. But, it is surrounded or framed by the actions of authorities within the political domain.

Model One—Patronage[16]

Because all ancient Mediterranean societies are characterized by a sharp social stratification and a relative and absolute scarcity of natural resources a system of patronage prevails.[17] This social institution, known as *clientele,* is established on a complex and variable system of socially fixed connections. "Patron-client relations," Eisenstadt and Roniger state, are "based on a very strong element of *inequality* and *difference in power"*— patrons having a "monopoly on certain positions and resources" essential to the client.[18] The institution, Elliot maintains, entails "issues of unequal power relations, pyramids of power, power brokers, protection, privilege, prestige, payoffs and tradeoffs, influence, 'juice,' 'clout,' 'connections,' . . . 'networks,' reciprocal grants and obligations, values associated with friendship, loyalty, and generosity, and the various strands that link this institution to the social system at large."[19] Halvor Moxnes describes this

15. Moxnes, *The Economy of the Kingdom,* 81.

16. Our model is described more fully because it is presented for the first time.

17. Gilmore, ed., *Honor and Shame and the Unity of the Mediterranean,* 192–93.

18. Eisenstadt and Roniger, eds., *Patrons, Clients and Friends,* 48–49.

19. Elliott, "Patronage and Clientage," 148.

association as a paradoxical blend of asymmetry in power and mutual solidarity.[20] Social connections, therefore, mean everything.[21] Patronage involves a whole range of social dyadic ties—whether it be father-son, God-man, lord-vassal, landlord-tenant (the list could go on)—that together establish and maintain patron-client interactions.[22]

Patrons control vital resources. They are persons who are able to render favors to clients based largely on personal knowledge and favoritism. They secure for their clients "a diversity of 'goods' including food, financial aid, physical protection, career advancement and administrative posts, manumission, citizenship, equality in or freedom from taxation, the inviolability of person and property, support in legal cases, immunity from expenses of public service, help from the gods, and, in the case of provincials, the status of *socius* or friend of Rome."[23] Such benefactions profit not only persons but villages and cities as well, resulting in a widespread and diverse social network of patron-client relations throughout a society.

A client subsists on the resources of a patron. In return, a client owes a variety of services and is obliged "to enhance the prestige, reputation, and honor of his or her patron in public and private life."[24] Such relations bind and solidify their ties to promote the personal honor of the patron.[25]

Between patrons and clients are brokers. They serve as mediators or go-betweens in a socially vertical relationship of patrons and clients. As patrons control first level resources such as land, jobs, goods, funds, and power, brokers provide critically important connections to those resources. For example, a city official might serve as a broker of the emperor's resources to the community.

Prophets or holy men serve as brokers of God's benefaction. Malina has demonstrated that in Matthew God is father/patron and the reign of God/heaven is "God's patronage and the clientele bound up in it."[26] As God's broker, Jesus goes throughout Galilee, "teaching in their synagogues

---

20. Moxnes, *The Economy of the Kingdom*, 42.
21. Malina and Rohrbaugh, *Synoptic Gospels*, 388–90.
22. Blok, "Variations in Patronage," 366; see Moxnes, "Patron-Client Relations," 242.
23. Elliott, "Patronage and Clientage," 149.
24. Ibid.
25. Eisenstadt and Roniger, *Patrons, Clients and Friends*, 48–49.
26. Malina, "Patron and Client," 9.

and proclaiming the good news of the kingdom and curing every disease and every sickness among the people" (4:23). As God's broker, Jesus calls disciples to follow him (4:18–22) and gives them "authority over unclean spirits, to cast them out, and to cure every disease and every sickness" (10:2). As clients of the kingdom's resources the disciples are to heal the sick, raise the dead, cleanse lepers, cast out demons knowing they have received without payment and they are to give without payment (10:8). In solidarity with Jesus, the disciples' righteousness is to exceed that of the scribes and Pharisees (5:20). In like fashion, the disciples are to practice "mercy over sacrifice" (9:13; 12:7). Merciful deeds imitate Jesus' brokerage and manifest God's patronage—the hungry receive food, the thirsty drink, strangers are welcomed, the naked are clothed, the sick are cared for, and those in prison are visited (25:31–46). In doing so, the righteous demonstrate loyalty to God as patron (1:19; 3:15–17; 6:33; see Isa 58:6–7) as well as solidify their ties to Jesus as God's broker. For that reason, the disciples are to pursue social justice by challenging the imperial system's hierarchy and exploitation through their merciful deeds. Their solidarity with Jesus requires that they not serve two patrons, God and Mammon (6:24).

Matthew describes numerous supplicants who seek out Jesus' benefaction. Examples include a leper (8:1–5), a centurion in behalf of his servant (8:5–13), a paralytic born by others (9:1–8), a father whose daughter has died and a woman who bleeds (9:18–26), two blind men (9:27–31), and a Canaanite woman who seeks her daughter's healing (15:21–28). Jesus as broker of God's mercy at times notes his client's faith (8:13; 9:2, 22, 28; 15:28).

The patronage system of the Roman Empire and the kingdom of heaven is illustrated in Matthew in the following diagram based on the work of Malina and Rohrbaugh[27] but adapted to the story of the centurion (8:5–13).

27. Malina and Rohrbaugh, *Synoptic Gospels* (1st ed.), 329.

FIGURE 7.1: PATRONAGE HIERARCHY

	General		*Matthew 5:8–13*	
	Roman Empire	Kingdom of Heaven	Sequence 1	Sequence 2
Patron	Caesar	God	Caesar	God
Broker	Elites	Jesus	Centurion	Jesus
Client	Citizens	Supplicants	Servant/Soldiers	Centurion
Benefit	Good	Good	Good	Good/Healing

Observe the following under the *General* portion of the diagram:

1. In the Roman Empire model, the patron is Caesar, brokers are from among the elite, clients are citizens, and benefactions are some form of good.

2. In the Kingdom of Heaven model, God is patron, Jesus is broker, supplicants are clients, and the benefaction is some form of good.

Observe the following under the *Matthew 8:5–13* portion of the diagram:

1. Sequence 1 follows the Roman Empire model—Caesar is patron, the centurion is a broker of imperial resources, his servant and soldiers are clients, and the benefaction is good.

2. Sequence 2 follows the model of the Kingdom of Heaven—God is patron, Jesus is broker, the centurion is client, and the benefit is the healing of his servant.[28]

We affirm that Jesus has been and is broker of the kingdom of heaven's resources to the woman. We do not know the form of good she previously received. But, as a grateful client she anoints Jesus.

28. What this means for Jesus and the centurion will be noted when we apply the patronage model.

Model Two—Degrees of Impurity

A summary of the purity/impurity model as previously discussed in chapter 3 features the following elements germane to the woman's story:[29]

1. Purity is defined as normality and wholeness, and pollution and taboo is defined as matter "dirt out of place"—a cultural system of order and disorder.[30] For example, the woman, from the disciples' point of view, is out of place. She has violated the orderly system of the meal at Simon's house.

2. Purity rules can also have symbolic meaning; that is, a rule beyond its expression of one-to-one discursive language can be also tensive and multivalent. The symbolic thrust constitutes a cultural language that expresses and reflects larger social concerns that work in concert with other structures of thought to deliver and support a common message.

3. Purity boundaries are fourfold: external, internal, at the margins, and marginal lines of internal contradiction. Crossing boundaries constitutes dangerous individual and social purity infractions. For example, Judas crosses a dangerous frontier, an external boundary, by going to the temple authorities. The woman's behavior involves danger pressing on several boundaries with significance for the kinship community of Jesus at the time of the Evangelist. Accordingly, boundary making, crossing, and breaking both externally and internally constitute a process and a social reality of pollution/taboo/"dirt out of order."

4. The human body is a center where purity issues are manifest—a microcosm of the social body. There is a correlation between socio-political strategy and bodily concerns.[31] This correlation is clarified through the use of purity "maps." In the case of the woman

---

29. Neusner, "History and Purity in First-Century Judaism"; Pilch, "Biblical Leprosy and Body Symbolism"; idem, "Sickness and Healing in Luke-Acts," 207; Malina, *New Testament World*; Neyrey, "The Idea of Purity in Mark's Gospel," 91–128; "The Symbolic Universe of Luke-Acts," 271–304.

30. Douglas, *Purity and Danger;* Isenberg, "Mary Douglas and Hellenistic Religions"; Isenberg and Owen, "Bodies, Natural and Contrived".

31. Neyrey, "Clean/Unclean," 93.

who anoints Jesus, the "map" originally set forth in the model is applicable.[32]

FIGURE 7.2: PURITY/POLITICAL MAP

	Social-Religious Political Elite	Jesus
Political Locus— Temple/Jerusalem/Rome	Network of control: from the Jerusalem temple to Galilee	No network of control: but a network mostly of rural villages and peasants of Galilee
God of Israel	*Core value*: God's holiness *Mission*: maintain political control	*Core value*: God's mercy *Mission*: inaugurate Israel's theocracy
Structural Implications	*Strong boundaries:* Exclusionary strategy	*Weaker boundaries:* Inclusionary strategy among Israelites
Legitimation in Scripture	Law, except Genesis Strong bodily control	Genesis and prophets Weaker bodily control
Strong Purity Concerns	Avoid public bodily contact with sick, demon-possessed, bodily deformed	Public, bodily contact with sick, demon-possessed, bodily deformed

Having set forth the two models, we now interpret the woman's story. However, we must as well include the other groups (26:3–5, 14–15)—the chief priests and elders of the people, the disciples, and Judas. This is so because the woman's story is woven inseparably with what precedes and follows. However, in light of our understanding of the political and kinship domains we will examine more closely the spatial locations of the palace and temple in Jerusalem and the house of Simon the leper at Bethany.

32. For the use of maps, see Neyrey, "Clean/Unclean," 91–95.

APPLICATION OF THE MODELS

The Locations

As previously noted, the palace, Jerusalem temple, and Simon's house are fundamentally different social locations. Following our understanding of the political and kinship domains, the temple environ is located at the spatial heart of the leading city of the region, Jerusalem, a hub of wealth and redistribution for the religious elite and Rome. This location meets the public space criterion for the time of Jesus' activity. Unlike the public space of the Jerusalem temple, the house of Simon situated in the village of Bethany is kinship space, Jesus' dwelling during his final week of public ministry in the temple (21:17).

In the palace, leading personages of the political-religious domain "gather" for counsel to plot, arrest, and kill Jesus (26:3–4). Matthew's use of the term "gathered" (26:3), as opposed to Mark's "were seeking," (14:1) punctuates a Matthean theme: the temple and/or palace are public, political spaces where Jesus' opposition *assembles* to kill him and/or to evaluate matters following his death. In these locations, Herod the Great calls "together" "all the chief priests and scribes of the people" (2:4) to gain information about the Messiah's birth place. After the question of the resurrection (22:23–33), Pharisees "gather" (22:34) and test Jesus concerning the greatest commandment. Following this challenge-riposte, the Pharisees remain "gathered together" (22:41) as Jesus questions them about David's son (22:41–46). Following Jesus' arrest, the scribes and the elders "gather" in the house of Caiaphas (26:67). Later, the religious elite persuade the crowd "gathered" before Pilate near the governor's head-quarters (27:17) to release Barabbas instead of Jesus. When the soldiers of the governor take Jesus into the praetorium, the whole cohort "gathers" to mock him (27:27). After Jesus dies, the religious elite "gather" before Pilate to demand a guard at the tomb (27:62). Finally, subsequent to the resurrection, the religious elite "gather" one last time to devise an explanation for the empty tomb (28:12). All of these assemblages take place in public space and address political/religious issues concerning Jesus (see Pss 2:2; 31:13). On the other hand, no one "gathers" at Simon' house because it is a hospitality space of reciprocity for Jesus' surrogate family. The woman "came" to Jesus.

Applying the Models to the Social-Religious-Political Elite

How do our two models, patronage and purity, cast light on the temple elite's conspiracy to kill Jesus? And how does the woman's behavior stand over and against that political plot? Following our purity model, the temple elite act as guardians of the social order. They are threatened by Jesus' recurrent violations of the temple's purity system. The most recent and defining incident is the temple cleansing, a prophetic action in which Jesus attacks both the temple's economy and its leadership (21:12–13). God's holiness, which includes the holy city, temple, and network of political control, is threatened immediately by pollution. Thus, two core values collide—the religious authorities' concern for maintaining God's holiness (Lev 11:44) and Jesus' commitment to uphold God's mercy. The practice of mercy is illustrated vividly by the healing of the blind and the lame after the temple cleansing (21:14). These persons are not permitted to draw near to the temple altar if holiness stipulations are upheld (Lev 21:16–24).[33] Healing the blind and the lame illustrates Jesus' inclusive strategy. Similarly, in our passage (26:6–13) the woman and Jesus follow the weaker boundaries of the kingdom that permit her to anoint his body. Ironically, while the religious-political leaders conspire to kill Jesus, her act of love prepares Jesus' body for burial.

Drawing from our understanding of the political social domain, the religious-political elite confront an intricate patronage dilemma devoid of a satisfactory solution short of Jesus' crucifixion. Jesus, on the other hand, gathers large crowds and recruits members for a new group loyal to the "kingdom of heaven." He makes radical statements about Roman taxation, the Jerusalem temple, and Herod Antipas. His healings and exorcisms raise rumors and open opposition. He resembles a social bandit even though he follows a strategy of non-violent resistance (5:38–42). He has village ties and associates with people adverse to norms of the Great Tradition. His statements about the temple and taxation are inflammatory to both Jerusalem and Rome. Some believe he is a messiah to the throne of Judea, a menace to the leaders of the high priestly families and the Roman rule of Palestine.[34] With good reason, the temple elite fear a possible riot (26:5; see John 11:48). Jesus is perceived as a challenge to Rome's rule, a social quandary that could terminate the tenuous solidarity of

---

33. See Malina and Rohrbaugh, *Synoptic Gospels*, 107.

34. Hanson and Oakman, *Palestine in the Time of Jesus*, 88.

patron/client ties between the empire and the temple elite. In contrast the woman as Jesus' client has received the resources of the kingdom. Thus, a broker/client relationship has been established between Jesus and the woman that is characterized by loyalty and the bestowing of honor, client to broker.

Following our understanding of the patronage model, in light of the political domain, Jesus threatens the redistributive network benefiting the few.[35] Beyond the immediate exchange of money or the selling and buying of animals for sacrifice (see Lev 1–7; Num 3:47), the act of temple cleansing could spiral out of control, posing possible loss of taxes and rents from peasants and a diminution of the economic surplus for Jerusalem and Rome. This is because all resources are in limited supply in a society of Limited Good. Finally, the norms and values of the Great Tradition, the ideological foundation for the elite, would be undermined by a new interpretation of the scriptures for the house of Israel underway in the activity of Jesus. Jesus calls those who follow him to a righteousness that exceeds that of the scribes and the Pharisees (5:20), a way of justice that fulfills the law and prophets (5:17). This righteousness, combining what is both old and new (13:52; 9:16–17; 5:17–20) as it accentuates mercy over sacrifice (9:12; 12:7), carries forward Hosea's ancient "Little Tradition" (Hos 6:6 [LXX]) among Israel's villages and peasants. The woman expends precious, costly resources that can never be recovered when she pours prized ointment on Jesus' head as he sits at table.

Applying the Models to the Disciples

All that transpires at Simon's house belongs to the kinship domain, which has bearing on the period of the Evangelist. Family members at this meal setting have no part in Palestine's redistributive power structure. Their reciprocal relations are characterized by a commitment to follow Israel's Little Tradition—a social vision of justice, mercy, and faith (23:23) interpreted and taught by Jesus.

Following the patronage model, Jesus is God's broker of the kingdom's resources to all those present: Simon, the disciples, and the woman. However, the woman's act angers the disciples,[36] because the ointment—

---

35. Ibid., 144.

36. Matthew redacts Mark's ambiguous "some" (14:4) to "the disciples," a character group in the gospel denoting the Twelve and connoting most probably teachers in the

the limited good—is valuable, but wasted; it could have been used for the care of the poor, a deed consistent with Jesus' core value of mercy as well as an established practice among Israelites during Passover week.[37] Matthew states, "But when the disciples saw this, they were angry and said, 'Why this waste? This ointment could have been sold for a large sum and the money given to the poor'" (26:8–9). We believe that when their response is weighed against Matthew's wider message their indignation evinces an ongoing divided loyalty and lack of wholehearted solidarity to God as patron and Jesus as broker. What is the basis for this assertion?

First, the Greek term *aganaktein*, translated "were angry," is used only three times in Matthew (20:24; 21:15; 26:8), twice in reference to the disciples—in the present text (26:3), and in the story of the request of the mother of James and John (20:24)—and once as a reference to the religious authorities who object to Jesus' healing of the blind and the lame (21:15). In the case of the mother's request all the disciples fail to comprehend that the kingdom of heaven is not about ambition, power, and domination (20:25), but merciful, life-giving service (20:26–27). Jesus rejects hierarchical domination within his kinship community.

Second, in similar fashion but in another setting, the disciples speak "sternly" to those who bring little children to Jesus for prayer and blessing (19:13). Here, the Greek term *epetimesan/epitmaō* is used in Matthew by Jesus to rebuke the winds and sea (8:26), to rebuke a demon (17:18), and to order that Jesus' identity be kept secret (12:16; 16:20). It is used by Peter to oppose Jesus' first passion prediction (16:20), and it is used by the crowd who "sternly" order the silence of the blind men who seek Jesus' mercy (20:31). In the children's example, the disciples do not perceive that the more inclusive community of sisters and brothers in the kingdom should by characterized by the children's social paradigm of a lack of power and privilege (12:46–50).

Third, as noted in earlier chapters, Matthew characterizes the disciples five times as having "little faith" (6:30; 8:26; 14:31; 16:8; 17:20), a matter of significance in patron/client relations. For example, in the account of deliverance in the storm (8:23–27) the disciples fail to see Jesus as God's broker who provides deliverance. Or, when Peter sinks like a rock

community at the time of the Evangelist.

37. Hare, *Matthew*, 294.

in the water (14:31), it is as God's broker that Jesus saves him.[38] Or, as a final example, Jesus tells the disciples that it is because of their *little faith* (17:20) that they are unable to dispense the kingdom's healing resources to a demon-possessed boy—that is, they are unable to broker God's patronage.

In light of this evidence we assert that the disciples' anger toward the woman at Simon's house is part of an ongoing divided loyalty, a struggle over the patronage of Rome supported and brokered by the temple authorities, and the patronage of God brokered by Jesus. Previous displays of the disciples' anger, indignation, power-seeking, inadequate comprehension, and little faith indicate a double clientage. Therefore, it is fair to ask whether the care of the poor is their ultimate concern or motivation in opposing the woman's costly act. Even though they have observed and heard Jesus' exchange with the rich young man (19:16–26) as well as his teaching concerning doing deeds of mercy (25:31–46), their objection to the woman's deed seems to be a pervasive and consistent behavioral pattern that shortly will lead Judas to join forces with the religious authorities (26:14–16),[39] prompt the other disciples to desert Jesus and flee (26:56), and finally, cause Peter under pressure to deny Jesus (26:69–75). The woman does not have a mixed clientage. Her single devotion, purity of heart (5:8), is for Jesus, her exclusive broker.

Applying the Models to Judas

Judas' betrayal of Jesus for money from the chief priests[40] (26:15) exemplifies issues of honor and shame as well as patronage. The chief priests' honor would be enhanced and their client ties with Rome possibly strengthened if a key follower of Jesus could be bribed. But for Judas, a member of the Jesus group honorably identified as "the Twelve," it is a matter of great shame.[41] His tragic betrayal and subsequent death have enduring social repercussions for the significance of the number Twelve because after the resurrection that symbolic number is reduced to "eleven," which becomes

---

38. For this theme, see Exod 3:20, 14:9–31; Ps 69, 107:23–32; Isa 43:15–16.

39. A lack of concern for the poor is applied directly to Judas in John 12:6. Certainly, Matthew's view is not that the disciples are thieves, but their commitment to the care of the poor is questioned.

40. A peculiarity found only in Matthew's redaction.

41. Malina and Rohrbaugh, *Synoptic Gospels,* 128.

the final numerical identity of this exalted group within the Evangelist's community.[42]

Further, only the Evangelist tells his community that Judas is paid "thirty pieces of silver" (26:15). His acceptance of silver stands over and against the Twelve's instruction that in their mission to Israel they are not to take with them "gold, or silver, or copper" in their belts (10:9).[43] It is true that a penitent Judas returns the money, admitting that he has betrayed innocent blood (27:4). But in the end, Matthew heightens Judas' shame—he hangs himself (27:5). The honored client has played the fool. The woman, in contrast, is honored by Jesus when he affirms that she is a prophet, for her prophetic act of anointing his body has prepared him for burial.

Applying the Models to the Woman

Little is said of the woman. She is unnamed and probably uninvited, an outsider to an insiders' inclusive meal: Simon, Jesus, and the disciples. It is probably a "luxury meal" because Jesus reclines at table. Such meals involve two stages. In the first stage servants wash the hands and feet of the guests and "anoint them with perfumed oils to remove body odors"[44] while appetizers or first courses are served. In the second stage main courses are eaten. Probably, it is during the first stage that the woman, without male agency, "crashes" this ceremonial event.

Following our purity model, she is probably a structurally marginal person, perhaps a woman of "questionable reputation."[45] At any rate, her movement from the outside public sector to the inside sphere of Jesus' surrogate kinship group involves a dangerous external boundary crossing that appears unacceptable to the disciples. However, Jesus upholds her behavior as a "good work" (26:10), a major purity theme in Matthew. For example, the disciples' transformative task is to let their light shine before others, "so that they see your good works and give glory to your Father in heaven" (5:16). Further, the community is given a rule; true and

---

42. "Eleven" appears only in the longer ending of Mark (16:14). Luke takes pains to restore the number twelve (Luke 24:9, 33; Acts 1:26; 2:14). John maintains the number "twelve" to the end (6:67, 70, 71; 20:24).

43. See Meier, *Matthew*, 313.

44. Malina and Rohrbaugh, *Synoptic Gospels*, 128.

45. Ibid.; Corley, *Private Women, Public Meals*, 104, traces the story to an encounter between Jesus and a prostitute.

false prophets are judged by their fruit—that is, their works.[46] That rule has antecedents in Israel's Little Tradition (Isa 5:2, 4; Sir 27:6)[47] and is presupposed by John's preaching of repentance—all Israelites need to get their lives in order because God's rule is near and requires bearing fruit worthy of repentance (3:8, 10). Accordingly, Jesus attacks Israel's religious leaders for their malicious words that demonstrate the depths of their evil (12:33, 34). A tree is known by its fruit; good fruit (righteous works) comes only from good trees, bad fruit (evil works) comes only from bad trees. In the parable of the wicked tenants Matthew alone declares that "the kingdom of God will be taken away" from Israel's powerful elite "and given" to a people that produce the fruits of the kingdom (21:43). As Meier points out, what holds true of Israel's religious leaders "holds equally true of community leaders in the Christian camp; Matthew constantly holds up the one group as a warning for the other group."[48] For that reason, the woman's "good work" demonstrates for Jesus' disciples what is whole, fitting, appropriate, and in place (Douglas' definition of purity), a lavish demonstration that typifies the economy of the kingdom and serves as a light to others and a good work that honors God (5:16). The woman is a good tree. She bears good fruit. Her deed stands over and against the religious elite's conspiracy to arrest and kill Jesus, Judas' deed to betray Jesus (26:14–16), and the disciples' indignation and badgering of the woman. The disciples believe, however, that, guided by God's core value of mercy in a world of Limited Good, the ointment should have been sold and its proceeds given to the poor. Thus, we have additional evidence that the community faces dangers of internal contradiction and only the authoritative words of the community's rabbi, Jesus, can resolve the incongruity—what she has done is a "good work."

Following the patronage model, the woman's "good work" substantiates her client relations with Jesus. Her lavish deed honors her broker and solidifies the dyadic bond between them even as it riles the disciples. Matthew does not tell us in what way Jesus is her broker. Her behavior by implication corroborates that she previously was a recipient of God's benefaction.

---

46. Luz, *Matthew 1–7*, 443.

47. Hauck, "καρπος κτλ.," 614.

48. Meier, *Matthew*, 136.

Finally, Jesus interprets the woman's anointing as a prophetic work that prepares his body for burial (26:12). Whether she understands this to be the case or whether she sees her deed as an anointing of God's chosen one who will die in God's service is unknown. The point is that Matthew's Jesus so interprets her work, a significant matter because Matthew later omits references stressed by Mark and Luke that the reason the women go to the tomb is to anoint Jesus' body (Mark 16:1; Luke 23:56; 24:1). Matthew, therefore, treats the deed as a singular prophetic act and the woman, accordingly, as an unwitting prophet.

What does it mean for the woman to be God's prophet for Matthew's community? As a prophet and client of God, she is juxtaposed to the religious elite who are descendants of those who murdered the prophets (23:31) and now plot to kill Jesus (12:14; 16:21; 26:3–5). As a prophet, her prophetic behavior in the house of Simon in the village of Bethany is juxtaposed with Jerusalem, the city which kills the prophets (23:37). As a prophet, she is harassed by the disciples and treated without honor within Jesus' surrogate family (13:57; 5:11, 12); but she is simultaneously approved and defended by Jesus as God's broker.

As a prophet who produces good fruit, she is juxtaposed to the false prophets within the community (7:15–20). As a prophet she stands alongside the great prophets, John the Baptist (3:1–12) and Jesus (21:11). She also stands alongside Joseph, a "righteous man," led by God's interventions set in motion by revelatory dreams (1:20; 2:13, 19, 22), and by Pilate's wife, a non-Israelite, who also has a dream and warns Pilate to have nothing to do with the "righteous" man, Jesus (27:19). As a prophet she belongs to one of three groups of Israel's community and perhaps within Matthew's community as well—prophets, sages, and scribes (23:34). As a prophet within Jesus' kinship group she will be remembered universally through a new oral tradition because of what she did for Jesus (26:13). In other words, she will be part of a new, developing Little Tradition of the kingdom of heaven that is connected organically and grows out of Israel's old Little Tradition cited fourteen times by Matthew[49] that includes the prophets Isaiah, Micah, Jeremiah, David, and Zechariah.[50]

49. 1:23; 2:5b–6, 15b, 17–18, 23b; 3:3; 4:14–16; 8:17; 12:17–21; 13:14–15, 35; 21:4–5; 26:56 [see 26:54]; 27:9–10.

50. Isaiah is cited at 1:23; 3:3; 4:14–16; 8:17; 12:17–21; 13:14–15; 21:4–5; Micah at 5:2; Hosea at 2:15b; Jeremiah at 2:17–18; David at Psalm 78:2; and Zechariah at 21:4–5; 27:9–10.

CONCLUSION

The woman's story carries forward the role of structurally and/or culturally marginal women in Matthew who behave courageously in the midst of extremity as they keep and advance values of Jesus' alternative community. The woman who bleeds is representative of those in Israel who were "harassed and helpless, like sheep without a shepherd." She demonstrates that the "harvest is plentiful" (9:36). The girl restored to life due to her father's plea for Jesus' help typifies how a "daughter" of a respected household also can be a "daughter" in Jesus' surrogate family. The Canaanite woman epitomizes the power of wisdom manifest in word and deed by an outcast non-Israelite woman. The woman at Bethany acts as a righteous prophet whose symbolic work triggers the passion of Jesus. Her good deed, as we will see in the next chapter, anticipates and participates in the status-changing ritual of the women who faithfully follow and serve Jesus in his ministry and at the cross and tomb.

In our final chapter a social-scientific reading is made of the three references to women as followers of Jesus in Matthew's passion and resurrection narratives (27:55–56; 27:61; 28:1–10). For this analysis a rites of passage model is employed, a combination initiation/death ritual, because we believe such a model best illumines why the women suddenly and inexplicably appear in Matthew's narrative and provide an essential linkage between Jesus and the disciples after his resurrection.

8

Jesus and the Women at the Cross and Tomb

[55] And there were many women there, watching from afar, who had followed Jesus from Galilee ministering to him; [56] among them were Mary Magdalene, and Mary the mother of James and Joseph, and the mother of the sons of Zebedee.
[57] When it was evening, there came a rich man from Arimathea, named Joseph, who also had become a disciple of Jesus. [58] He went to Pilate and asked for the body of Jesus; then Pilate ordered it to be given to him. [59] And Joseph took the body, wrapped it in a clean linen cloth [60] and placed it in his own new tomb, which he had cut in the rock, and departed. [61] Mary Magdalene and the other Mary were there, sitting opposite the tomb. . . .
[1] But after the Sabbath, at the dawning of the first day of the week, Mary Magdalene and the other Mary went to see the tomb. [2] And look, there was a great earthquake! For an angel of the Lord, having descended from heaven, came and rolled back the stone and sat on it. [3] His appearance was like lightning and his clothing white as snow. [4] And for fear of him the guards shook and became like dead men. [5] But the angel said to the women, "Do not be afraid; I know that you look for Jesus who was crucified. [6] He is not here; for he has been raised, as he said. Come see the place where he was lying. [7] Then go quickly and tell his disciples, 'He has been raised from the dead, and look he is going ahead of you to Galilee; there you will see him.' Look, I have told you." [8] So they departed from the tomb quickly with fear and great joy and ran to tell his disciples. [9] Suddenly Jesus met them and said, "Greetings!" And they came to him, took hold of his feet, and worshiped him. [10] Then Jesus said to them, "Do not be afraid; go and tell my brothers to go to Galilee; there they will see me." (Matt 27:55–61; 28:1–10, author's translation)

INTRODUCTION

IN OUR FINAL STORY a social-scientific reading is made of the three references to women as followers of Jesus in Matthew's passion and resurrection narratives (27:55–56; 27:61; 28:1–10). The first citation (27:55–56) stipulates that "many women" were present "looking on" at Jesus' crucifixion "from a distance." Among the "many" three are identified: Mary Magdalene, Mary the mother of James and Joseph, and the mother of the sons of Zebedee, James and John (20:20). All of these women followed Jesus from Galilee and ministered to him (27:55).

The second reference (27:61), at the tomb of Jesus (27:57–61), narrows the number to two, Mary Magdalene and the other Mary, and identifies them alongside a wealthy male from Arimathea named Joseph, a new figure in the narrative who boldly asks Pilate for Jesus' body, makes the necessary arrangements for Jesus' internment, and provides his own new (unused) rock tomb for Jesus' burial. Identified as a "disciple" (27:57), Joseph is the only such named person other than the Twelve so designated anywhere in Matthew (see 10:2–4).[1] After Joseph leaves the tomb, the two women, Matthew concludes, remained "sitting opposite the tomb" (27:61).

The third account is more extensive and as at the scene of the tomb only the two women who witness Jesus' burial, Mary Magdalene and the other Mary, are present. They come "to see" the tomb (28:1) but not to anoint Jesus (see Mark 16:1). For Matthew, this already has been accomplished by the anonymous woman at Simon's house in Bethany (26:6–13). Guided by the angel who invites them to "see the place where he lay" (28:6), the women are instructed to hasten and tell his disciples that Jesus is resurrected and he will precede them to Galilee where they should meet (28:6–7). Leaving the tomb the women are greeted by Jesus. They clasp his feet, worship him, and hear similar words from Jesus as they heard from the angel, "Do not be afraid; go and tell my brothers to go to Galilee; there they will see me" (28:10). The striking exclusion from all of these scenes is Jesus' twelve male disciples who have deserted and betrayed or denied him (26:14–16, 56, 69–75).

---

1. Joseph, like Simon the leper (26:6; see 8:2–3), and the woman who anoints Jesus for his burial (26:6–13), are not only new figures to Matthew's narrative, but appear only in the passion account and then disappear.

ESTABLISHING THE MODEL

For our analysis a rite of passage model is employed. "Rites of passage," known also as "life crisis" ceremonies (from the French term *rites de passage*), constitute multifaceted practices and/or training related to critical life moments of status transitions.[2] Arnold van Gennep, a pioneer in the comparative study of folk knowledge and culture,[3] first examined at length passage ceremonies and defined them as "rites which accompany every change of place, state, social position, and age."[4] Van Gennep discovered "a wide degree of general similarity among ceremonies of birth, childhood, social puberty, betrothal, marriage, pregnancy, fatherhood, initiation into religious societies, and funerals."[5] Consequently, the folklorist devoted five chapters respectively to pregnancy and childbirth, birth and childhood, initiation rites, betrothal and marriage, and funerals.[6] Victor Turner, building on the work of van Gennep, maintains that the basic model of society is a "structure of positions."[7] Another anthropologist, Terence Turner, holds that rituals which mark structural transitions of position can involve "temporal periods, spatial zones, social states, or relations of various kinds."[8]

---

2. Auslander, "Rites of Passage," 2022.

3. Van Gennep first published his work *Les rites de passage* in 1908. It was translated into English as *The Rites of Passage*.

4. V. Turner uses the term "state" as "a metonym for other terms; it refers to any type of stable or recurrent condition that is culturally recognized." See Turner, "Variations on a Theme of Liminality," 36.

5. Van Gennep, *The Rites of Passage*, 3.

6. Rituals and ceremonies are not the same. In distinguishing the two, McVann states, "In the course of routine daily living, individuals take special time, either to pause from routine or to intensify aspects of it. When the pause occurs irregularly, or as a break in the routine, it is call *ritual*. When the pause happens predictably it is a *ceremony*. These pauses, moreover, are under the care of specific people. Those who preside over or direct ritual pauses, the irregular breaks, are *professionals*, such as physicians, judges, and clergy. Those who preside over or direct *ceremonies* on the other hand, are *officials*, such as the father or mother presiding at a meal, a priest conducting a temple sacrifice, or a politician officiating at a Fourth of July picnic. *Rituals* . . . unlike ceremonies are concerned with status transformation and passage from one role or status to another." See McVann, "Rituals of Status Transformation," 334, 335–36. See also K. C. Hanson, "Transformed on the Mountain," 147–50. Hanson's study is a ritual study of the Gospel of Matthew.

7. V. Turner, *The Forest of Symbols*, 93.

8. T. Turner, "Transformation, Hierarchy and Transcendence," 53.

Thus, a rite of passage is a ritual or series of rituals in which participants cross an array of boundaries such as from being single to being married or from being a lay person to becoming a priest. In a rite of passage the normal conditions of life are changed or transformed because every society, K. C. Hanson reminds us, "employs means of creating, maintaining, and celebrating its group identity."[9] With the completion of the status transition the person takes on new tasks appropriate to her/his new identity. If we use the biblical theme of sanctification to describe this ritual process, a person (or group) is set apart or consecrated from the normal "profane" condition of a lay person, for example, to the "sacred" (sanctified, set apart) condition of a priest.[10]

In these rites, van Gennep identifies three transitional phases (more technically a tripartite procedural structure)—(1) separation, (2) margin (or *limen*),[11] and (3) aggregation (sometimes called re-aggregation) or incorporation (re-incorporation).[12] V. Turner maintains that the first and the last phases "speak for themselves; they detach ritual subjects from their old places in society and return them, inwardly transformed and outwardly changed, to new places."[13]

Let us examine these three transitional phases a little more closely.

Step one is a formal separation from the larger society. For example, persons preparing for baptism are separated from others for the moment of baptism.

Step two is the "liminal" state (margin/boundary/threshold phase). In this phase persons to be baptized, using our same illustration, are on the margin of society—neither outside nor inside, but in process. During this threshold phase a baptismal candidate may study the theological meaning of baptism and engage in various spiritual disciplines to prepare for the rite. This phase might involve a number of preliminary acts of preparation and/or training such as study, prayer, and fasting. By

9. Hanson, "Transformed on the Mountain," 147–70.

10. The theme of sanctification is appropriated from Malina, *New Testament World*, 180–83.

11. V. Turner (*The Ritual Process*, 95) notes that a *limen* is a threshold. During the liminal period, initiates are in a threshold.

12. When the ritual process is finished, neophytes "return to society with new roles and statuses, and new rights and obligations.... Their status in the community has been redefined" (McVann, "Rituals of Status Transformation," 340–41).

13. V. Turner, "Variations," 36.

engaging in these acts, the initiate is on the threshold of transformation—
that is, of entering a new state and status.

Step three is the aggregation of the participant(s) to the larger
group. Once baptized, the person in the marginal or liminal state now
rejoins society, in this case the community, but with a new status. Using
the language of Paul the newly baptized person has been "clothed" with
Christ (Gal 3:27). We might depict this process as follows:

FIGURE 8.1: RITUAL STEPS

Step One: Separation	**Step Two:** "Liminal State" (marginal condition)	**Step Three:** Aggregation
Normal condition Profane to you	Potentially yours	Normal condition Sacred to you

The Three Steps

Let us differentiate these three steps with the twelve disciples in
Matthew.

Step one (separation) is identified in three passages: the recruitment
of the two sets of brothers (4:18–22), the severance of Matthew from his
toll booth (9:9), and the summons of Jesus' "twelve disciples" at the opening of the missionary discourse (10:1–4). In this phase Jesus' disciples
experience separation in three ways: "separation of people, place, and
time."[14] For example, when Jesus calls the two sets of brothers (4:18–22)
and Matthew (9:9) they are separated from people (their families, fishing
workers, persons paying tolls) and places (fishing on the Sea of Galilee, a
toll booth) and time (they leave the normal flow of secular time and participate with Jesus in the *sacred* "timelessness" of the "kingdom of heaven"
that "has come near") (4:17).

Step two (the "liminal" state) is fully underway with the beginning of
the missionary discourse (chap. 10). Jesus is training his disciples as scribes
of the kingdom of heaven (13:52), an initiation that continues until they
desert him just before his death (26:56). Shortly, we will examine seven
characteristics of the liminal stage for the disciples. This step is the middle

---

14. McVann, "Rituals of Status Transformation," 338.

threshold phase, a critically ambiguous period, V. Turner argues, that has "implications for a general theory of sociocultural processes."[15] The use of V. Turner's thought on liminality is set forth especially in two essays, the first examines initiation rites in primitive societies in Central Africa,[16] and the second analyzes post-tribal societies—larger pre-industrial societies and "complex, large-scale civilizations" that feature the categories of work, leisure, play, flow, and what Turner refers to as "*communitas*."[17] For our model we draw primarily from both of V. Turner's studies, with the occasional use of other sources. It is important to note that V. Turner's earlier groundbreaking piece, *The Forest of Symbols,* has its limitations in making comparisons to first-century Greco-Roman society due to its focus on primitive tribal societies south of the Sahara, Africa. Also, Turner's efforts are "synoptic" accounts. Not all preindustrial societies have lengthy rites of passage and some stress, as Turner admits "particular themes and symbolic processes, and play down others."[18] Our model does not reflect so much a compendium of status transformation rituals; rather, it incorporates components appropriate to Jesus' activity with his disciples in the social world described in the Gospel of Matthew.

The middle phase, as noted, is one of marginality or "liminality"—an inter-structural process, a time of transition or "becoming." As V. Turner observes, initiation rites can be protracted, "having a long threshold, a corridor almost, or a tunnel which may, indeed, become a pilgrim's road or passing from dynamics to statics, may cease to be a mere transition and become a set way of life, a state, that of the anchorite, or monk."[19] In other words, this dangerous path is an intermediate segment, a phase that Turner identifies as "betwixt and between." Transitional beings, Turner states, "are neither one thing nor another; or may be both; or neither here nor there; or may even be nowhere (in terms of any recognized cultural topography), and are at the very least 'betwixt and between' all the recognized fixed points in space-time of structural classification."[20]

---

15. V. Turner, "Variations," 36.

16. V. Turner, "Betwixt and Between," 93–111.

17. V. Turner, "Variations," 36–52.

18. Ibid., 38.

19. Ibid., 37, 39.

20. V. Turner, *Forest of Symbols,* 97.

Persons or groups in the liminal phase are defined by names and by a set of symbols associated with the process of transformation. In his first essay Turner designates such persons as initiates or neophytes. In his second essay he often refers to them as "liminaries."[21] Matthew's label for such persons is "disciples" (10:1, 24; 11:1 et al.) or his "twelve disciples" (10:1, 2, 5; 11:1; 19:28; 20:17; 26:14, 20),[22] the number twelve being symbolic of the twelve tribes of Israel (19:28). Matthean scholarship has recognized the Gospel's distinctive treatment of the disciples as a group called by Jesus and designated "disciples."[23]

Following Victor Turner, Warren Carter has dealt with the disciples as a liminal group that follows an "alternative existence" and lives a "marginalized alternative social existence, though they cannot withdraw from society."[24] Our analysis is more far-reaching than Carter's in three ways. First, it develops an extensive anthropological model based not only on Victor Turner's work but also the studies of Terence Turner[25] and Arnold van Gennep. Second, it bonds Victor Turner's views of liminality with some of van Gennep's insights on burial rituals (the initiatory transition of Jesus' disciples is grounded in the Matthean funerary process of death/resurrection). Third, it integrates the story of the woman who anoints Jesus for burial (26:6–13) with the women who witness his death (27:55–56), wait opposite the tomb (27:61), and go to the tomb (28:1–10). This integration is critically essential to the disciples' liminal journey (26:31, 56; 69–75; 27:3–10). These women unlike other undesignated followers of Jesus in Matthew fulfill essential roles in the liminal stage. They are temporal and geographical/spatial bridges to the disciples' re-aggregation with Jesus.[26]

Step three (the rite of aggregation) may be identified as the commissioning scene on the mountain in Galilee (28:16–20) for the new task of making disciples as Jesus previously had instructed the Twelve. We will

21. V. Turner, "Variations," 37.

22. After the suicide of Judas (27:3–10), the designation changes from "twelve disciples" to "eleven disciples" (28:16).

23. Carter, *Households and Discipleship*; idem, "Matthew 4:18–22 and Matthean Discipleship," 58–75; Edwards, "Uncertain Faith: Matthew's Portrait of the Disciples," 47–61; Kingsbury, *Matthew as Story*; "The Verb ἀκολουθεῖν ('To Follow')," 56–73; Luz, "The Disciples in the Gospel According to Matthew"; Wilkins, *The Concept of Discipleship in Matthew's Gospel*.

24. Carter, *Households and Discipleship*, 52–55.

25. T. Turner, "Transformation, Hierarchy and Transcendence," 53–70.

26. We will demonstrate this shortly.

demonstrate that with minor modifications the women at the crucifixion and the tomb of Jesus also undertake a parallel rite of passage. This rite of passage model also is a combination initiation/death ritual. It best illumines why the women suddenly and inexplicably appear in Matthew's narrative and provide an essential linkage between Jesus and the disciples after his resurrection.

Previous Models as a Presupposition

Our use of a rite of passage model does not mean that our earlier insights about social domains are irrelevant to the women's accounts. Indeed, most of the events of Matthew 27—Jesus before Pilate (vv. 1–2), the suicide of Judas (vv. 3–10), Jesus' condemnation by the Romans (vv. 11–31), and his crucifixion and death (vv. 32–56)—are set in the public, political sphere. Moreover, the narrative units that immediately precede and include chapter 28 alternate public, political, and private, surrogate kinship settings, beginning with the burial of Jesus (27:57–61), the guard at the tomb (27:57–61), the resurrection of Jesus (28:1–20), the report of the guard (28:11–15), and the commissioning of the disciples (28:16–20).

FIGURE 8.2: PUBLIC AND PRIVATE SPHERES

Public, Political Sphere	Private, Kinship Sphere
Guard at the tomb (27:62–66)	Burial of Jesus by Joseph (27:57–61)
Report of the guard (28:11–15)	Resurrection of Jesus (28:1–10)
	Commissioning of the disciples (28:16–20)

Neither does our rite of passage model obviate the potential for a model of degrees of purity. Jesus' death abounds with purity problems. Pollution issues, we will show, are at the heart of the liminal phase of a rite-of-passage model. Thus, much that transpires in initiation and/or burial rites (the two rituals combined in this study) fits Mary Douglas' contention that the concept of pollution "is a reaction to protect cherished principles and categories from contradiction."[27]

---

27. Douglas, *Purity and Danger*, as quoted in V. Turner, *The Forest of Symbols*, 97.

Finally, our rite-of-passage model is best understood within the "pivotal value of Mediterranean society of the first century,"[28] honor and shame. It is a critically important social reality for the personages of our passages—preeminently for Jesus who dies in disgrace but is honored by his resurrection, his return to Galilee, and the commissioning of the Eleven. The women join in Jesus' shame and honor; the disciples are shamed by their desertion and/or betrayal and denial but, with the exception of Judas, are ascribed honor by Jesus on the mountain in Galilee. The religious and political personages initially acquire honor in putting Jesus to death but subsequently are shamed by the events associated with the unoccupied tomb.

Rites of Passage and a Narrative Genre

Before we present the liminal phase for the twelve disciples in more detail, it is legitimate to ask whether such a model is too dissimilar to the nature of a gospel such as Matthew that is basically a narrative genre. We certainly want to avoid "forcing," or "arbitrarily or whimsically"[29] altering the meaning of the First Evangelist. Stated in other words, we do not want the rhetorical strategy of Matthew to be compromised by our use of another strategy that is inconsistent with the writing itself. It is true that our model depends greatly on the concept of *liminality* as set forth in the work of V. Turner in primitive Central African societies and in post-tribal societies. How then do we justify the use of such a model as an interpretive tool for Matthew's gospel?

Most if not all rites of passage are rooted in individual and group narratives, established by and in the stories of persons and/or groups in which a *change* in status takes place, whether it be circumcision, baptism, graduation, marriage, anointing the sick, bar/bat mitzvah, confirmation, ordination, or a bishop's consecration. All such transformational rituals involve the crossing of a variety of boundaries that are rooted in actual life scripts—from being single to being married, from being a layperson to becoming a priest, from being an outsider to becoming an insider, from being unclean to being clean. Such stories can be described explicitly

---

28. Malina and Rohrbaugh, *Synoptic Gospels*, 369–70.

29. See chapters 1 and 4 in Rohrbaugh, *The New Testament in Cross-Cultural Perspective*, for a healthy warning of the problem we are describing. The wording "forcing" or "arbitrarily or whimsically" is that of Rohrbaugh.

(consciously) or implicitly (unconsciously) by an author by means of a narrative genre. For example, van Gennep recognizes that in all cultures he observed death rituals were a transformational process of separation. A written description of a particular death ritual might be done in a variety of ways, but the memory of the deceased and the lives of the living might be couched implicitly in a narrative genre. Therefore, we do not affirm that the First Evangelist set out to write a rite of passage narrative; we simply acknowledge that the trained eye can discern such rites within the author's narrative.[30] Certainly the Gospel of Matthew is a transformational piece of literature. And when rites of passage are identified justifiably they deepen and widen our understanding of the author's narrative intent.

We draw the reader's attention to the fact that a central and distinctive purpose of the Gospel of Matthew is to train disciples as scribes for the kingdom of heaven (13:52). An informed reader, we believe, can see in the author's stated purpose the possibility of an initiation/burial rite of passage. To train scribes for the kingdom of heaven is fundamental to Matthew and is reinforced by the inclusion of five major teaching discourses (chap. 5–7, 10, 13, 18, 24–25) that are set individually within the larger context of the story or narrative of Jesus. This combination of narrative and teaching organizational structure is not accidental and reaches its culmination in the commissioning of the disciples as teachers that Jesus has trained (28:18–20). Thus, we believe a rite of passage model can inform a narrative sequence such as the Gospel of Matthew. In the end, only the reader will be the final judge of the legitimacy and value of using this model to illumine the place of the women at the cross and tomb in Matthew.

The Disciples' Desertion and the Women's Indispensable Function

Let us summarize our central idea. In brief, the disciples leave their traditional roles and statuses and are in transition (state of *liminality*) from the time of their call by Jesus (state of *separation*) ultimately until the return of the Son of Man—but more immediately until they are recommissioned

30. Three examples come to mind: (1) Carter's treatment of the disciples as a liminal group (*Households and Discipleship*, 52–55); (2) McVann's handling of Jesus's transformative ritual process "from private person to public teacher" ("Rituals of Status Transformation"); and (3) Hanson's ritual analysis tied to mountains in Matthew ("Transformed on the Mountain").

(state of *aggregation*) as teachers by Jesus for their mission (28:16–20; see 10:5–6). But, the temporal (from call, 4:18–22, to commission, 28:6–10) and geographical/spatial (from Galilee, 4:12, to Galilee, 28:16) lines of this transitional process are decisively broken/interrupted shortly before the death of Jesus (26:56). At this critical juncture, the disciples' desertion, a significant break in their initiation/death rite, takes place. This creates a vacuity that is filled by the women who alone provide the indispensable temporal and geographical/spatial connection to the disciples' aggregation on the mountain in Galilee. Within this process the women also undergo their own liminal transition and aggregation.

A Geographical Bridge

How do the women provide a geographical/spatial bridge? How are they unlike other "undesignated disciples"[31] such as Joseph (1:18–25), the magi (2:1–11), the centurion (8:5–13), the ruler and hemorrhaging woman (9:18–31), the two blind men (9:27–31; 20:29–34), and the Canaanite woman (15:21–28)? Certainly, like the others, they are never "called" by Jesus as the "Twelve" are (4:19; 9:9; 10:1). However, apart from the woman who anoints Jesus (26:6–13 [her case will be examined momentarily]), these women not only minister to Jesus, they also "follow" him from Galilee (27:55), a matter that both Matthew and Luke emphasize up front (Luke 23:49) but Mark includes almost as a postscript (15:41). Matthew also adds "many women" indicating that there were more than the three named.[32]

Galilee is especially significant to Matthew. It is the place of the beginning of Jesus' activity (4:12) and it attracts crowds not only from Galilee but also Syria (4:24) and ". . . the Decapolis, Jerusalem, Judea, and from beyond the Jordan" (4:25). Matthew underscores this geographical feature with a quotation from Isaiah 9:1–2 (Matt 4:14–16). Luz, commenting on the Galilean aspect of this gospel unit, points out that "Galilee was after 70 the heartland of Israel. Thus the designation 'Galilee of the Gentiles' has a fictive character."[33]

Further, Galilee is the place where the disciples are called (4:18) and the location where the community has its beginning (28:16). Matthew

31. Here I make use of Carter's terminology (*Matthew: Storyteller, Interpreter, Evangelist*, 215–16).

32. Typical of Matthew, the Evangelist shortens Mark's account; it is more precise.

33. Luz, *Matthew 1–7*, 194–95.

alone mentions that the disciples are "gathering in Galilee" (17:22). This is admittedly a difficult phrase to interpret, but it appears to be a statement that points to the inauguration of Jesus' activity in Galilee (4:13–17) and to the place where Jesus' task ends (28.16). Not to be forgotten are two other distinctive Old Testament quotations, in 2:23, "He shall be called a Nazorean," and 12:18–21, which cites Isaiah 42:1–4 [LXX], "And in his name the Gentiles will hope." Luz believes that these quotations "also indicate this hidden perspective" of Israel.[34] Only Matthew tells his auditors when Jesus enters Jerusalem in 21:11 that the crowds identify him as, "the prophet Jesus from Nazareth in Galilee." At the announcement of the disciples' impending desertion (26:30–35), Jesus tells them that after the events surrounding his death he will go before them to Galilee to greet them when they arrive (26:32). Finally, both the angel and Jesus instruct Mary Magdalene and the other Mary to tell the disciples to go to Galilee where they will see Jesus (28:7, 10). This the Eleven do. They go "to the mountain where Jesus had directed them" (28:16). Also, except for the suicide of Judas (27:3–10), the "disciples" are perceptibly absent in chapter 27. Consequently, a critical link in the geography of the disciples' *liminal* state is reserved for and/or taken up by the women. They alone connect the disciples to the death, burial, and resurrection of Jesus.

In this light, the woman who anoints Jesus at Bethany (26:6–13) also participates in the heart of this *liminal* journey. She alone prepares Jesus' body for burial and, perhaps, in so doing recognizes his "divinely authorized role."[35] What she does stands over and against the disciples' behavior. Luz states, ". . . this woman and then later the women at the cross and at Jesus' tomb . . . stand by Jesus precisely in his suffering."[36] Thus, they are witnesses and participants in the disciples' initiatory, transformative process.[37]

A Temporal Bridge

Similarly, the women simultaneously provide a temporal bridge to the disciples' *liminal* transformation. We begin with the ritual process of Jesus. McVann has shown through the use of Luke's account (3:1—4:30)

34. Ibid., 195.

35. Carter, *Matthew: Storyteller, Interpreter, Evangelist*, 224.

36. Luz, *Matthew 21–28*, 337.

37. This connection will be elaborated shortly.

that Jesus undergoes a transformative ritual process of separation, liminality, *communitas*, confrontation, and aggregation.[38] The transformative movement is "from private person to public teacher."[39] In Jesus' case, John the baptizer serves as ritual elder. Separation for Jesus' prophetic role takes place at his baptism (3:21–22). The *liminal* state then follows in the temptation story (4:1–11) and aggregation occurs when Jesus returns to Galilee in the power of the Spirit (4:14–15). McVann's analysis seems to parallel Matthew: Jesus' baptism marks his separation (3:13–17); his temptation signals the marginal, *liminal* state (4:1–11); and the report of John's arrest pinpoints the beginning of his ministry in Galilee, his aggregation. Matthew's temporal formula, "from that time" (4:17), signals the beginning of Jesus' new role identified by his own proclamation, "'Repent, for the kingdom of heaven has come near.'"

After Jesus' status transformation, Matthew then turns to the ritual modification process of the disciples. If John the baptizer serves as "Jesus' elder,"[40] Jesus now acts as "elder" for the disciples.[41] We have already described step one (separation) of their transformation. The ambiguous *liminal* state for the disciples is fully underway with the beginning of the missionary discourse.[42] The model illustrates several facets of initiation in this discourse (10:1—11:1) and its corresponding narrative (4:17—11:1),

38. McVann, "Rituals of Status Transformation," 333–60.

39. Ibid., 341.

40. Ibid., 343–45.

41. V. Turner designates persons in charge of the ritual process as "elders." They supervise and socialize "by exhibiting and explaining" to the neophytes the process of their transformation. McVann ("Rituals of Status Transformation," 337) refers to the elders as "limit breakers" or "boundary jumpers." He states, "They are immune to the powers harmful to those outside the process because they have been appointed to conduct the ritual and have themselves been transformed by it." See V. Turner, *The Forest of Symbols,* 97. In this process elders may beat, withhold food and sleep, taunt and insult the neophytes, strip them, and say or do things to humiliate and disorient them (McVann, "Rituals of Status Transformation," 335–36).

42. The instruction process is underway in the Sermon on the Mount (5:1—7:29) and in the collection of ten miracle stories (8:1—9:34). The latter section returns Matthew's auditors to 4:25, "And great crowds followed him from Galilee, the Decapolis, Jerusalem, Judea, and from beyond the Jordan." Discipleship units appear at strategic points in the miracle section (8:18–22; 9:9–17). With the summons of the "twelve" disciples (10:1), corresponding to the twelve tribes of Israel (19:28), Matthew seems to indicate that the "missionary discourse" is entirely about Israel (10:6), a point not previously made in the previous separation stories (4:18–22; 9:9). The First Evangelist did not set out to write a rite-of-passage narrative.

and in the parable discourse (13:1–53) and its corresponding narrative (11:2—16:20). In 16:20 Jesus commands silence on the part of his initiates, a directive that follows on the heels of the special knowledge they received in the second Son of God confession and subsequent promise to Peter (16:13–20). At this critical point (16:21), as in 4:17, a second temporal bridge is identified. *"From that time on,"* the disciples now enter the heart of a mid-*liminal* phase related to Jesus' passion predictions and corresponding teachings to his neophytes (16:21; 17:22–23; 20:17–19; 26:1–2). During this phase in which Jesus' passion is anticipated, the adumbration of a burial ritual can be identified in concert with the initiation ritual.[43] The blending of these two rituals reaches its fulfillment in the death and resurrection of Jesus, but the termination of the mid-*liminal* phase for the disciples takes place at the close of the Lord's Supper account when Jesus announces, "You will all become deserters because of this night" (26:31), which then takes place (26:56).[44] Thereafter, the Twelve are absent from the ritual process but return as the "eleven disciples" on the mountain in Galilee for their *aggregation* (28:16).

How does one account for this temporal gap? It is carried forward by the women who prepare Jesus' body for burial (26:12), "look on from a distance" when he is crucified (27:55), sit opposite the tomb when Jesus is buried (27:61), "see the tomb" after his resurrection, and accept the summons of the angel to instruct the disciples that Jesus would meet them in Galilee (28:7). Then, they witness the risen Jesus, take "hold of his feet," worship him (28:9), and accept Jesus' encouragement not to be afraid but to "go and tell my brothers to go to Galilee; there they will see me" (28:10). Both the angel and Jesus have entrusted them with a message and a task. Without the participation of these women in the temporal line of the ritual process the fruition of the transformative goal would have been aborted by the disciples' desertion.

At this point we examine seven characteristics of the *liminal* state of the disciples.

---

43. I will demonstrate how these two rites combine shortly. However, I cite first just one example of the initiation process. Jesus tells James and John that they will share in his destiny, his suffering and death—"You will indeed drink my cup" (19:23)—as he instructs them about the reversal of hierarchical leadership among his disciples.

44. It is true that Peter's threefold denial takes place thereafter (26:69–75), but he remembers at that time "what Jesus said (26:34) and departs and weeps bitterly (26:75). At this point Judas has already agreed to betray Jesus (26:14–16).

DEATH TO THE WORLD—Initiates are "in a sense 'dead' to the world." The state of "liminality has many symbols of death."[45] In Matthew, the plot of Jesus' mission and that of his disciples necessitates death and resurrection both in a real and symbolic sense—the loss of life for the sake of the Messiah as the means of finding life (16:21–23; 17:22–23; 20:17–19; 26:2). Jesus' initiates are taught to "deny themselves," to "take up their cross and follow" him (16:24; see 10:37–39; 19:29; 20:22–23). The cross, a metaphor of death and life, is not a trifling symbol because it signifies the ignominy, anguish, social rejection, brutality, mortification, and marginalization of Roman crucifixion. This initiation process is combined with a death ritual, a transformative union of two rites of passage, both being essential to the third phase—the aggregation of the disciples and the beginning of the community (28:16–20).

But how is this possible? In 16:21, immediately after the second temporal marker (16:21a; see 4:17), Matthew incorporates for the first time instruction to Jesus' neophytes about matters pertaining to his future suffering, death, burial, and resurrection. Four times in subsequent materials Jesus makes predictions to his initiates of his impending death (16:21; 17:22–23; 20:17–19; 26:1–2). The last instruction, peculiar to Matthew, is located at the beginning of the passion and resurrection narratives (26:1—28:10) and coincides with the Passover celebration of Israelites (the death of Egypt's firstborn son) (26:2).[46] Van Gennep, writing on funeral ceremonies, demonstrates that in all cultures he observed death rituals are a transformational process of separation, transition, and incorporation.[47] This involves not only the person who dies but those who closely attend the "deceased's social transition out of the living world."[48] The mourners are a separate "collective social unit out of ordinary life, placing them

---

45. V. Turner, "Variations," 37.

46. Jesus' deliberate prediction of his passion only to the disciples is underscored in 20:17: "While Jesus was going up to Jerusalem, he took the twelve disciples aside by themselves . . ."

47. Van Gennep, *The Rites of Passage*, 146.

48. Auslander, "Rites of Passage," 2024. Auslander states, "The dead person may be thought of as moving from initial separation (through special treatment, including embalming), into the ambiguous liminal status of funeral corpse, to a final state of integration in the domain of the dead (signified by burial or cremation)." For more in-depth analysis see Geertz, *Local Knowledge*; and Huntington and Metcalf, *Celebrations of Death*.

into an ambiguous interstitial space and time."[49] As we might expect, van Gennep notes that "funerary rites vary widely among different peoples."[50]

The death of Jesus has at least four identifiable ritual components: (1) repeated preparatory announcements of his death to his neophytes (16:22; 17:22–23; 20:17–19; 26:2), (2) a burial anointing rite while Jesus still lives (26:5–13), (3) descriptions of his death and burial, and (4) a unique element, a resurrection story (28:1–8). Here, only Jesus' death announcements to his initiates are addressed. The other three elements are taken up when the model is applied to the women.

After the first passion prediction Peter seizes the role of instructor and rebukes Jesus in the form of a divine oath, "God forbid it, Lord! This must never happen to you" (16:22). Both his behavior and language betray that he is in a state of denial. Jesus interprets Peter's actions as satanic and as a stumbling block to his own divine destiny. Peter's mind is set on "human things" and not "divine things." Thus, the neophytes, Peter being representative, are ill-prepared for Jesus' subsequent instructions about the cross paradigm and self-denial (16:24–26). The second passion prediction (17:22) takes place in the context of Jesus' disciples "gathering in Galilee." After the prediction, Matthew indicates that the disciples are greatly distressed (17:23). The third prediction (20:17–19) is followed by the request of the mother of James and John that her two sons hold preeminent positions of power and honor in Jesus' future kingdom (20:20–28). Jesus' answer, directed not to the mother but to her sons, affirms quite to the contrary. Their destiny with Jesus will entail suffering and death (20:22). The fourth prediction (26:2) is made two days before the Israelite celebration of the death/life, slavery/freedom festival of Passover (Exod 12:14–27; 34:18). It is followed immediately by the religious authorities' plot to kill Jesus (26:3–5), an extravagant and costly anointing of Jesus' body for burial by an unnamed woman, a ritual opposed by the disciples under the pretext of concern for the poor (26:6–13), and Judas' betrayal of Jesus for money (26:14–16). The disciples' misunderstanding and resistance to Jesus' instructions ill equip them for their mentor's death. As Jesus predicted, when the shepherd is struck, the sheep of the flock will be scattered (26:31).

49. Ibid.

50. Van Gennep, *The Rites of Passage,* 146.

An Occasional Loss of Names—Liminaries can lose their "prelimi-nal names."[51] The example in Matthew is of "Simon, who is called Peter" (4:18), "Simon, also known as Peter" (10:2), "Simon, son of Jonah." He is commissioned by Jesus and renamed by his instructor as "Peter" a term from the Greek *petros*, meaning rock or stone, which functions as a sym-bolic appellation that corresponds to Peter's confession of Jesus as Israel's Messiah (16:16)[52] and his apparent imminent leadership role in the com-munity's establishment and prolongation.

An Engagement in Tasks that Involve Prohibitions, Pain, Humil-iation, and Risk—Neophytes often are given special tasks, are subject to unusual prohibitions and precautions, and subjected to pain, humilia-tion, and heightened risks.[53] This is evidenced frequently in Matthew but especially is apparent in the missionary discourse (10:1—11:1). There, the "twelve disciples," are summoned, commissioned, and sent out by Jesus to follow his example as a wandering beggar, preacher, and healer (10:1–15). In doing their tasks only among the "lost sheep of the house of Israel" (10:5), Jesus' neophytes live out what V. Turner refers to as a "sacred poverty."[54] Turner explains,

> A further structurally negative characteristic of transitional beings is that they *have* nothing. They have no status, property, insignia, secular clothing, rank, and kinship position, nothing to demarcate them structurally from their fellows. Their condition is in deed the very prototype of sacred poverty. Rights over property, goods, and services inhere in positions in the politico-jural structure. Since they do not occupy such positions, neophytes exercise no such rights. In the words of King Lear they represent "naked unaccom-modated man."[55]

The disciples are to travel without money, a journey bag, two tunics, and even sandals (10:9–10). This is a thoroughgoing austere subsistence previ-ously taught and grounded in the culture of the Sermon on the Mount (6:25–34).[56] Their task includes a sacred urgency. They are to depend on

51. V. Turner, "Variations," 37.
52. See 14:33 for an earlier confession of all the disciples.
53. Auslander, "Rites of Passage," 2023.
54. V. Turner, *The Forest of Symbols*, 98–99.
55. Ibid.
56. The separation accounts of the two sets of two brothers (4:18–22) and Matthew the toll collector (9:9) demonstrates that they left their economic means of support to

the hospitality (or the lack thereof) of households in towns and villages of Israel (10:11). Their instructor warns them of impending suffering and persecution. They will be handed over to councils, flogged in synagogues, and dragged before governors and kings (10:18, 22; 5:10–12). In preparation for harassment Jesus' initiates are taught not to fear their persecutors or to be anxious but to trust in the Spirit's guidance (10:20). Instruction to "fear not" maltreatment appears three times in the space of six verses (10:26, 28, and 31). They are to fear only the one "who can destroy both soul and body in hell" (10:28). Jesus' initiates are commanded to be faithful to Jesus, their teacher. Those who do so will be acknowledged in the future judgment but those who deny his demanding instructions will be denied by "my Father in heaven" (10:32–33). In summation, Matthew 10 specifies the initiates' itinerant and outsider status (10:5–6), their indigence (10:9–10), their dependence on hospitality (10:11–15), their trials and persecutions as they face a hostile world and risk their lives (10:17–23, 28–29), and their extended hospitality to other wandering brothers (10:40–42). They are reminded that "whoever receives" them, "receives" their teacher (10:40). Matthew 10 parallels Turner's description of a "grinding down process" . . . "accomplished by ordeals."[57] Turner states, "Liminal entities, such as neophytes in initiation rites, demonstrate that as liminal beings they have no status. Their behavior is normally passive or humble. It is as though they are being ground down or reduced to a uniform condition to be fashioned anew and endowed with additional powers to enable them to cope with their new station in life."[58] But Turner then adds, "reducing down overlaps with reconstruction" a process achieved in multiple ways such as training and the development of practical skills, evidenced as well in the missionary discourse.[59] Matthew 10 illustrates how Jesus' neophytes engage in tasks and experience rigorous hardships as they are being prepared for the outcome of their work.

---

follow Jesus. In 4:20, the word "follow," a key Matthean disciple/liminality word (Kingsbury, "The Verb ἀκολουθειν ('To Follow')," 56–73), is used for the first time in Matthew. Their nets are not even pulled up on the land. Further, the rich young man is told that if he desires to be "perfect," he should "go, sell" his possessions, and "give the money to the poor, and you will have treasure in heaven; then come, follow me" (19:21), after which Peter states, "Look, we have left everything and followed you" (19:27).

57. V. Turner, "Variations," 37.

58. Ibid., 95.

59. Ibid.

Jesus, as instructor, also shames or humiliates his initiates in their *liminal* walk. On four different occasions he makes one of his disciples or all of them self-conscious of their "little faith" (6:30; 14:31; 16:8; 17:20). When taught not to worry about life's necessities Jesus shames them, "But if God so clothes the grass of the field, which is alive today and tomorrow is thrown into the oven, will he not much more clothe you—you of little faith?" (6:30). When Peter becomes frightened, sinks in the water, and cries out for help, Jesus saves him but then chides him, "You of little faith, why did you doubt?" (14:31). Peter is singled out for humiliation but increasingly becomes representative of all of the disciples (15:15; 16:16). Further, Jesus warns his neophytes of the "yeast of the Pharisees and Sadducees" (16:6). The initiates, however, misunderstand their teacher evidenced by their response, "It is because we have brought no bread" (16:7), to which Jesus scolds them through a series of belittling questions: "You of little faith, why are you talking about having no bread? Do you still not perceive? . . . How could you fail to perceive that I was not speaking about bread?" (16:8b–11a). When the disciples ask why they are unable to heal a boy with a demon Jesus' answer is disparaging, "Because of your little faith. For truly I tell you, if you have faith the size of a mustard seed, you will say to this mountain, 'Move from here to there,' and it will move; and nothing will be impossible for you" (17:20).

INTERSTRUCTURAL ASSOCIATION MARKED BY SIMPLICITY—A fourth characteristic is the interstructural association among liminaries. A "set of relations" constitutes a specific kind of social structure marked by simplicity. Turner states, ". . . between instructors and neophytes there is often complete authority and complete submission; among neophytes there is often complete equality" as opposed to the intricate networks, hierarchical arrangements, rights and duties "proportioned" to "rank, status, and corporate affiliation" outside the group and/or the larger society.[60] A goal of the ritual process is to emphasize "an essential and generic human bond, without which there could be no (status differentiating) society."[61] Turner continues: ". . . the bonds of *communitas* (formed among initiates undergoing a rite of passage are anti-structural in that they are undifferentiated (and) egalitarian."[62] Degrees of "superordination and subordination" tend

60. V. Turner, *The Forest of Symbols,* 99–100.

61. V. Turner, *The Ritual Process,* 97.

62. V. Turner, *Dramas, Fields, and Metaphors,* 46. Terence Turner argues that the intermediate or liminal phase of such rites is characterized not so much by "anti-structure," as

to be eliminated. The neophytes' elders (in Matthew this would be Jesus) have absolute authority over the liminaries—an authority, however, not predicated on legal sanctions but on "the self-evident authority of tradition . . ." Authority is unqualified "because it represents the absolute, the axiomatic values of society" that convey the "'common good' and the common interest." In their persons, the elders (Jesus) represent "the total community."[63] Perhaps in Matthew this would be the *ideal* community of which the disciples are a representative transparency.

This kind of inter-structural order can be detected especially in Matthew 23. Jesus' neophytes are taught to reject the hierarchical, dominating social order evidenced by the leaders of Israel in favor of an alternative community (23:8–12). Titles such as "rabbi" (literally "my great one," see 26:25, 40), "father," and "instructor" are to be eschewed because the initiates have one rabbi (great one) and teacher, Jesus, and one "Father— the one in heaven" (23:9). Instead, Jesus' initiates are "brothers," students of Jesus and servants of one another (23:11, 12). Self-exaltation is condemned. Here, the story of the mother's request for her sons, James and John, is germane (20:20–28). Her wish that her sons be hierarchical rulers like the Romans cannot be granted by Jesus among his disciples. Further, Jesus instructs his initiates in the parable of the laborers in the vineyard (20:1–16) that all of the laborers receive "equal" pay whether they toiled one hour or all day (20:12). The householder's behavior illustrates a reversal of the social-structural expectations of an advanced agrarian society. Finally, Jesus' absolute authority as teacher for his disciples is illustrated by his six legal interpretations concerning anger, adultery, divorce, swearing oaths, retaliation, and hating one's enemies that alter or radicalize the meaning of the law in contrast to Israel's religious leaders (5:17–48). Jesus as the neophytes' instructor gives the "right" interpretation of the will of God, and his absolute teaching authority stands over and against that of the scribes and Pharisees (7:28–29).

PARTICIPATION IN A REALM WITHOUT STRUCTURE IN WHICH SEXUAL DISTINCTIONS DO NOT APPLY—In societies structured by kinship institutions, the "structureless realm" of the neophytes often is one in which

---

by a kind of hyper-structuration, enabling a kind of regimenting or reconceptualization of the opening and closing phases of the ritual process. See T. Turner, "Transformation, Hierarchy, and Transcendence," 53–70; Auslander, "Rites of Passage," 2024.

63. V. Turner, *The Forest of Symbols*, 100.

typical kinship sexual distinctions do not apply. V. Turner states, "It is consistent with this to find that in liminal situations (in kinship-dominated societies) neophytes are sometimes treated or symbolically represented as being neither male and female. Alternatively, they may be symbolically assigned characteristics of both sexes, irrespective of their biological sex."[64] Although gender specificity obviously is evident for the "twelve disciples," Matthew does not seem to view them as androgynous, or as males "assigned characteristics of both sexes." Still, the notion of kinship and sexual identity is so radically reformulated that Jesus' new surrogate family is identified as "whoever does the will of my Father" (12:50; see 10:34–39; 23:9).[65] Jesus instructs his liminaries that his mission thoroughly divides families and that his initiates constitute a new kin group defined not by biology, ancestry, or hereditary wealth but by the doing of God's will in the face of scribal and Pharisaic opposition and Roman hegemony (10:37–39; 4:18–22; 8:21–22; 12:46–50). These instructions parallel what V. Turner refers to as a paradoxical language of "being *both* this *and* that," and neither.[66] As novices the disciples are "being 'grown' into a "new postliminal state of being."[67] This represents an identity shift, using one of V. Turner's images, from being children to becoming adults. "The novices at times may be treated as embryos in a womb, as infants being born, as sucklings, and as weanlings. Usually, there are words and phrases which indicate that they are 'being grown' into a postliminal state of being."[68]

Jesus uses the child/adult metaphor but reverses it.[69] When the disciples ask their elder, "Who then is the greatest in the kingdom of heaven?" (18:1), Jesus unexpectedly and unconventionally tells them that they must become like children. To do this, they must "turn" (18:3), that is, be subjected to an inverse transformation. The disciples' old role as "adults" is thoroughly defective and must be rejected and replaced by "a completely new one pressed permanently upon them."[70] Returning to the symbol

64. Ibid., 98.

65. Perhaps here, the larger circle of Jesus' disciples, including women, fits the categorization. If so, the Gospel sets forth both an uncompromising gender inclusion but a community led by males.

66. Ibid.

67. V. Turner, "Variations," 37.

68. Ibid.

69. See also Matt 11:25; 19:13–15; 21:15–16.

70. McVann, "Rituals of Status Transformation," 340.

of the new surrogate family, the movement of language in 12:46–50 is striking. First, Jesus' mother and brothers (biological family) seek to speak with him. When this becomes apparent, Jesus asks what seems to be obvious, "Who is my mother, and who are my brothers?" Pointing to his male disciples, he declares, "Here are my mother and my brothers!" (12:49). Following Turner, the disciples apparently are "symbolically represented as being neither male nor female." Sexual distinctions based on biological kinship ostensibly do not matter for the true kindred of Jesus.

PARTICIPATION IN SACRED PLACES OF CONCEALMENT THAT LINK THE INITIATES WITH DEITY—Sixth, neophytes can be brought into "close connection with deity or with superhuman power," often regarded as the "unbounded, the finite, the limitless." V. Turner states, "Since neophytes are not only structurally 'invisible' (though physically visible) . . . they are very commonly secluded, partially or completely, from the realm of culturally defined and ordered states and statuses." If they are not removed to a "sacred place of concealment they are often disguised, in masks or grotesque costumes or striped with white, red, or black clay, and the like."[71] The disciples are not continually secluded or disguised but their intermittent and purposeful seclusion with Jesus can be documented. In the parables Jesus gives private instruction to the disciples (13:10–23). In the privacy of Caesarea Philippi, Peter confesses Jesus to be the Messiah (16:13, 16). Warren Carter summarizes what takes place in this sheltered setting. "Jesus affirms that the basis of this confession is the revelation of God (16:17) and gives instructions about the future community of disciples, the community (16:18–19). But he forbids the disciples from proclaiming that he is the Christ (16:20)."[72] Revelation, instruction, and a stern injunction to silence (16:20; see 8:4; 9:30) characterize this isolated setting.

In the transfiguration scene (17:1–8) Jesus takes Peter, James and his brother John to what Matthew describes as a "high mountain by themselves" (17:1), a sacred place of revelation (see 4:8; 5:1; 8:1; 14:23; 15:29; 17:9; 24:3; 28:16).[73] There, the transfiguration unfolds replicating the appearance of God to Moses on Mount Sinai (Ex 24:15). Jesus' altered manifestation reveals his future glory (see 16:27; Ex 34:29);

71. V. Turner, *The Forest of Symbols,* 103.

72. Carter, *Matthew: Storyteller, Interpreter, Evangelist,* 147.

73. For a treatment of this mountain through a ritual analysis, see Hanson, "Transformed on the Mountain," 147–60.

Jesus' radical transformation along with the unexpected appearance of Moses and Elijah evokes great fear in the disciples (17:6; see 8:25–26; 14:26; 28:8–10). In addition, God's presence symbolized in the "bright cloud" (17:5) further underscores the presence of the *sacra* along with the divine confirmation of Jesus' identity (17:5). On the "great mountain" the three neophytes are in another place, an altered state of consciousness. They are hidden from others, even the other disciples, because they see what "ought not to be there!"[74] Hanson distinguishes between the inner circle and the Twelve as neophytes in what he refers to as "the mountain of epiphany."[75] Peter, James, and John, we are reminded, are separated by Jesus "not only from society generally, but also from the other nine disciples . . ." When they fall on their faces awestruck (17:6) they do what is "appropriate and expected" (Ezek 1:28). Hanson continues, "But more than simply a literary motif, this is the appropriate *ritual action and posture*. The disciples have been taken further along their journey of discipleship in being granted this vision in which Jesus' unique status as God's son is revealed to them. Thus, their status as disciples is heightened even as Jesus' exalted status is revealed."[76]

Finally, the celebration of the Passover with the disciples and the institution of the Lord's Supper (26:17–30) apparently take place with Jesus and the Twelve alone (26:20). In the unfolding events, Jesus announces his imminent death and that this would be his last Passover with his initiates (26:18). In the meal Jesus announces that one of the neophytes will betray him (26:21). The initiates then become "greatly distressed" and one after another say to him, "Surely not I, Lord?" (26:22). Judas dips his hand in the bowl which is proof that he has broken the bond (*communitas*) of those who eat together (Ps 41:9). He then addresses Jesus as "Rabbi" (26:25), a title used of Jesus only by his opponents and Judas. The meal proceeds, which is a covenant meal that symbolizes the body and blood of Jesus in his death. The initiates' teacher instructs his neophytes about his death as a sacrificial atonement referenced by his words "for this is my blood of the covenant, which is poured out for many for the forgiveness of sins" (1:21;

74. V. Turner, *The Forest of Symbols*, 103.

75. Hanson, "Transformed on the Mountain." The inner circle is not only separated from society, but also from the other nine disciples. Hanson states, "This highly significant event is reserved for the innermost circle."

76. Ibid., 159.

6:12, 14–15; 9:6; 18:21). A sacred meal of Israel is reinterpreted privately among Jesus' initiates.

DANGEROUS BOUNDARY AMBIGUITIES INVOLVING PURITY INFRACTIONS— Finally, purity issues are at stake in the liminal phase. Utilizing the work of Mary Douglas,[77] V. Turner asserts that liminality is a phase in which there is "a reaction to protect cherished principles and categories from contradiction."[78] Dangerous ambiguity is about "what is unclear and contradictory. . . . The unclear is the unclean."[79] For example, Jesus' neophytes are polluted from a conventional perspective because "they transgress classificatory boundaries."[80] They are called from unclean occupations, fishing and toll collecting (4:18–22; 9:9), to follow their teacher. They eat with "toll collectors and sinners" alongside their teacher (9:10), taboo behavior to Pharisees (9:11) but evidence of God's greater concern for mercy over sacrifice according to their teacher (9:12–13). They engage in their instructor's healing ministry—practices that often place them in contact with the unclean (10:1, 8). They harvest grain on the Sabbath, a violation of what is lawful (12:1, 2). Again, their teacher interprets such polluting behavior as evidence of the importance of mercy over sacrifice (12:7) and cites Hosea 6:6, seemingly making mercy not only greater than sacrifices but also superior to Sabbath observances 12:5, 7).[81]

They are being trained (literally, "discipled") as scribes of the kingdom of heaven (13:52) who, like their teacher, "bring out" of their treasure chest "what is new and what is old"—old scriptures newly fulfilled in Jesus' ministry (13:52; 5:17–20; 9:16–17; 28:18–20).[82] Their calling as scribes (13:52) places them over and against scribes in confederation with the chief priests and Pharisees.[83] This ambiguity concerning scribal authority is further evidenced by the way the initiates' teacher is disingenuously or contemptuously addressed as "teacher" by his critics (9:11; 12:38; 17:24; 22:15–18, 24, 36; cf. 23:8). Following their instructor, the liminaries break

---

77. See V. Turner, *The Forest of Symbols*, 97.

78. Ibid.

79. Ibid.

80. V. Turner, "Variations," 37.

81. See Duling, "Matthew," 1682.

82. Ibid., 1692.

83. Matt 2:4; 5:20; 7:29; 9:3; 12:38; 15:1; 16:21; 17:10; 21:15; 23:2, 13 [14], 15, 23, 25, 27, 29; 26:57; 27:41.

the "tradition of the elders" and eat without washing their hands (15:2). Their teacher instructs them instead to emphasize purity of heart (15:17; 5:8), which is the seat of thought, intention, and moral disposition (9:4; 11:29; 12:34). In these and other examples that could be cited evidence exists in Matthew for what V. Turner identifies as static and dynamic situations of pollution.[84] Having set forth the disciples' paradoxical and dramatic reversals of ordinary behavior in their liminal passage, they are prepared, except for their desertion, for the third phase of the initiation rite, aggregation.

Third Phase—Aggregation

In the rite of aggregation the ritual subjects return to "their old places in society"…"inwardly transformed and outwardly changed, to new places."[85] For Jesus' initiates this takes place in the re-commissioning[86] scene on the mountain in Galilee (28:16–20) based on the instructions they received from the women (28:7, 10, 16). Reunited, the Eleven manifest a mixed reaction, worship and doubt (28:17; see 14:31), but at this point they are prepared for a different and more significant social role than before they began the "tripartite" status transition. Because Jesus' prophetic/teaching task is completed he announces that "all power in heaven and on earth" has been given to him (28:18). The disciples, transformed by the rituals of separation and liminality are given a new task as they actually are going to another place in society—to the non-Israelites. This new task of teaching (never before in Matthew do the disciples teach) consists of making disciples by means of a ritual passage, baptism (not circumcision) done in the name of the Father, Son and Holy Spirit, that echoes Jesus' own baptismal passage (3:16–17). Following baptism new initiates are then to be taught as Jesus trained the disciples "to obey everything that I have commanded you" (28:19). In other words, with the absence of their instructor Jesus' initiates are to engage in a teaching mission carried out by their teacher's unparalleled power. As Hanson notes, "The commissioning, then changes the status of the Eleven from disciples to apostles, matching the nature of their changed mission."[87] They are to be the new "elders" whose task is

---

84. V. Turner, *The Forest of Symbols*, 94.

85. V. Turner, "Variations," 36.

86. The disciples are first commissioned in chapter 10 for their mission to Israel.

87. Hanson, "Transformed on the Mountain," 161.

to train neophytes as Jesus had served as their elder. Finally, through the process of memory they are assured of their instructor's ongoing presence (1:23; 28:20). At this point, their aggregation is almost complete. Still missing is an actual scene of the disciples reentering society; the incident ends with them still on the mountain. Hanson observes, "This lack of closure provides the gospel with a sense of open-endedness: the success of the Eleven is left undeveloped. Jesus remains standing within the community, the future is uncertain except for Jesus' vow of continued presence."[88] Having set forth the model using the disciples as a primary example, the model is now applied to the women following the tripartite procedural structure of separation, margin (or *limen*), and aggregation.

APPLYING THE MODEL TO THE WOMEN

First Phase—Separation

Even though we have no explicit evidence of the origins of the women's ritual separation (a call scene), these women did "follow" Jesus from Galilee to minister to him in the sense that Kingsbury has defined.[89] At the moment of Jesus' crucifixion they are separated from other people (their biological kinship ties), their place of origins (Galilee), and their temporal ties (day-to-day private, domestic kinship duties). This corresponds to McVann's observation that "individuals undergoing status transformation tend to experience separation in three ways: separation of people, place, and time."[90]

Second Phase—Liminality

When the women are first mentioned (27:55–56) they are in the ambiguous liminal initiatory/funerary process, a protracted "long threshold, a corridor almost, or a tunnel" which becomes a "pilgrim's road or passing from dynamics to statics."[91] Following the dangerous path of transitional beings, the women lack expected recognizable points in their space-time cultural topography. They are neither here nor there, but "betwixt and

---

88. Ibid.

89. Kingsbury, "The Verb ἀκολουθεῖν ('To Follow')."

90. McVann, "Rituals of Status Transformation," 338.

91. V. Turner, *The Ritual Process*, 95; "Variations," 37, 39.

between." I draw evidence to support this observation from six of the characteristics of the liminal transition of the disciples.

Death to the World

Matthew provides little evidence that the women at the cross were present and/or involved in Jesus' repeated preparatory announcements of his death to his neophytes (16:22; 17:22–23; 20:17–19; 26:2). There is the example of the mother of James and John—the sons of Zebedee—who is with Jesus on the way to Jerusalem (20:20–23). Also, if Luke's summary statement (8:2–3) is applicable, the women accompanied Jesus and the Twelve, heard his message, were willing to act on it, and now are in attendance at his death. If so, following V. Turner, the women have undergone Jesus' instruction to his neophytes of his impending crucifixion and are "in a sense 'dead' to the world . . ." a symbolic phrase especially applicable to women structurally marginalized in Greco-Roman, Palestinian culture. They would have been exposed to Jesus' teachings pertaining to the meaning of the cross and self-denial, and the necessity to "lose" their lives for their teacher's sake in order to find them (16:25). Further, even if they weren't present, they probably would have been aware of Jesus' interpretation of the anointing of his body by the woman in Bethany as preparation for burial (26:12).

At any rate, now at his death "many women" observe what takes place including Mary Magdalene, Mary the mother of James and Joseph, and the mother of the sons of Zebedee (27:56). The identification of "the mother" is a peculiarly Matthean reference and carries forward a previous situation (20:20).[92] The first notation supports the perception that women did follow Jesus for some time in Galilee. However, only Mary Magdalene and the other Mary carry forward the complete funerary ritual through the burial and resurrection stages. It is true that Matthew probably follows Mark (Matt 26:61//Mark 15:47). However, Mark never mentions the "mother" which makes Matthew's double inclusion a matter of interpretive concern, especially since the author provides no explanation. How then does one account for the presence of the mother of James and John and her subsequent absence at least in part in light of the funerary rite? It should not be forgotten that the "mother" requested that her two sons hold preeminent positions of power and honor—motivated by

92. My concern is not whether the mother of Zebedee's sons is the "Salome" of Mark 15:41 or "Mary the wife of Clopas" of John 19:25.

earthly prominence—in Jesus' future kingdom in a passage that features suffering and service (20:20–28), and which follows immediately Jesus' third instruction to his neophytes of his impending passion (20:17–19). Both the mother and her sons apparently do not understand that "death to the world" is essential to leadership among the teacher's initiates. For the women to observe the crucifixion of Jesus would have had the effect, as Donald Hagner states, that "all seemed to have come to an end . . ." that they would "have no more hope than do the men."[93] For the "mother" of Zebedees' sons that reality might have been insurmountable knowing most probably that her sons had deserted Jesus.[94] Even so, she is present at Jesus' death and has at least an initial part in the disciples' re-aggregation in 28:16–20. There is no evidence that she deserted Jesus as did the male disciples.

Engagement in Tasks that Involve Prohibitions, Pain, Humiliation, and Risk

As Jesus' initiates, the women have the task of "ministering to him." Their ministry should not be interpreted necessarily as performing traditional women's roles but in the sense of their shared ministry of the gospel (20:26–28) according to the model of Christ. This is so because the phrase "ministering to him" is closely aligned to the term "follow" having the wider sense as an expression of discipleship. They are not designated as disciples but they function as women who follow Jesus in pursuance of the kingdom of heaven. In performing their tasks, the women subject themselves to the risks associated with Jesus' Galilean ministry.

Interstructural Association Marked by Simplicity

Following our model the social structure among neophytes is marked by simplicity, that is, "between instructors and neophytes there is often complete authority and complete submission; among neophytes there is often complete equality" as opposed to an intricate network of hierarchical arrangements.[95] A goal of the ritual process is to emphasize "an essential

---

93. Hagner, *Matthew 14–28*, 855.

94. In making these observations, I do not speculate on her future role as a follower after the resurrection. However, I cannot agree with Luz that "Matthew does not portray her in a negative light" (*Matthew 8–20*, 543).

95. V. Turner, *The Ritual Process*, 97.

generic human bond," *communitas.*[96] The women's loyalty to Jesus as their authoritative leader can be assumed in all three Matthean passages. Their faithful submission is implied as they observe his death from afar, as they sit opposite the tomb, and as they take "hold of his feet" and worship him in the resurrection account (26:55; 61; 28:9). The bonds of *communitas* may also be assumed in all three passages. There is no evidence that the women's horizontal ties are structured in any way, let alone by a hierarchical arrangement.

Participation in a Realm without Structure in which Sexual Distinction Do Not Apply

According to V. Turner, in kinship-dominated societies "neophytes are sometimes treated or symbolically represented as being neither male nor female."[97] Our prior observations concerning the male disciples are relevant as well for the women. Matthew does not regard them as androgynous but as members of Jesus' radically reformulated surrogate family (12:50; see 10:34–39; 23:9). In their liminal passage the women do not perform women's traditional domestic tasks. Instead, they carry forward Jesus' instruction that his initiates do the will of "my Father" (12:50).

Participation in Sacred Places of Concealment that Link the Initiates to Deity

The women's passage reaches its climax in the resurrection story (28:1–10). Here, following our model, Mary Magdalene and the other Mary are brought into "close connection with deity or with superhuman power" that often is regarded as the "unbounded, the infinite, the limitless."[98] The women go "to see the tomb" (28:1) and enter into an altered state of consciousness. What they witness first in seclusion with the angel (the guards become "like dead men" [28:4]) is an angelophany. Then, with Jesus alone on the way they witness a christophany (28:9–10). The angelophany is manifest in the form of "a great earthquake" in which "an angel of the Lord descended from heaven and came and rolled back the stone, and sat upon it" (28:2). Variously, the account parallels the transfiguration of Jesus (17:1–8), an earlier example of the *sacra* in the disciples' liminal journey.

---

96. V. Turner, *Dramas, Fields, and Metaphors,* 46.

97. V. Turner, *The Forest of Symbols,* 98.

98. V. Turner, "Variations," 37.

First, the angel's appearance, described "like lightning," and his clothing as "white as snow," corresponds to Jesus whose face "shone like the sun, and his clothes became dazzling white" (17:2). Second, in both accounts the initiates' response is punctuated by fear; the disciples' fear is a critical factor in the transfiguration of Jesus (17.6–7); in the resurrection story the term appears four times (28:4–5, 8, 10):

1. The guards fear the angel's presence and become like dead men (28:4)

2. The angel instructs the women to not be afraid (28:5)

3. The women quickly leave the tomb with "fear and great joy" (28:8)

4. Jesus instructs the women not to be afraid (28:10)

Finally, in both accounts there is an emphasis on Jesus' resurrection (17:9; 28:6–7). This marks the close of the liminal process, that is, the angelophany and christophany (their altered state of consciousness) are followed by the giving of their new task (28:7, 10).

Purity Issues

Following V. Turner, those in the liminal process are polluted.[99] Dangerous ambiguity is about "what is unclear and contradictory. . . . The unclear is the unclean."[100] The first indicator of a purity issue for the women is found in the perplexing phrase, "There were also many women there, looking on from afar" (27:55a). Following the model, this phrase[101] possibly connotes a boundary question related to the women's location—an unknown distance from the place of crucifixion. Why would this be the case? The women are "betwixt and between" in the sense that they are "neither here nor there, or may even be nowhere (in terms of any recognized cultural topography)."[102] The location is unclear and ambiguous—"looking on from afar." We would add, however, that in the death scene, the entire cultural setting is characterized by ambiguity and contradiction, "a reaction to

---

99. Ibid.

100. V. Turner, *The Forest of Symbols*, 103.

101. It may refer to potential danger the women face in being too close to the crucified person identified as "King of the Jews." Or, perhaps, less likely, the phrase may be a reminder of Peter, who follows Jesus "from a distance" into the palace of the high priest (26.58). For a discussion see Luz, *Matthew 21–28*, 572–73.

102. V. Turner, *The Forest of Symbols*, 97.

protect cherished principles and categories."[103] If purity is defined as normality and wholeness,[104] the "order of a social system,"[105] and if pollution and taboo refer to matter "out of place" and to a social system of disorder,[106] the death of Jesus is a thoroughgoing cultural environment of pollution. If Douglas is correct in identifying pollution as a violation of boundary crossing,[107] the women's position—observing "at a distance"—signifies and particularizes their precarious location. They are present to the death of Jesus but also separate from it. They are "betwixt and between"—their location is a neutral zone separated from his death. They are perilously close but at a distance. They observe his death but are protected from it. They are at the margins, a boundary location of dangerous uncertainty. Apparently, this is even how Matthew treats the text; it is an independent section, a "short notice . . . like a postscript"[108] after the crucifixion scene. Their behavior, unlike that of the centurion and the soldiers, is to watch, and only watch, a Roman crucifixion in a public, politically polluted space. Their impurity as initiates is separate from but dangerously close to the impure cultural setting where absurdity and contradiction abound and where no righteous person stands with Jesus at the cross.[109]

In the burial scene (27:57–61), only two women, Mary Magdalene and the other Mary, are present. As in the previous passage, Matthew's auditors know of their presence only after the burial is completed and Joseph of Arimathea has left (27:61). Purity issues surround Joseph's burial task—handling the body, wrapping it in a clean linen cloth, and laying it in his own new tomb (27:59–60). The women are not involved in any of these proceedings. Then why are they present? They are not needed as witnesses to the location of the tomb (see Mark 15:47). However, their presence maintains an essential liminal conduit to their initiatory pilgrimage that encompasses the impurity of the crucifixion, burial, and

---

103. Ibid.

104. Douglas, *Purity and Danger*; Isenberg, "Mary Douglas and Hellenistic Religion," 179–85; Isenberg and Owen, "Bodies, Natural and Contrived," 1–17.

105. Ibid., 274.

106. Douglas, *Purity and Danger*; Isenberg, "Mary Douglas and Hellenistic Religions"; Isenberg and Owen, "Bodies, Natural and Contrived."

107. Douglas, *Purity and Danger*, 122.

108. Luz states, "In Matthew, unlike Luke and John, there are no good people who stand with him at the cross" (*Matthew 21–28*, 572).

109. Ibid., 552.

the resurrection settings. Mary Magdalene and the other Mary simply sit across from the tomb as the final and only faithful neophytes of those who followed Jesus from Galilee.

Thus, six of the seven characteristics of the disciples' liminal passage pertain to the women. Both the male disciples and the women experience the following:

1. Death to the world

2. Engagement in tasks that involve prohibitions, pain, humiliation, and risk

3. Interstructural association marked by simplicity

4. Participation in a "structureless realm" in which sexual distinctions do not apply

5. Participation in sacred places of concealment that link the initiates with deity

6. Dangerous boundary ambiguities involving purity infractions

The only missing feature is the change of a neophyte's name, a characteristic applicable only to one male disciple, Peter.

Third Phase—Aggregation

The women's aggregation—their return to "their old places in society" "inwardly transformed and outwardly changed, to new places"—overlaps the completion of their liminal journey as they are brought into "close connection with deity or with superhuman power" by the angel's epiphany and Jesus' greeting on the way (28:1–10). In this "close connection with deity" and "sacred concealment" (the final phase of liminality), they are then commissioned to a new task (aggregation). Their task is to hasten and tell the disciples that Jesus is raised and that he will precede his "brothers" to Galilee (28:7, 10). There is no documentation that the women were commissioned for their previous task of ministering to Jesus (27:55). Now, however, they are assigned a specific, distinctive, and essential mission that grows out of but also separates them from their liminal state. The funerary/initiatory rite is over. Now the "gathering," of Jesus and his disciples can take place in Galilee (17:22) where the community began. This gathering constitutes a bonding, a *communitas*, and is made possible only because the women faithfully fulfilled the tripartite transitional phases of the gospel's initiatory/funerary rite of passage—separation, *limen,* and aggregation.

CONCLUSION—DIFFERENCES THAT MATTER

The use of a rites of passage model illumes the sudden and inexplicable appearance of the women. They are not isolated figures that abruptly appear in the narrative or women who simply travel to Jerusalem with Jesus to serve his needs in a traditional sense.[110] In their role as neophytes it has been shown that the women are followers of Jesus in their own right who remain close to him at his death for a distinguishing reason. They alone supply the vital and indispensable tie to their own and the male disciples' re-aggregation both temporally ("from that time," 4:17; 16:21) and geographically to Galilee, which is the central location necessary to achieve Matthew's purpose. This transformative assignment at the pivotal point of Jesus' crucifixion begins with the woman who anoints Jesus at Bethany (26:6–13) and is carried forward by the women and especially by Mary Magdalene and the other Mary.

The use of a rites of passage model refines, expands, or negates two scholarly perspectives concerning Matthew's treatment. First, the women do stand by Jesus as faithful initiates precisely in his death journey. In doing so, as Elaine Wainwright affirms, they devotedly "watch" (27:55; 28:1), but this loyal undertaking belongs to a larger enterprise, their liminal pilgrimage.[111] And second, the women's presence at Jesus' death does not parallel the witness of the centurion and those with him as affirmed by Donald Senior. The centurion does not participate in the disciples' rite of passage, but the women do (27:54, 55–56).[112]

Following Victor Turner's assessment, in the phase of aggregation the women return to "their old places in society . . . inwardly transformed and outwardly changed, to new places."[113] The old places involve social realities of an advanced agrarian society, but the women's inward and outward change cannot be understood separate from a radical inclusion in and a

110. Melzer-Keller, *Jesus und die Frauen.*

111. Wainwright, *Towards a Feminist Critical Reading of the Gospel.*

112. I agree with Luz (*Matthew 21–28,* 572) against Senior (*The Passion Narrative according to Matthew,* 333).

113. V. Turner, "Variations," 36.

belonging to the new surrogate family of the kingdom of heaven. This reality provides the vision that the Matthean community is to espouse but apparently struggles to keep.

Finally, we close with an observation of Victor Turner, "During the liminal period, neophytes are alternately forced and encouraged to think about their society, their cosmos, and the powers that generate and sustain them. Liminality may be partly described as a stage of reflection."[114] Unquestionably, this is true for both the disciples and the women as they are trained by Jesus.

In the conclusion we will sum up our findings and reflect hermeneutically on the tasks of preaching and teaching what we have learned about the women's stories for contemporary American churches.

114. V. Turner, *The Forest of Symbols*, 105.

9

Conclusion

A T THIS POINT OUR study is essentially complete. We now summarize our findings and engage in some hermeneutical reflection about what we have learned that is applicable for teachers and preachers who use the Gospel of Matthew today.

SUMMARY OF FINDINGS

Jesus and the Household

Gender status and roles of women in Matthew cannot be understood separate and apart from the household, the basic social unit of Greco-Roman society beginning at the level of the empire but including as well in a descending order the city, village, and family. But, we discovered that there were two households in Matthew—the typical household of an advanced agrarian society and the new surrogate household of the kingdom of heaven. Evidence for the advanced agrarian household was found on nearly every page with its contours readily identifiable among actual households, Jesus' teachings (especially his use of parables), and among examples of the embedded status of wives in relation to their husbands. The social world of Matthew at both the macro and the micro levels mirrored advanced agrarian household expectations both as a reality and as an ideological societal metaphor, a social reality that Gerhard Lenski has identified as the "agrarian mould."

Manifest at numerous points in the writing as well was the new surrogate household of Jesus. This kin group was not based on biological blood ties but on a commitment to do the will of God. Fundamental to its ideology was an opposition to the archetypal hierarchical societal leadership authority of human domination so pervasively prevalent in the advanced agrarian example. Accordingly, Jesus advocated a paradigm reversal (bottom/up rather than top/down) exemplified preeminently by the social position of children within typical agrarian households. This model of leadership power reversal was consistent as well with Jesus' passion predictions and his teachings on discipleship. Those who sought greatness and power in Matthew's community were to do so by becoming "servants" and "slaves."

Jesus' paradigmatic reversal, however, did not entail the flattening of hierarchy or the abandonment of advanced agrarian household structural patterns. Jesus' expectation for exclusive allegiance to God in the new surrogate family was not a summons to societal egalitarianism or a condemnation of the advanced agrarian household per se. By definition, the new family of God was not a-familial or anti-structural. Such interpretations of the data did not square with the societal assumptions of Jesus' teaching on divorce, the care of parents, or examples of actual households within the writing. At all of these points the reality of advanced agrarian households was made explicit and/or assumed. Neither did it square with societal assumptions documented among Jesus' teachings on discipleship or in his parables about the kingdom of heaven. Thus, one should not confuse the doing away of top/down leadership patterns of authority with an abandonment of the agrarian household per se. No societies in the ancient world were egalitarian by definition because the ideology for egalitarianism as a possibility for all human society "did not arise until the 18th century C.E. with its altered economic, social, and political conditions and its secular optimism concerning the possibility of social transformation."[1]

Yet, the disciples were to be known as "brothers" (23:8) and Jesus acknowledged them as his brothers (28:10). Brothers, notwithstanding, could be and often were unequal in terms of position or privilege within the advanced agrarian family. Perhaps the interpretive differences between scholars like Carter and Elliott on the issue of equality could be ameliorated if the character group designated as "disciples" in Matthew was perceived as participating in the liminal (marginal) step of an initiatory rite of passage. If so, one of the critical characteristics of their inter-structural association was marked by simplicity—complete authority and submission between instructors and neophytes but often complete equality among fellow "neophytes" (in this case the disciples). This

---

1. Elliott, "Jesus Was not an Egalitarian," 77.

marginal phase was designed to separate the disciples from the intricate networks, hierarchical arrangements, rights and duties related to rank, status and affiliation within the society at large. Consequently, in their liminal phase, the disciples would have been "neither here nor there," but "betwixt and between," a marginal step characterized by the term *communitas*, "a status-less, role-less phase marked by spontaneity, concreteness, intense comradeship, and egalitarianism."[2] But even in a state of *communitas*, one cannot assume that *spontaneous* communitas or anti-structure would have prevailed. Over time, *normative* communitas probably would have developed and would have been characterized by the need to mobilize and organize resources as well as the necessity for social control, a process documented in Matthew by Duling. Further, the liminal phase was not characteristically permanent. At its completion, the disciples entered the third and final step of their ritual progression, aggregation, a step in which they "rejoined society." They returned to the larger group with a new vision and mission. Of necessity this would have included societal realities indigenous to advanced agrarian societies, in this case a Galilean, Greco-Roman social world.

But if the new surrogate family was a reverse hierarchical (bottom/up rather than top/down) structure, what societal model did it incorporate (an issue apparently not spelled out by Matthew)? Two anthropologists, Victor Turner and Meyer Fortes, provided us a possible option. Turner affirmed that all societies were composed of two models—a patrilineal model and a matrilineal model. The patrilineal example emphasized jural, political and economic positions, offices, statuses, and roles. The matrilineal example concentrated on society as an undifferentiated, homogenous totality, in which individuals confronted one another integrally and not as a group fragmented into statuses and roles. The matrilineal option was based on ties associated with spiritual characteristics, mutual interests and concerns that were "counterpoised to exclusiveness and material interests." Fortes identified this structural connection as the "bond of uterine descent," a relationship that opposed exclusiveness but upheld inclusiveness. If Matthew's new surrogate community followed the matrilineal option, even though it was embedded in a male dominant social model, it would have been taught by Jesus not to follow the jural domination of patrilineal patriarchy. In view of this, the nondominant side, the matrilineal,

2. V. Turner, *The Ritual Process,* 127, 132.

feminine side of society, might have been an appropriate model for the new surrogate household. As Jacobs-Malina has argued, the Gospels set forth the roles recommended by Jesus for his potential leaders, and they grew out of the domestic domain—the social world of women, children, servants, and slaves—and not the political sphere of the empire, temple, and synagogue. Thus, the domestic sphere may have provided within the social realities of advanced agrarian societies a social model appropriate for both men and women in the new surrogate household based on their shared belief in God as Father, their care and nurture of God's children, and their stewardship of his creation.

Jesus and Men and Women in Public Settings

Having explored the household, we then examined the place of women among three character groups, the disciples, the crowds, and the religious leaders, as they were taught by Jesus or interacted with him in three representative public settings: the mountain in the Sermon on the Mount, the boat in the Parables Discourse, and the temple in the clash between Jesus and the authorities. The religious authorities and disciples were male teachers, but in their preparation to be teachers, the disciples, unlike their counterparts, were not to exalt themselves. Rather, they were to follow the model of greatness found in children, and the paradigm of faith and service epitomized among the marginal women and other such persons scattered throughout the writing. At this point Matthew's community ran counter to the crystallized social stratification of the synagogue and mishnaic cultures.

The crowds opened a real alternative for women in Matthew because examples of women from among the crowds as well as those who followed Jesus from Galilee were noted for their faith and/or faithfulness to Jesus. Their "faith" and "great faith" was juxtaposed within the writing to the disciples' "little faith." At this critical juncture Matthew's community stood opposite to the synagogues of the Pharisees because the women's inclusion and acceptance by Jesus demonstrated that men no longer were the only ones who could come before the Lord. Their standing within the Evangelist's group ran counter to the standing of women in mishnaic culture. Apparently, women as well as men underwent the rite of baptism. Both women and children probably participated with men in the eucharistic meals. In other words, men, women, children, as well as non-Israelites belonged to the God of Israel's new household. No longer was ancestry, family role, religious patronage, or socio/economic status the basis for religious standing before Israel's God. What counted was obedience to the word of God as the basis of belonging to the new surrogate kin group.

Jesus, the Hemorrhaging Woman, and the Ruler's Daughter

We have examined four accounts of women beginning with the story of the ruler's daughter and the hemorrhaging woman (9:18–26). First, we affirmed that the healing of the hemorrhaging woman took place during the historical period of Jesus. Such an affirmation was based on a combination of four factors: the woman's faith, her identity as an Israelite outcast, the location of the healing in open, public, political space, and the implicit violation of the Second Temple's purity boundaries. These factors validate the woman's identity as a structurally marginal Israelite woman in need of healing—a representative of the lost sheep of the house of Israel (10:1–16). Put in other words, she was illustrative of those helpless Israelites without a shepherd (9:36). Matthew's redaction of Mark highlighted the healing as a distinctive Israelite event. The woman symbolized the "house of Israel" in the new theocratic kingdom in contrast to the "house of Israel" that would be left desolate (23:38). The consequences of her healing were mostly positive except for the implicit political boundary violation of the temple's holiness standards and its far-reaching influence throughout Palestine. The consequences for Jesus were mixed. His reputation among peasants was magnified—they would praise the God of Israel for his mercy. But most likely his relationship with the center of Israelite political, economic, and religious power—the Jerusalem Temple—would have deteriorated even further.

The story's social/theological challenge for the Matthean community was also significant. First, it heightened the image of the woman's "faith" over and against the disciples' "little faith." Second, her standing as a rural, outcast Israelite probably posed a social problem for an urban, relatively prosperous group that needed to be warned about the dangers of wealth. A failure to welcome without reservation rural outcast women such as the hemorrhaging woman violated the commitment of Jesus' surrogate, kinship group to include all Israelites who did the will of God. Third, the discipleship *logia* that surrounded her story and other accounts like hers in chapters 8 and 9 underscored the implementation of weaker social boundaries that embraced an inclusive strategy among all Israelites. This served as a contrast to the Pharisees who, motivated by God's holiness and need for political power among their synagogues, practiced an exclusionary strategy of social separation among their fellow Israelites.

The importance of the girl's story revealed first the hostility between Matthew's group and the synagogue. This was evidenced in Matthew's redaction of Mark (as well as Luke) that identified the father not as a synagogue ruler but as an aristocratic, high official—a ruler of the people. The father, unlike the Pharisees, did not criticize Jesus at the tax collector's banquet (9:10–13) if for no other reason than his need for Jesus' mercy far outweighed any purity issues pertaining to eating with sinners and fasting.

Second, the ruler's implied trust in Jesus' ability to restore his daughter's life paralleled the faith of the hemorrhaging woman. In other words, when the Matthean community heard the two stories simultaneously they were reminded that both framed a praiseworthy social paradigm for those committed to Jesus' Israelite mission. Quite distinct from the hemorrhaging woman, the daughter belonged to an honorable household; her father was a respected male household leader. The good news of the kingdom of heaven required a significant social leveling. Both the ruler and his daughter and the hemorrhaging woman had parallel standing within the Matthean community. Both were recipients of the God of Israel's mercy. Therefore, the community needed to resist traditional purity taboos and to treat as whole what previously had been thought of as "dirt out of place."

Jesus and the Canaanite Woman and Her Daughter

The healing story of the Canaanite woman's daughter (15:21–28) had significant points of comparison with the hemorrhaging woman. Both were structurally marginal individuals but for different reasons. The hemorrhaging woman was an Israelite outcast, probably due to her continuous physical impurity. The Canaanite woman's outsider status was due to her non-Israelite heritage, the probability that she was a prostitute, and her daughter's demon possession. Both women were commended for their faith. Both stories, located in open, outdoor space, were rooted in the historical activity of Jesus that also conveyed a social message for the time of the First Evangelist. In the case of the hemorrhaging woman the social challenge involved the inclusion of outcast Israelites. In the case of the

Canaanite woman the challenge involved the acceptance of non-Israelite expendables who sought the mercy of the God of Israel.

In addition, the Canaanite woman's story raised the question of whether Matthew ever envisioned a non-Israelite mission. Did Jesus' explicit and distinctive affirmation that he was sent *only* to the house of Israel (15:24) rule out such an effort? Or, did it mean that in spite of the statement, the First Evangelist ultimately envisioned a mission to all peoples? We affirmed with reservation that the evidence seemed to tilt in favor of a non-Israelite mission. However, in the end the pivotal concern of the Canaanite woman's story was not over a non-Israelite mission but whether Jesus in his historical activity granted a non-Israelite woman's appeal for mercy and pronounced her as a woman of "great faith." If so, the implications for the Matthean community were significant. The community following the example of Jesus needed to receive and to serve those who sought the God of Israel's pity but were culturally marginalized because they were not Israelites.

Finally, the Canaanite woman probably was a rural prostitute and not a destitute widow, a divorced person, or an individual who never married. But even if she was, for example, a widow, she probably would have become a prostitute with the passage of time because this would have been the only viable means of survival for women in similar social circumstances in advanced agrarian societies. She certainly was not a matron or wealthy widow with an urban household at her disposal. She ventured into male space without male agency. Ethnocentric issues were challenged, overcome, and/or suspended by the distinctive nature of her encounter and exchange with Jesus. She acted wisely, and as a wise woman she taught Jesus.

Jesus and the Woman Who Anoints His Body for Burial

The account of the woman who anointed Jesus at Simon's house was of consequence because it took place in a private setting situated between two public, political settings: (1) the plot to kill Jesus by the religious authorities in the palace and (2) the agreement between Judas and the religious authorities in the temple to betray him. Her story, positioned as it was in the larger context, also involved four points of view concerning Jesus' death: conspiracy and murder (the chief priests and elders), pre-death anointing (the woman), misunderstanding and critique of the woman's behavior (the disciples), and betrayal (Judas). Her significance for Matthew also was manifest in that she alone, not the women who went to the tomb as in Mark and Luke, anointed Jesus' body for burial. Thus, she proleptically participated in the status changing ritual of the women at the cross and tomb who faithfully followed and served Jesus in his ministry. The deed was a singular prophetic act, and the woman, accordingly, was an unwitting prophet.

The social-religious-political elite, acting as guardians of the social order, faced an intricate patronage dilemma without any satisfactory solution short of Jesus' crucifixion. Jesus was a challenge to Rome's rule. He represented a political quandary that could threaten the tenuous patron/client solidarity that tied the temple elite with Rome. But for the woman, a broker/client relation was established with Jesus characterized by loyalty and the bestowal of honor. In contrast to a social world of Limited Good, the woman anointed Jesus with costly resources that could never be recovered.

The woman's movement from the public sector to the private sphere of Jesus' surrogate group involved a dangerous external boundary crossing that appeared unacceptable to the disciples. Their indignation over the apparent waste was prompted by their conviction that the ointment's proceeds could have been sold and the money given to the poor. However, when viewed by other evidence their response evinced an ongoing divided loyalty and lack of wholehearted solidarity to God as patron and Jesus as broker. The disciples' behavior parallels their previous displays of anger, indignation, power-seeking, inadequate comprehension, and little faith tied to a double clientage: (1) Rome—brokered by the temple authorities and (2) God—brokered by Jesus. On another note, Judas's betrayal of Jesus was a matter of great shame. The honored client in the end played the fool and committed suicide. From that moment the Twelve became the Eleven.

Opposite to the disciples, the woman's single devotion (clientage) was to Jesus, her exclusive broker. Even though she acted inadvertently, the symbolic import of her actions triggered the passion of Jesus. In turn, Jesus upheld her behavior as a "good work," a major purity theme in Matthew. Her "good work" riled the disciples but substantiated her client relations with Jesus. As a prophet she was juxtaposed to (1) the religious elite, (2) Jerusalem, the city which killed the prophets, and (3) the disciples who harassed her. As a prophet she stood alongside the great prophets who belonged to Matthew's Little Tradition. Perhaps, as well as any individual, the woman behaved courageously in the midst of extremity.

Jesus and the Women at the Cross and the Tomb

In our final chapter we made use only of a rite of passage model that was applied both to the disciples and to the women at the cross and the tomb. It was applied to the disciples because they were trained by Jesus as scribes for the kingdom of heaven. In that initiatory, transformational process they (1) were separated (called) by Jesus to be his disciples, (2) trained by Jesus through a transitional process (state of *liminality*) of instruction, and (3) aggregated by Jesus on the mountain for their mission (28:18–20). Two critically important lines of the transitional process, however, were broken and/or interrupted simultaneously by the male disciples' desertion shortly before Jesus' death (26:56). The first break was a geographical/spatial path, from Galilee (4:12) to Galilee (28:16), a geographical bridge especially significant to Matthew because it marked the place of the beginning of Jesus' activity, the disciples' call, and the location where the community had its beginning. Only the women at the cross and the tomb supplied this geographical linkage because they alone were present at the climactic element of that journey, the death, burial, and resurrection of Jesus, and they alone in the persons of Mary Magdalene and the other Mary were given the task by the angel and Jesus to tell the disciples to go to Galilee where they would see Jesus. Similarly, the women alone supplied an uninterrupted temporal bridge to the disciples' *liminal* transformation marked by Matthew's usage of the phrases "from that time" (4:17) and "from that time on" (16:21). Once more, the temporal gap was disrupted by the disciples but carried forward by the women who prepared his body for burial (26:12), witnessed his crucifixion (27;55), sat opposite the tomb when Jesus was buried (27:61), saw the tomb after his resurrection (28:1–10), and instructed his brothers to meet him in Galilee (28:10). Without the participation of these women in the temporal line of the ritual process the fruition of the transformative goal would have been aborted by the disciples' desertion.

Thus, the only "followers" of Jesus who ministered to him from Galilee other than the Twelve were these women. Even though there was no separation (call scene) for the women in the text, at the time of Jesus' crucifixion they were separated from other people (their biological kinship ties), their place of origin (Galilee), and their temporal ties (day-to-day, private, domestic duties). By making their pilgrim's journey with Jesus and the twelve disciples, the women experienced six of the seven characteristics of the disciples' marginal transition. Both the male disciples and the women underwent the following:

1. Death to the world

2. Engagement in tasks that involved prohibitions, pain, humiliation, and risk

3. Inter-structural association marked by simplicity

4. Participation in a "structureless realm" in which sexual distinctions did not apply

5. Participation in sacred places of concealment that linked the initiates with deity

6. Participation in dangerous boundary ambiguities that involved purity infractions

The only characteristic missing in their initiation from their male counterparts was the change of a neophyte's name, a characteristic applicable only to Peter.

Finally, the task of their aggregation, to quickly tell the disciples that Jesus was raised and that he would precede his "brothers" to Galilee (28:7, 10), was commissioned by the angel and Jesus. In the accomplishment of that new and original task they were separated from their *liminal* pilgrimage. The funerary/initiatory rite was over. Because of the women's faithfulness to their task, the "gathering" of Jesus and the Eleven took place in Galilee where the community had its beginning. They alone faithfully fulfilled the tripartite transitional phase of the writing's initiatory/funerary rite of passage. Having summarized our findings we now consider some hermeneutical matters for communicating Matthew's message today.

HERMENEUTICAL REFLECTION FOR TODAY

We live in a very different social world than the one described in the preceding chapters. Any discussion of the contemporary status and role of women based on the Gospel of Matthew must take into account the ideological and societal structural changes brought about by democratization and industrialization within contemporary American society.

Those changes are far greater than what is usually meant by the phrase "it's cultural." Rather, the modifications we speak of had their ideological origins in the Enlightenment; and today technological breakthroughs over about a 225-year period have led to societal alterations that have shaped the very structural foundations of human existence. This shift is so great that sociologists identify it as a major transformation—from a societal type labeled "advanced agrarian" to a societal type labeled "advanced industrial." Among numerous social reversals are those that impinge on the way age, gender, and family are viewed, especially manifest in gender-specific public/private behavioral expectations.[3]

Thus, the advent of industrialization has brought about a revolution of "new societies" with "distinct life patterns," including the changing status and roles of men and women. From the perspective of social stratification prior to the Industrial Revolution, every major technological advance led to an increase in the degree of social inequality within societies. In contrast, advanced industrialization indicates that "this 9,000-year trend toward inequality has begun to falter, even to show signs of a reversal."[4] For the first time we can speak realistically of societal equality. Further, the Lenskis state,

> Nowhere are the effects of industrialization on society's norms, values, and sanctions seen more clearly than in the changing role of women. Throughout recorded history most women were destined to spend their prime years bearing children, nursing them, caring for them when they were sick and dying, and rearing them if they survived; doing domestic chores; tending a garden; and often helping in the fields. It is hardly surprising, therefore, that women seldom played significant roles outside the home or made outstanding contributions to the arts.[5]

Let us consider three interrelated topics where striking consequences in the changing status and roles of women has taken place.

---

3. We refer the reader to Lenski and Lenski, *Human Societies* (1987), 176; Aitchison, *A History of Metals*, vol. 1; Boserup, *Women's Role in Economic Development*; Childe, *Man Makes Himself*; Goldschmidt, *Man's Way*, chap. 6; Harris, *The Rise of Anthropological Theory*, chap. 2; Nisbet, *Social Change and History*, chap. 4.

4. Lenski and Lenski (1987), 313. The reference to nine thousand years includes the eras of historical dominance for horticultural (simple and advanced) as well as agrarian societies (simple and advanced).

5. Ibid., 340.

Technology

Technological innovations have affected the size of families and the domestic workload. Birth control, effective substitutes for breast feeding, and household appliances reduce family size and the time required to care for the home. For example, British marriages contracted around 1860 produced a median of six children. Two generations later, the median had dropped to two. Families with eight or more children declined from 33 percent of the total to only 2 percent.[6]

A number of laborsaving devices such as refrigerators, freezers, automatic washing machines and dryers, vacuum cleaners, electric irons, frozen foods, and microwave ovens have greatly reduced the time and effort necessary to maintain a household. The Lenskis describe what this means in doing the laundry, recalling that laundry required numerous time-consuming activities including the transporting and boiling of water as well as the starching and ironing of clothes. Today, technological advances have reduced the expenditure of time and energy by 95 percent, even as standards of cleanliness have risen.[7] Technological innovation is essential to societal change, and every major technological alteration modifies a society. One of the effects of domestic technological change, especially in birth prevention, has freed women, especially from middle and upper classes, to exercise wider choices in determining their expectations in society. Sjoberg states,

> With industrialization and its attendant high degree of social and spatial mobility, not only does the extended family splinter but, most revolutionary of all, woman's role and status change dramatically. Educational and economic opportunities, once considered illusionary, now become a reality, and in conformance with the disintegration of sharp status distinctions within the total society, those between men and women begin to fade as well.[8]

Sjoberg's observations were published in 1960. In the opening years of the twenty-first century, the necessity of choosing domestically determined lives has rapidly disappeared, and those who select homemaking as a career are relatively free to involve themselves in a variety of community, leisure, and social activities. The Lenskis may overstate the influence of

---

6. Ibid.

7. Ibid., 341.

8. Sjoberg, *Preindustrial City,* 170.

technological change, but their point is well taken, "Without modern techniques of contraception, and without modern machine technology most women would still be confined to the nursery and the kitchen."[9] The social values of a culture shape the life styles of its members.

Household Structure

The Greco-Roman household is no longer the basic social unit of advanced industrial societies. Although the traditional family exists (but should not be confused with the advanced agrarian household), it is diminishing in number. In addition to the variety of family structures that are present, our society has a large number of single persons. In agrarian societies, the single life would have rendered one vulnerable and outcast and is advocated in the Bible apparently only in 1 Corinthians 7:8 and Matthew 19:12. Or, let us consider the example of widows. Becoming widowed in industrial cultures generally occurs later in life, because of increased life expectancy. In 1970 the probability of one spouse dying between the ages of twenty and forty-five was only 0.11.[10] Widowhood in advanced agrarian societies recurrently takes place while children are still at home, especially when women experience child bearing for as long as twenty-five years. In such circumstances repeated marriages create complicated economic obligations in family relationships.

Education and Employment

An increasing number of women have opportunities for higher education and professional training. This includes academic doctorates and first-level professional degrees in fields such as medicine, dentistry, law, politics, theology, veterinary medicine, and optometry. Sociologists believe that a college-educated population serves as a social barometer for both the workforce and marriage and family relationships. For example, college graduates are often recruited for management positions. Accordingly, an increasing number of women are breaking through the industrial "caste" system, which magnifies the number of dual-career marriages and, in turn, breaks down gender-specific labor practices. More husbands and wives are joint providers and share in household responsibilities including the rearing of children. One of the social elites of an advanced industrialized

9. Lenski and Lenski, *Human Societies,* (1974), 401.
10. Ibid., 404.

society is the educated. For women, a college education and/or professional training is a powerful influence for sexual equality. Technology also plays a role. Physical strength is no longer a foremost criterion for job performance. Thus a gender-based division of labor tends to break down advanced agrarian female/male, inside/outside, private/public social distinctions. Women and men today do not consider themselves bound by the public/private expectations of agrarian societies.

Without precedent, the above societal shift has affected the underlying social ideology and societal structures of advanced industrialized societies. Hereditary monarchies and the proprietary theory of the state have given way to the will of the masses, including women. Luke Timothy Johnson describes both the ancient and modern situation. In terms of what we refer to as the advanced agrarian social ideology of the household, Johnson writes,

> Visions of alternative societies were not totally unknown in the ancient world: Plato's *Republic* was thoroughly utopian and reformist. But under the empire—which was by the time of Paul the only real political fact in the world for over three hundred years, much longer than the whole history of the United States—such alternatives were not seriously entertained. The most massive fact available was this: A single hierarchical order reached from the top to the bottom of the "human family," an order in which authority moved downward and submission moved upward. Moralists had further solidified this symbolic world by taking it as given, and asking "What are the duties (*kathēkonta*) of the various members of society within this structure?"[11]

Johnson then summarizes the radical societal shift we have experienced today:

> It is difficult for us who live in fragile if not fragmented social worlds to appreciate the sheer facticity of that ancient order. It was generally regarded, in fact, as part of the *oikonomia theou*—the dispensation of God. Nature and society were part of the same continuum, all of which was governed by God's will, or "providence." To deviate from the norms of the social order, then, was really to deviate from "nature" and from God's ordering of the world. The point of these observations is simple: It was as impossible for Paul to have envisaged a Jeffersonian democracy as it was for him to have imagined the contemporary nuclear family with

11. Johnson, *1 Timothy, 2 Timothy, Titus*, 63–64.

dual-career spouses. His instructions were for a world not only different from ours structurally, but even in conception. Part of the "symbolic world" we live in, after all, is the concept that society *is* in fact a changeable thing. Precisely that perception would not have been Paul's as a human being of the first century. There may have been good or bad emperors but surely there would always be emperors![12]

Johnson lays open the practical impossibility of foreknowing the future of our social world or of returning to the past. The advanced agrarian social order found so prominently in the Gospel of Matthew simply does not mix and match with a democratic societal structure of an advanced industrialized society like contemporary America.

Therefore, can a hermeneutical bridge be established between two such different social worlds for the purpose of preaching and teaching? Put another way; is it possible or impossible for Matthew's message to be read largely freed from the evolved values of contemporary American life? We must admit that one possibility is that the context of Matthew's social world and our own is so vastly different that a sociological transference and/or transposition of his message are blocked. For this reason we delineate criteria of comparability and incomparability between Matthew's social world and the writing's message from our own. Three possibilities are conceived:

1. Some material may automatically transfer from the Matthean community to American society. However, we believe this would be a rare phenomenon.

2. Other matters may be nontransferable. An obvious example would be slavery.

3. Other material may be extracted and transposed legitimately from the Matthean environ to an American industrial culture. This is the more realistic option but the most difficult to conceive of and achieve.

It must be kept in mind that Matthew's message cannot be separated from its own past, rooted in what we referred to in chapter 6 as the Little Tradition of ancient Israel's prophets.

12. Ibid.

To facilitate our undertaking we will limit ourselves to three evaluative theological/social-ethical ideas of Matthew's message: justice, mercy,
and faith (23:23). These themes are treated by Matthew as "heavier matters
of the law"[13] and become for him evaluative criteria for community life
governed by the kingdom of heaven. Although "heavier" can refer to what
is difficult to fulfill, it more fundamentally rests on what is important,
such as the importance of first cleansing "the inside of the cup" (23:26).
Already, we see an example of an Israelite practice that is blocked—the
tithing of agricultural produce given to support the temple and its priests
(Lev 27:30–33; Num 18:8–32; Deut 14:22–29; 25:1–15; Tob 1:7–8). As
we consider the weightier matters then, justice finds its parallels in the
prophetic language of the Little Tradition, the "just verdict" that everyone
has by right.[14] "Mercy" is used twice within Matthew based on Hosea 6:6
(9:13; 12:7) and refers to "works of love."[15] The first reference (9:13) is most
evident in Jesus' healing ministry and in the final judgment (25:35–39,
42–44). The second reference (12:7) contrasts Sabbath observance of the
Pharisees to the neglect of addressing human needs. "Faith" probably
equates to "faithfulness."[16]

The three matters viewed together amplify Matthew's meaning of
the highest commandment of love (22:34–40; cf. 5:21–26, 43–48; 7:12).
What Matthew's Jesus calls for is the foundation of the prophetic message
(Mic 6:8). This means that Matthew's hermeneutical criteria are rooted
in the prophetic heritage of Israel's Little Tradition and constitute the es-
sence of the Old Testament. We now apply the criteria to aspects of our
considerations of the disciples and the four stories of women. Our treatment represents only an initial venture into this most difficult interpretive
process.

The Disciples

There can be little doubt that the twelve male disciples in Matthew are
accorded an honored teaching role within the Matthean community.

13. Matthew's purpose was to denigrate the Pharisees through the creation of negative stereotypes. Scholars know today that Pharisees were quite capable of self-criticism
(see the seven classes of Pharisees in *b. Sot.* 22; see Str.B. IV 338–39). See Luz, *Theology of
the Gospel of Matthew*, 123–24.

14. See Isa 1:17; Jer 22:3.

15. Beyond Hos 6:6 see Zech 7:9–10.

16. See Hab 2:4.

Jesus called them not long after his ministry began, honored them as "his brothers," and sent them to teach others whatever Christ had commanded them.[17] This group was viewed by later church fathers such as Irenaeus,[18] Origin,[19] Hippolytus,[20] Methodius,[21] John Chrysostom,[22] Justin,[23] Ignatius,[24] and Cyril of Jerusalem[25] as constituting the beginnings of the church and its foundation. As a whole the early church fathers believed the apostles had received an endowment of divine power, a commission for a universal mission, and an authority for church governance. Their appeal was to follow the apostles' teaching as the criterion for the church's ministry and church order. These cherished ideas and practices had their inception within the social ideological framework and structures of advanced agrarian societies.

But to conclude that teachers in the American church today can only be male—based on the twelve male disciples, the rationale of the Pastoral Letters, and the practice of the early church fathers—is largely blocked from a sociological perspective. Reasons for that blockage include the following:

1. Women freely take part in the public sectors of advanced industrial societies whether the sphere be political or religious, which is a matter rarely documented in advanced agrarian societies. A public/private social world still exists but participation within each sphere is not based on gender. Women lead and contribute in public arenas. Men are involved in the domestic realm. Outsiders within the social world of Matthew would have raised their eyebrows at a new religion that permitted women to teach in public settings. But outsiders within our social world see it strange that churches and worship services are led only by men. To recognize the views of outsiders in any given society is only realistic. Of course there are social settings in the contemporary world where agrarian practices

17. See Eusebius *Church History* 1.10.5(7).

18. Irenaeus *Against Heresies* 3.1.1.; 3.12.7; 4.21.3.

19. Origin *Commentary on John* 10.39.228; *Against Celsus* 1.62; 3.28; 8.47; *On First Principles* preface 1; 3.3.4; *Homilies on Jeremiah* 10.1.

20. Hippolytus *Commentary on Daniel* 4.9.2.

21. Methodius *On Things Created* 1.

22. John Chrysostom *Homilies on the Beginning of Acts* 3.4.

23. Justin *Dialogue with Trypho* 119.6.

24. Ignatius *Trallians* 7.1; cf. *Magnesians* 13.1 quoted at n. 44.

25. Cyril of Jerusalem *Catechetical Lectures* 17.29.

may still be viable. This is especially true among Third World countries and within certain cultures of our own society. But that cannot be labeled as normative. More and more, it is a difficult task to live out the social past in the social present.

2. Women in advanced industrial societies have opportunities for educational advancement and training, including theological studies, in our leading universities and seminaries, which represent a reversal of prevailing educational expectations and practices for women in advanced agrarian societies.

3. In our social world, educated and professionally trained women are hired by churches, schools, and other ministry-based institutions to teach, preach, and fill pastoral leadership positions. We recognize that these practices vary among and within Christian denominations. Change, however, is taking place rapidly especially when compared to the approximately three thousand years in which advanced agrarian societies were the dominant societal type.

4. Given these social realities and following Matthew's theological criteria of justice, mercy, and faith, it would be a breach of justice to deny women in our cultural setting the privilege of theological training. It is also a breach of justice to encourage women to receive theological training and subsequently block their access to participation in ministry as vocation.

The Stories of Women in Matthew

The women's stories cluster around issues of social/religious marginality. The basic issue for Matthew was the social inclusion of Israelite and non-Israelite women within the community. To facilitate our thinking, we defined four concepts of marginality (structural, social role, ideological, and cultural) of which three of the concepts were applicable to our study (structural, ideological, and cultural). Among the four stories of women, marginal issues were at stake for the hemorrhaging woman, the Canaanite woman, the woman who anointed Jesus for burial, and the women at the cross and tomb. These women suffered social inequities because their situation in life prevented them from participating in normative social statuses and roles. The sole exception was the ruler and his daughter, who had community respect and social standing. Structural marginality, inequities in the social system, most probably was experienced by all the women except the ruler's daughter. In addition, the Canaanite woman experienced cultural marginality. She was a woman caught between two competing cultures, Canaanite and Israelite. Three instances (the hemorrhaging woman, the Canaanite woman, and the woman who anointed Jesus) illustrated involuntary marginality. The women who followed Jesus from Galilee experienced voluntary, structural, and ideological marginality along with Jesus and the disciples. The following figure illustrates these relationships.

FIGURE 9.1: ILLUSTRATION OF CONCEPTS OF MARGINALITY

Concepts of Marginality and the Stories of Women

Example	Structural	Ideological	Cultural	Voluntary	Involuntary	Not an Issue
Hemorrhaging woman	x				x	
Ruler and his daughter						x
Canaanite woman	x		x		x	
Woman who anoints Jesus	x				x	
Women at the cross and tomb	x	x		x		

For most of the examples, marginality issues required greater acceptance and a social leveling within the community. The issue was multifaceted. It involved difficulties for rural peasant women to find mercy and acceptance within an urban and relatively wealthy community. It also involved non-Israelite women, possibly prostitutes, who sought the God of Israel's mercy. These women demonstrated significant faith as opposed to the disciples' (the community's teachers) little faith. It involved holding up the women at the cross and tomb as individuals who kept faith with Jesus in his passion when the disciples failed. The one warning highlighted by our study was that the acceptance and inclusion of these women was not because the community was egalitarian. At any rate, the theological themes of justice, mercy, and faith cut to the heart of the communal relationships and composition of the Evangelist's community.

The stories of women do not transfer automatically to our social setting. Neither, unlike the example of the public/private issue, are they blocked. Rather, they require extraction and transposition to our social world.

Why is this so? First, there is the question of healing. In Matthew healing is accomplished within an ideological framework that includes illness and healing as belonging to patterns of social relations and cultural expectations within the community. This is quite different from the biomedical approach largely operative in advanced industrial societies. Therefore, many in our social world simply do not readily identify or understand how Jesus' healing activity would have social-political implications. Also, many are wary of the topic because of the practices of faith healers in our social world.

Second, a number of persons in our social setting question whether there is a connection between illness and marginality. Certainly, there are illnesses like AIDS that attach great social stigma for some (but attitudes toward AIDS are changing). Very few in our social world affix social shame to those who for example are paralyzed, blind, or epileptic.

However, when other attendant issues such as the inclusion of outcast, rural persons or poor, lower-class, inner-city persons into an urban, well-to-do church are considered, the social disparities underlying the Matthean stories take on force. For example, churches often ignore or struggle to establish rich, thick, vertical demographic patterns of membership inclusive of ethnicity, race, and economic factors. It is much easier "to grow" a mega-church, for example, based on a horizontal slice of upper-middle class suburbanites. It remains a social/theological challenge for wealthy urban churches or middle-class groups to accept readily those from marginal walks of life. For our world it is not only an issue of acceptance and inclusion, but one of equality, as well. Thus, transposition of the women's healing stories requires a careful crafting of germane analogies for women (and others) in our social world. But when it is accomplished the themes of justice, mercy, and faith cast light both on the community and its outer environment and provide a bridge from Matthew's social setting to our own.

A few more thoughts on ethnic and racial differences (cultural marginality) are in order. Churches that build almost exclusively around ethnic and racial particularism continue to be a social problem in advanced industrial settings. We may not readily identify with Israelite/non-Israelite ethnocentric social/religious issues. Most of us have not been to Israel for the purpose of seeing first hand the social, economic, political, and economic issues that separate Israelis and Palestinians. But we do know of persons who are forced to live between two different, antagonistic social worlds—persons and groups caught between competing cultures. We have long understood that the most segregated hour in American religious life is 11:00 am on Sunday. We also know that within many of our churches boundaries still exist that keep women in silent roles. Somehow we, too, need to be challenged by women of "great faith," teachers of wisdom, and prophets who call us to good works. In other words, the stories of women in Matthew address perennial social challenges that teachers in the church cannot ignore.

SOME PERSONAL OBSERVATIONS

Finally, I make three personal, unscientific observations. First, the good news of the kingdom of heaven critiques all social ideologies and social structures of any given societal type. Second, of necessity the gospel of the kingdom of heaven is always operative within a given society. Third, no societal type or human social order can be co-defined with the kingdom of heaven. In other words, the kingdom of heaven is not synonymous with the ideologies or structures of either agrarian or industrial societies. Rather, the "household of the kingdom" is composed of "whoever does the will of my Father in heaven" (12:50).

Living out the demands of the kingdom of heaven takes place in the social world in which we find ourselves. The Gospel of Matthew and, in particular, the stories of women within the gospel, teach us that we live in a very different world. Certainly, the social order found on every page of Matthew and the social order of our own democratic advanced industrial world do not mix and match. Yet, the Gospel's message of justice, mercy, and faith transcends the boundaries of social ideology and cultural particularity and calls all who have ears to hear and eyes to see to do the will of their Father who is in heaven.

Bibliography

Abel, E. L. "The Genealogies of *Jesus ho Christos.*" *NTS* 20 (1974–1975) 203–10.

Abu-Lughod, Lila. *Veiled Sentiments: Honor and Poetry in a Bedouin Society.* Berkeley: University of California Press, 1986.

Abu-Zeid, A. "Honour and Shame among the Bedouins of Egypt." In *Honour and Shame: The Values of Mediterranean Society,* edited by J. G. Peristiany, 243–59. London: Weidenfeld and Nicholson, 1966.

Aitchison, Leslie. *A History of Metals.* Vol. 1. London: MacDonald, 1960.

Albeck, Charles. *Introduction to the Mishna.* Tel Aviv, et al.: 1971–1974. Albeck, Chanoch. Jerusalem: Bialek Institute, 1959.

Albright, W. F., and C. S. Mann. *Matthew.* AB 26. Garden City, NY: Doubleday, 1971.

Allbaugh, Leland G. *Crete: A Case Study of an Underdeveloped Area.* Princeton: Princeton University Press, 1953.

Anderson, Judith A. "Matthew: Gender and Reading." The Bible and Feminist Hermeneutics. *Semeia* 28 (1983) 3–27.

———. "Mary's Difference: Gender and Patriarchy in the Birth Narratives." *JR* 67 (1987) 183–202.

Applebaum, Shimon. "The Organization of the Jewish Communities in the Diaspora." *Compendia* 1:464–503.

Arndt, W. F., and F. W. Gingrich. *A Greek-English Lexicon of the New Testament.* Chicago: University of Chicago Press, 1957.

Auslander, Mark. "Rites of Passage." In *EncAnth* 5:2022–25.

Baab, Otto J. "Marriage." In *IDB* 3:278–87.

Baby, Parambi. *The Discipleship of the Women in the Gospel according to Matthew.* Rome: Pontifica Università, 2003.

Bahr, Gordon J. "The Seder of Passover and the Eucharistic Words." *NovT* 12 (1970) 181–202.

Balch, David L. "Household Codes." In *Greco-Roman Literature and the New Testament: Selected Forms and Genres,* edited by David E. Aune. Atlanta: Scholars, 1988.

———. *Let Wives Be Submissive: The Domestic Code of 1 Peter.* SBLMS 26. Chico, CA: Scholars, 1981.

———, editor. *The Social History of the Matthean Community: Cross-Disciplinary Approaches.* Minneapolis: Fortress, 1991.

Balch, David L., and Carolyn Osiek. *Families in the New Testament World: Households and House Churches.* FRC. Louisville: Westminster John Knox, 1997.

Balch, David L., and Carolyn Osiek, editors. *Early Christian Families in Context: An Interdisciplinary Dialogue.* Grand Rapids: Eerdmans, 2003.

Balsdon, J. P. V. D. *Roman Women: Their History and Habits.* London: Bodley Head, 1962.

Barbour, Ian G. *Myths, Models, and Paradigms: A Comparative Study in Science and Religion.* New York: Harper & Row, 1974.

Barth, Gerhard. "Matthew's Understanding of the Law." In *Traditions and Interpretation in Matthew,* edited by Gerhard Barth et al., translated by P. Scott. NTL. Philadelphia: Westminster, 1963.

Barth, Gerhard, et al. *Tradition and Interpretation in Matthew.* Translated by P. Scott. NTL. Philadelphia: Westminister, 1963.

Barton, Stephen C. *Discipleship and Family Ties in Mark and Matthew.* SNTSMS 80. Cambridge: Cambridge University Press, 1994.

Berger, Klaus. "Die könighlichen messiastradition des Neuen Testaments." *NTS* 20 (1973) 1–44.

Biale, Rachel. *Women and Jewish Law: An Exploration of Women's Issues in Halakhic Sources.* New York: Schocken, 1984.

Billson, J. M. "No Owner of Soils: The Concept of Marginality Revisited on Its Sixtieth Birthday." *IRMS* 18 (1988) 183–204.

Bird, Phyllis. "Images of Women in the Old Testament." In *Religion and Sexism: Images of Woman in the Jewish and Christian Traditions,* edited by R. R. Ruether, 41–88. New York: Simon & Schuster, 1974.

————. "'To Play the Harlot': An Inquiry into an Old Testament Metaphor." In *Gender and Difference in Ancient Israel,* edited by P. Day, 75–94. Philadelphia: Fortress, 1989.

————. "Women (OT)." In *ABD* 6:951–57.

Black, Max. *Models and Metaphors.* SLP. Ithaca, NY: Cornell University Press, 1962.

Blok, Anton. "Rams and Billy-Goats: A Key to the Mediterranean Code of Honour." *Man* 16 (1981) 427–40.

————. "Variations in Patronage." *SG* 16 (1969) 365–78.

Blum, Richard, and Eva Blum. *Health and Healing in Rural Greece: A Study of Three Communities.* Stanford, CA: Stanford University Press, 1965.

Bornkamm, Günther, Gerhard Barth, and Heinz Joachim Held. *Tradition and Interpretation in Matthew.* Translated by P. Scott. NTL. Philadelphia: Westminster, 1963.

Boserup, Ester. *Women's Role in Economic Development.* New York: St. Martin's, 1970.

Bourdieu, Pierre. "The Sentiment of Honour in Kabyle Society." In *Honour and Shame: The Values of Mediterranean Society,* edited by J. G. Peristiany, 191–241. London: Weidenfeld & Nicholson, 1966.

Brandes, Stanley H. "Reflections on Honor and Shame in the Mediterranean." In *Honor and Shame and the Unity of the Mediterranean,* edited by David D. Gilmore, 121–24. AAASP 22. Washington, DC: American Anthropological Association, 1987.

Brooten, Bernadette. "Jewish Women's History in the Roman Period: A Task for Christian Theology." *HTR* 79 (1986) 22–30.

————. *Women Leaders in the Ancient Synagogue: Inscriptional Evidence and Background Issues.* Providence, RI: Brown University Press, 1982.

Brown, Raymond E. *The Birth of the Messiah: A Commentary on the Infancy Narratives in Matthew and Luke.* Garden City, NY: Doubleday, 1979.

————. *An Introduction to the New Testament.* New York: Doubleday, 1997.

Brown, Schuyler. "The Matthean Community and the Gentile Mission." *NovT* 22 (1980) 193–221.

————. "The Mission to Israel in Matthew's Central Section (Mt. 9:35—11:1)." *ZNW* 69 (1978) 73–90.

―――. "Universalism and Particularism in Matthew's Gospel: A Jungian Approach." In *SBLASP* 28 (1989) 388–99.

Brunt, P. A. *The Fall of the Roman Republic and Related Essays*. Oxford: Clarendon, 1988.

―――. *Roman Imperial Themes*. Oxford: Clarendon, 1990.

Burkill, T. Alec. "The Historical Development of the Story of the Syrophoenician Woman." *NovT* 9 (1967) 161–77.

Camp, Claudia V. *Wisdom and the Feminine in the Book of Proverbs*. Decatur, GA: Almond, 1985.

―――. "The Wise Women of 2 Samuel: A Role Model for Women in Early Israel?" *CBQ* 43 (1981) 14–29.

Campbell, J. K. "Honour and the Devil." In *Honour and Shame: The Values of Mediterranean Society*, edited by J. G. Peristiany, 139–70. London: Weidenfeld and Nicholson, 1966.

Cantarella, Eva. *Pandora's Daughters: The Role and Status of Women in Greek and Roman Antiquity*. Baltimore: Johns Hopkins University Press, 1987.

Carcopino, Jérôme. *Daily Life in Ancient Rome: The People and the City at the Height of the Empire*. Translated by E. O. Lorimer. New Haven: Yale University Press, 1940.

Carney, Thomas F. *The Shape of the Past: Models and Antiquity*. Lawrence, KS: Coronado, 1975.

Caro Baroja, Julio. "Honour and Shame: A Historical Account of Several Conflicts." In *Honour and Shame: The Values of Mediterranean Society*, edited by J. G. Peristiany, 79–137. London: Weidenfeld and Nicholson, 1966.

―――. "Religion, World Views, Social Classes and Honor During the Sixteenth and Seventeenth Centuries in Spain." In *Honour and Grace in Anthropology*, edited by J. G. Peristiany and J. Pitt-Rivers, 91–102. Cambridge: Cambridge University Press, 1992.

Carroll, Berenice A., editor. *Liberating Women's History: Theoretical and Critical Essays*. Urbana: University of Illinois Press, 1976.

Carter, Warren. *Households and Discipleship. A Study of Matthew 19–20*. JSNTSS 103. Sheffield: JSOT Press, 1994.

―――. "Matthew 4:18–22 and Matthean Discipleship: An Audience Oriented Perspective." *CBQ* 59 (1997) 58–75.

―――. *Matthew: Storyteller, Interpreter, Evangelist*. Rev. ed. Peabody, MA: Hendrickson, 2004.

Chaney, Marvin L. "Ancient Palestinian Peasant Movements and the Formation of Premonarchic Israel." In *Palestine in Transition: The Emergence of Ancient Israel*, edited by David Noel Freedman and David F. Graf, 39–90. Sheffield: Almond, 1983.

―――. "Systematic Study of the Sociology of the Israelite Monarchy." Paper presented at the SBL Annual Meeting, San Francisco, CA, 1981.

Chao, B. Yang. *Autobiography of a Chinese Woman, Buwei Yang Chao*. New York: John Day, 1947.

Childe, V. Gordon. *Man Makes Himself*. Rev. ed. New York: Mentor, 1951.

Christensen, D. L. "Huldah and the Men of Anathoth: Women in Leadership in the Deuteronomic History." In *SBLSP* 23 (1984) 399–404.

Clark, Elizabeth A., and Herbert Richardson, editors. *Women and Religion: A Feminist Sourcebook of Christian Thought*. San Francisco: Harper & Row, 1977.

Cohen, Shaye J. D. "The Significance of Yavneh: Pharisees, Rabbis, and the End of Jewish Sectarianism." *HUCA* 40 (1984) 27–53.

―――. "Women in the Synagogues of Antiquity." *CJud* 34 (1980) 23–29.

Cope, O. Lamar. *Matthew, A Scribe Trained for the Kingdom of Heaven*. Washington, DC: Catholic Biblical Association of America, 1976.

Corley, Kathleen E. "The Egalitarian Jesus: A Christian Myth of Origins." *Forum* 1–2 (1998) 291–325.

―――. *Private Women, Public Meals: Social Conflict and Women in the Synoptic Tradition*. Peabody, MA: Hendrickson, 1993.

―――. "Were the Women around Jesus Really Prostitutes? Women in the Context of Greco-Roman Meals." In *SBLASP*, 487–521. Atlanta: Scholars, 1989.

Cowling, G. "The Biblical Household." In *Wünschet Jerusalem Frieden: Collected Communications to the XIIth Congress of the International Organization for the Study of the Old Testament, Jerusalem 1986*, edited by M. Augustin and K. Schnunck, 179–92. New York: Lang, 1988.

Craven, Toni. "Women Who Lied for the Faith." In *Justice and the Holy: Essays in Honor of Walter Harrelson*, edited by Douglas A. Knight and Peter J. Paris, 35–49. Atlanta: Scholars, 1989.

Cresswell, R. "Lineage Endogamy among Maronite Mountaineers." In *Mediterranean Family Structures*, edited by J. G. Peristiany, 101–14. Cambridge: Cambridge University Press, 1976.

Crosby, Michael H. *Church, Economics, and Justice in Matthew*. Maryknoll, NY: Orbis, 1988.

―――. *House of Disciples: Church, Economics, and Justice in Matthew*. Maryknoll, NY: Orbis, 1988.

Crossan, John Dominic. *The Essential Jesus: Original Sayings and Earliest Images*. San Francisco, HarperSanFrancisco, 1994.

―――. *The Historical Jesus: The Life of a Mediterranean Jewish Peasant*. San Francisco: HarperSanFrancisco, 1991.

―――. *Jesus: A Revolutionary Biography*. San Francisco: HarperSanFrancisco, 1994.

Cumont, Franz. *The Mysteries of Mithra*. New York: Dover, 1956.

D'Angelo, Mary Rose. "Theology in Mark and Q: Abba and 'Father' in Context." *HTR* 85 (1992) 149–74.

Danker, Frederick W. *Benefactor: Epigraphic Study of a Graeco-Roman and New Testament Semantic Field*. St. Louis: Clayton, 1982.

Darity, William A., Jr., editor. *International Encyclopedia of the Social Sciences*. 2nd ed. Macmillan Social Science Library. Detroit: Macmillan Reference USA, 2002.

Davies, W. D. *The Setting of the Sermon on the Mount*. 1964. Reprint, Atlanta: Scholars, 1989.

Davies, W. D., and Dale C. Allison, Jr. *A Critical and Exegetical Commentary on the Gospel according to St. Matthew*. Vol. 2. Edinburgh: T. & T. Clark, 1988.

Davis, John. "Family and State in the Mediterranean." In *Honor and Shame and the Unity of the Mediterranean*, edited by David D. Gilmore, 22–34. AAASP. Washington, DC: American Anthropological Association, 1987.

Delaney, Carol L. "Mortal Flow: Menstruation in Turkish Village Society." In *Blood Magic: The Anthropology of Menstruation*, edited by T. Buckley and A. Gottlieb, 75–93. Berkeley: University of California Press. 1988.

Douglas, Mary. *Implicit Meanings: Essays in Anthropology*. London, Boston: Routledge & Kegan Paul, 1975.

―――. *Natural Symbols: Explorations in Cosmology*. New York: Pantheon, 1973.

————. *Purity and Danger: An Analysis of the Conceptions of Pollution and Taboo.* London: Routledge & Kegan Paul, 1966.

Dube, S. C. *Indian Village.* Ithaca, NY: Cornell University Press, 1955.

Dubisch, Jill. "Culture Enters through the Kitchen: Women, Food, and Social Boundaries in Rural Greece." In *Gender and Power in Rural Greece,* edited by J. Dubisch, 195–214. Princeton: Princeton University Press, 1986.

Duling, Dennis C. "Egalitarian Ideology, Leadership, and Factional Conflict in the Gospel of Matthew." *BTB* 27 (1997) 124–37.

————. "Ethnicity, Ethnocentrism, and the Matthean *Ethnos.*" *BTB* 35 (2005) 125–43.

————. "The Matthean Brotherhood and Marginal Scribal Leadership." In *Modelling Early Christianity: Social-Scientific Studies of the New Testament in Context,* edited by Philip F. Esler, 159–82. London: Routledge, 1995.

————. "Matthew." In *The HarperCollins Study Bible, New Revised Standard,* edited by Harold W. Attridge. Rev. ed. San Francisco: HarperSanFrancisco, 2006.

————. "Matthew 18:15–17: Conflict, Confrontation, and Conflict Resolution in a 'Fictive' Kin Association." *BTB* 29 (1999) 4–22.

————. "Matthew and Marginality." In *SBLSP,* edited by Eugene H. Lovering, 642–71. Atlanta: Scholars, 1992.

————. "Matthew as a Marginal Scribe in an Advanced Agrarian Society." *HvTSt* 58 (2002) 520–75.

————. "Matthew's Plurisignificant 'Son of David' in Social Science Perspective: Kinship, Kingship, Magic, and Miracle." *BTB* 22 (1992) 99–116.

————. "Social Theory, Social Models, and the Gospel of Matthew." In *The Gospel of Matthew in its Roman Imperial Context,* edited by John Riches and David C. Sims, 49–74. London: T. & T. Clark, 2005.

————. "Solomon, Exorcism, and the Son of David." *HTR* 68 (1975) 235–52.

————. "The Therapeutic Son of David: An Element in Matthew's Apologetic." *NTS* (1978) 392–410.

Edwards, R. A. "Uncertain Faith: Matthew's Portrait of the Disciples." In *Discipleship in the New Testament,* edited by Fernando Segovia, 47–61. Philadelphia: Fortress, 1985.

Eisenberg, Leon. "Disease and Illness: Distinctions between Professional and Popular Ideas of Sickness." *CMP* 1 (1977) 9–23.

Eisenberg, Leon, and Arthur Kleinman. *The Relevance of Social Science for Medicine.* Dordrecht, Neth.: Reidel, 1981.

Eisenstadt, S. N., and Louis Roniger, editors. *Patrons, Clients and Friends: Interpersonal Relations and the Structure of Trust in Society.* New York: Cambridge University Press, 1984.

Elliott, John H. *A Home for the Homeless: A Sociological Exegesis of 1 Peter, Its Situation and Strategy.* Philadelphia: Fortress, 1981.

————. "Jesus the Israelite Was Neither a Jew Nor a Christian: On Correcting the Nomenclature." *JSHJ* 5 (2007) 119–55.

————. "The Jesus Movement Was Not Egalitarian but Family-Oriented." *BibInt* 11 (2003) 173–210.

————. "Jesus Was Not an Egalitarian. A Critique of an Anachronistic and Idealist Theory." *BTB* 32 (2002) 75–91.

————. "Matthew 20:1–15: A Parable of Invidious Comparison and Evil Eye Accusation." *BTB* 22 (1992) 52–65.

————. "Patronage and Clientage." In *The Social Sciences and New Testament Interpretation,* edited by Richard R. Rohrbaugh, 144–56. Peabody, MA: Hendrickson, 1996.

————. *1 Peter.* AB 37B. New York: Doubleday, 2000.

————. "Social-Scientific Criticism of the New Testament and Its Social World: More on Method and Models." *Semeia* 35 (1986) 1–33.

————. "Temple versus Household in Luke-Acts: A Contrast in Social Institutions." In *The Social World of Luke-Acts: Models for Interpretation,* edited by Jerome H. Neyrey, 211–40. Peabody, MA: Hendrickson, 1991.

————. *What is Social-Scientific Criticism?* Guides to Biblical Scholarship. Minneapolis: Fortress, 1993.

Elshtain, Jean B. *Public Man, Private Woman: Women in Social and Political Thought.* Princeton: Princeton University Press, 1981.

Emmerson, Grace I. "Women in Ancient Israel." In *The World of Ancient Israel: Sociological, Anthropological, and Political Perspectives,* edited by R. E. Clements, 371–94. Cambridge: Cambridge University Press, 1989.

Estévez López, Elisa. *El poder de una mujer creyente: Cuerpo, identidad y discipulado en Mc 5.24b–34: Un studio desde las ciencias sociales.* ABE 40. Estella, Spain: Verbo Divino, 2003.

Fei, John. "Peasantry and Gentry: An Interpretation of Chinese Social Structure and Its Changes." *AJS* 52 (1945) 4–5.

Ferguson, Everett. *Backgrounds of Early Christianity.* Grand Rapids: Eerdmans, 1987.

Filson, Floyd V. "The Significance of the Early Christian House Churches," *JBL* 58 (1939) 105–12.

Finley, M. I. "The Silent Women of Rome." In *Aspects of Antiquity,* edited by M. I. Finley, 124–36. 2nd ed. Harmondsworth, UK: Penguin, 1985.

Fisher, Loren R. "Can This Be the Son of David?" In *Jesus and the Historian: Written in Honor of Ernest Cadman Colwell,* edited by E. T. Trotter, 82–97. Philadelphia: Westminster, 1968.

Flandrin, Jean L. *Families in Former Times: Kinship, Household, and Sexuality.* Translated by R. Southern. Cambridge: Cambridge University Press, 1979.

Fontaine, Carole R. "The Sage in Family and Tribe." In *The Sage in Israel and the Ancient Near East,* edited by J. Gammie and L. Perdue, 155–64. Winona Lake, IN: Eisenbrauns, 1990.

Fortes, Meyer. *The Dynamics of Clanship among the Tallensi.* London: Oxford University Press, 1945.

Foster, George M. "Disease Etiologies in Non-Western Medical Systems." *AmAnth* 78 (1976) 773–82.

————. "The Image of Limited Good." In *Peasant Society: A Reader,* edited by J. Potter et al., 300–323. Boston: Little, Brown, 1967.

————. "Peasant Society and the Image of the Limited Good." *AmAnth* 67 (1965) 293–315.

Fox, Robin. *Kinship and Marriage: An Anthropological Perspective.* Harmondsworth, UK: Penguin, 1967.

Frankemölle, Hubert. *Jahwe-bund und Kirche Christi: Studien zur Form- und Traditionsgeschichte des Evangeliums nach Matthäus.* 2nd ed. Neutestamentliche Abhandlungen 10. Münster: Aschendorff, 1984.

————. *Matthäus: Kommentar.* Vol. 2. Düsseldorf: Patmos, 1997.

Franzmann, Martin H. *Follow Me: Discipleship according to Saint Matthew.* St. Louis: Concordia, 1961.

Freedman, David Noel, editor. *Anchor Bible Dictionary.* 6 Vols. New York: Doubleday, 1992.

Freedman, Maurice. *Lineage Organization in Southeastern China.* MSA 18. London: University of London, Athlone, 1958.

Friedl, Ernestine. "The Position of Women; Appearance and Reality." *Anthropological Quarterly* 40.3 (1967) 97–108. Reprinted in *Gender and Power in Rural Greece,* edited by J. Dubisch, 42–52. Princeton, NJ: Princeton University Press, 1986.

———. *Women and Men: An Anthropologist's View.* New York: Holt, Rinehart and Winston, 1975.

Gardner, Jane F. *Women in Roman Law & Society.* Bloomington: Indiana University Press, 1986.

Gardner, Jane F., and Thomas E. J. Wiedemann. *The Roman Household: A Sourcebook.* London: Routledge, 1991.

Garland, Robert. *The Eye of the Beholder: Deformity and Disability in the Greco-Roman World.* Ithaca, NY: Cornell University Press, 1995.

Geertz, Clifford. *The Interpretation of Cultures: Selected Essays.* New York: Basic Books, 1973.

———. *Local Knowledge: Further Essays in Interpretive Anthropology.* New York: Basic Books, 1983.

Gellner, Ernest, and John Waterbury, editors. *Patrons and Clients in Mediterranean Societies.* London: Duckworth, 1977.

Gennep, Arnold van. "Arnold van Gennep on the Rites of Passage." In *Frontiers of Anthropology,* edited by Ashley Montagu, 315–19. New York: Putnam, 1974.

———. *The Rites of Passage.* Translated by Monika B. Vizedom and Gabrielle L. Caffee. Chicago: University of Chicago Press, 1960.

Germani, Gino. *Marginality.* New Brunswick, NJ: Transaction Books, 1980.

Geus, J. C. de. *The Tribes of Israel: An Investigation into Some of the Presuppositions of Martin Noth's Amphictyony Hypothesis.* Studia Semitica Neerlandica 18. Assen: Van Gorcum, 1976.

Gilmore, David D. "Honor, Honesty, Shame: Male Status in Contemporary Andalusia." In *Honor and Shame and the Unity of the Mediterranean,* edited by David D. Gilmore, 90–103. AAASP 22. Washington, DC: American Anthropological Association, 1987.

———, editor. *Honor and Shame and the Unity of the Mediterranean.* AAASP 22. Washington, DC: American Anthropological Association, 1987.

———. "Introduction: The Shame of Dishonor." In *Honor and Shame and the Unity of the Mediterranean,* edited by David D. Gilmore, 2–21. AAASP 22. Washington, DC: American Anthropological Association, 1987.

Giovannini, M. J. "Female Chastity Codes in the Circum-Mediterranean: Comparative Perspectives." In *Honor and Shame and the Unity of the Mediterranean,* edited by David D. Gilmore, 61–74. Washington, DC: American Anthropological Association, 1987.

Goldschmidt, Walter R. *Man's Way: A Preface to the Understanding of Human Society.* New York: Holt, 1959.

Goody, Jack. "The Evolution of the Family." In *Household and Family in Past Time,* edited by P. Laslett and R. Wall, 103–24. Cambridge: Cambridge University Press, 1972.

Gottwald, Norman K. *The Tribes of Yahweh: A Sociology of the Religion of Liberated Israel, 1250–1050 B.C.E.* New York: Orbis, 1979.

Grant, Elihu. *The People of Palestine: The Life, Manners and Customs of the Village.* 1907. Reprinted, Eugene, OR: Wipf & Stock, 2005.

Grassi, Joseph A. *The Hidden Heroes of the Gospels: Female Counterparts of Jesus.* Collegeville, MN: Liturgical, 1989.

Gregory, James R. "Image of Limited Good, or Expectation of Reciprocity?" *CAnth* 16 (1975) 73–92.

Guijarro Oporto, Santiago. "The Family in First Century Galilee." In *Constructing Early Christian Families: Family as Social Reality and Metaphor,* edited by Halvor Moxnes, 42–65. London: Routledge, 1997.

———. "The Family in the Jesus Movement." *BTB* 34 (2004) 114–21.

———. "Kingdom and Family in Conflict: A Contribution to the Study of the Historical Jesus." In *Social Scientific Models for Interpreting the Bible: Essays by the Context Group in Honor of Bruce J. Malina,* edited by John J. Pilch, 210–38. BIS 53. Leiden: Brill, 2001.

Gundry, Robert H. *Matthew: A Commentary on His Literary and Theological Art.* Grand Rapids: Eerdmans, 1982.

Hagner, Donald. *Matthew 1–13.* WBC 33A. Dallas: Word, 1993.

———. *Matthew 14–28.* WBC 33B. Dallas: Word, 1995.

Hahn, Robert A. *Sickness and Healing: An Anthropological Perspective.* New Haven: Yale University Press, 1995.

Halsey, A. H. "Equality." In *The Social Science Encyclopedia,* edited by Adam Kuper and Jessica Kuper, 260–63. London: Routledge, 1989.

Hamerton-Kelly, Robert. *God the Father: Theology and Patriarchy in the Teaching of Jesus.* OBT. Philadelphia: Fortress, 1979.

Hanson, K. C. "BTB Readers Guide: Kinship." *BTB* 24 (1994) 183–94.

———. "The Herodians and Mediterranean Kinship, Part I: Genealogy and Descent." *BTB* 19 (1989) 75–84.

———. "The Herodians and Mediterranean Kinship, Part II: Marriage and Divorce." *BTB* 19 (1989) 142–51.

———. "The Herodians and Mediterranean Kinship, Part III: Economics." *BTB* 20 (1989) 10–21.

———. "Transformed on the Mountain: Ritual Analysis and the Gospel of Matthew." *Semeia* 67 (1994[95]) 147–70.

Hanson, K. C., and Douglas E. Oakman. *Palestine in the Time of Jesus: Social Structures and Social Conflicts.* 2nd ed. Minneapolis: Fortress, 2008.

Hare, Douglas R. *The Theme of Jewish Persecution of Christians in the Gospel according to Matthew.* London: Cambridge University Press, 1967.

Harrington, Daniel J. *The Gospel according to Matthew.* Collegeville, MN: Liturgical, 1983.

Harris, Marvin. *The Rise of Anthropological Theory: A History of Theories of Culture.* New York: Crowell, 1968.

Harris, William V. *Ancient Literacy.* Cambridge: Harvard University Press, 1989.

Hauck, Friedrich. "καρπός κτλ." In *TDNT* 3 (1965) 614–16.

Hearon, Holly. "The Story of 'the Woman Who Anointed Jesus' as Social Memory: A Methodological Proposal for the Study of Tradition as Memory." In *Memory, Tradition, and Text: Uses of the Past in Early Christianity,* edited by Alan Kirk and

Bibliography

Tom Thatcher, 99–118. Society of Biblical Literature Semeia Studies. Atlanta: Society of Biblical Literature, 2005.

Held, Heinz Joachim. "Matthew as Interpreter of the Miracle Stories." In *Tradition and Interpretation in Matthew*, edited by Gerhard Barth et al., translated by P. Scott, 165–99. NTL. Philadelphia: Westminster, 1963.

Hengel, Martin. *Nachfolge und Charisma*. BZNW 34. Berlin: Töpelmann, 1968.

———. "On the Exegesis of Mt 8.21–22: 'Let the dead bury their dead.'" In *The Charismatic Leader and His Followers*, 3–15, translated by J. Grieg. New York: Crossroad, 1981.

Herzfeld, M. "'As in Your Own House': Hospitality, Ethnography, and the Stereotype of Mediterranean Society." In *Honor and Shame and the Unity of the Mediterranean*, edited by D. D. Gilmore, 75–89. Washington, DC: AAASP, 1987.

Hobbs, T. R. "Man, Woman, and Hospitality—2 Kings 4:8–36." *BTB* 23 (1993) 91–100.

Hoens, D. "Rites of Initiation: A Contribution to the Methodology of Comparative Religion." In *Explorations in the Anthropology of Religion: Essays in Honour of Jan van Baal*, edited by W. E. A. van Beek and J. H. Scherer, 29–45. The Hague, Netherlands: Nijhoff, 1975.

Hollenbach, Paul W. "Jesus, Demoniacs, and Public Authorities: A Socio-Historical Study." *JAAR* 49 (1981) 567–88.

Hood, R. T. "The Genealogies of Jesus." In *Early Christian Origins. Studies in Honor of Harold R. Willoughby*, edited by Allen P. Wikgren, 1–15. Chicago: Quadrangle, 1961.

Hopkins, M. K. "The Age of Roman Girls at Marriage." *PSt* 19 (1965) 309–27.

Horsley, Richard A. *Jesus and the Spiral of Violence: Popular Jewish Resistance in Roman Palestine*. Minneapolis: Fortress, 1993.

Hull, John M. *Hellenistic Magic and the Synoptic Tradition*. SBT 2/28. Naperville, IL: Allenson, 1974.

Hulse, E. V. "The Nature of Biblical 'Leprosy' and the Use of Alternative Medical Terms in Modern Translations of the Bible." *PEQ* 107 (1975) 87–105.

Hummel, R. Die *Auseinandersetzung zwischen Kirche und Judentum im Mattäusevangelium*. BEvT 33. Munich: Kaiser, 1966.

Huntington, R. and P. Metcalf. *Celebrations of Death: The Anthropology of Mortuary Ritual*. Cambridge: Cambridge University Press, 1991.

Isenberg, Sheldon K. "Mary Douglas and Hellenistic Religions: The Case of Qumran." In *SBLSP* (1975) 179–85.

Isenberg, Sheldon K., and Dennis E. Owen. "Bodies, Natural and Contrived: The Work of Mary Douglas." *RSR* 3 (1977) 1–17.

Jacobs-Malina, Diane. *Beyond Patriarchy: The Images of Family in Jesus*. New York: Paulist, 1993.

Jackson, Ralph. *Doctors and Diseases in the Roman Empire*. Norman: University of Oklahoma Press, 1988.

Jeremias, Joachim. *The Sermon on the Mount*. Translated by Norman Perrin. Facet Books. Philadelphia: Fortress, 1963.

Johnson, Luke Timothy. *1 Timothy, 2 Timothy, Titus*. Knox Preaching Guides. Atlanta: John Knox, 1987.

Johnson, Marshall D. *The Purpose of the Biblical Genealogies with Special Reference to the Setting of the Genealogies of Jesus*. SNTSMS 8. Cambridge: Cambridge University Press, 1969.

Judge, Edwin A. "The Household Community: *Oikonomia*." In *The Social Pattern of the Christian Groups in the First Century: Some Prolegomena to the Study of New*

Testament Ideas of Social Obligation, edited by Edwin A. Judge, 30–39. London: Tyndale, 1960.

―――. *Rank and Status in the World of the Caesars and St. Paul.* UCP 29. Canterbury: University of Canterbury, 1984.

Jules-Rosette, Bennetta. "Faith Healers and Folk Healers: The Symbolism and Practice of Indigenous Therapy in Urban Africa." *Religion* 11 (1981) 315–48.

Karris, Robert J. *Jesus and the Marginalized in John's Gospel.* Collegeville, MN: Liturgical, 1990.

Kay, Margarita A. *Anthropology of Human Birth.* Philadelphia: Davis, 1982.

Kee, Howard Clark. *Medicine, Miracle, and Magic in New Testament Times.* SNTSMS 55. Cambridge: Cambridge University Press, 1986.

Kendall, Paul Murray. *The Yorkist Age: Daily Life during the Wars of the Roses.* New York: Norton, 1962.

Keuls, Eva C. *The Reign of the Phallus: Sexual Politics in Ancient Athens.* New York: Harper & Row, 1985.

Kilpatrick, George Dunbar. *The Origins of the Gospel according to St. Matthew.* Oxford: Clarendon, 1946.

King, Philip J., and Lawrence E. Stager. *Life in Biblical Israel.* LAA. Louisville: Westminster John Knox, 2001.

Kingsbury, Jack Dean. *Matthew.* 2nd ed. PC. Philadelphia: Fortress, 1986.

―――. *Matthew as Story.* 2nd ed. Philadelphia: Fortress, 1988.

―――. "Observations on the 'Miracle Chapters' of Matthew 8–9." *CBQ* 40 (1978) 559–73.

―――. "The Title 'Son of David' in Matthew's Gospel." *JBL* 95 (1976), 591–602.

―――. "The Verb ἀκολουθεῖν ('To Follow') as an Index of Matthew's View of the Old Testament." *JBL* 97 (1978) 56–73.

Kleinman, Arthur. "Concepts and a Model for the Comparison of Medical Systems as Cultural Systems." In *Concepts of Health, Illness, and Disease: A Comparative Perspective,* edited by C. Currer and M. Stacey, 29–47. New York: Berg, 1986.

―――. *Patients and Healers in the Context of Culture: An Exploration of the Borderland between Anthropology, Medicine, and Psychiatry.* CSHSMC 3. Berkeley: University of California Press, 1989.

Kloppenborg, John S. "Blessing and Marginality: The 'Persecution Beatitude' in Q, Thomas, and Early Christianity." *Forum* 2 (1986) 36–56.

Kopas, Jane. "Jesus and Women in Matthew." *ThTo* 47 (1990) 13–21.

Kraemer, Ross S. "Hellenistic Jewish Women: The Epigraphical Evidence." In *SPSBL* 25, 183–200. Decatur, GA: Scholars, 1986.

―――. *Her Share of the Blessings: Women's Religions among Pagans, Jews, and Christians in the Greco-Roman World.* New York: Oxford University Press, 1992.

―――. "Monastic Jewish Women in Graeco-Roman Egypt: Philo Judaeus on the Therapeutrides." *SJWCS* 14 (1989) 342–70.

―――. "A New Inscription from Malta and the Question of Women in Diaspora Jewish Communities." *HTR* 78 (1985) 431–38.

―――. "Non-Literary Evidence for Jewish Women in Rome and Egypt." In *Rescuing Creusa: New Methodological Approaches to Women in Antiquity,* edited by Marilyn B. Skinner, 85–109. Lubbock, TX: Texas Tech University Press, 1986.

―――. "Women in the Religions of the Greco-Roman World." *RSR* 9 (1983) 133–39.

Kraemer, Ross S., editor. *Maenads, Martyrs, Matrons, Monastics: A Sourcebook on Women's Religions in the Greco-Roman World.* Philadelphia: Fortress, 1988.

Lamaire, André. "The Sage in School and Temple." In *The Sage in Israel and the Ancient Near East,* edited by John G. Gammie and Leo G. Perdue, 165–81. Winona Lake, IN: Eisenbrauns, 1990.

Lenski, Gerhard. *Power and Privilege: A Theory of Social Stratification.* MHSS. New York: McGraw-Hill, 1966.

Lenski, Gerhard, and Jean Lenski. *Human Societies: An Introduction to Macrosociology.* 2nd ed. New York, et al.: McGraw-Hill, 1974.

———. *Human Societies: An Introduction to Macrosociology.* 4th ed. New York: McGraw-Hill, 1982.

———. *Human Societies: An Introduction to Macrosociology.* 5th ed. New York: McGraw-Hill, 1987.

Levine, Amy-Jill. "Discharging Responsibility: Matthean Jesus, Biblical Law, and Hemorrhaging Woman." In *Treasures New and Old: Recent Contributions* to *Matthean Studies,* edited by D. R. Bauer and M. A. Powell, 379–97. SBLSymS 1. Atlanta: Scholars, 1996.

———. "Matthew." In *The Women's Bible Commentary.* Edited by Carol Newsom and Sharon H. Ringe. Louisville: Westminster John Knox, 1992.

———. "Second Temple Judaism, Jesus and Women: Yeast of Eden." *BibInt* 2 (1994) 8–33.

———. *The Social and Ethnic Dimensions of Matthean Salvation History.* SBEC 14. Lewiston, NY: Mellen, 1988.

Loewe, Raphael. *The Position of Women in Judaism.* London: SPCK, 1966.

Love, Stuart L. "Gender Status and Roles in the Church: Some Social Considerations." *RQ* 36 (1994) 251–66.

———. "The Household: A Major Social Component for Gender Analysis in the Gospel of Matthew," *BTB* 23 (1993) 21–31.

———. "Jesus, Healer of the Canaanite Woman's Daughter in Matthew's Gospel: A Social-Scientific Inquiry," *BTB* 32 (2002) 11–20.

———. "Jesus Heals the Hemorrhaging Woman." In *The Social Setting of Jesus and the Gospels,* edited by Wolfgang Stegemann et al., 83–91. Minneapolis: Fortress, 2002.

———. "The Place of Women in Public Settings in Matthew's Gospel: A Sociological Inquiry," *BTB* 24 (1994) 52–65.

———. "Women's Roles in Certain Second Testament Passages: A Macrosociological View." *BTB* 17 (1987) 50–59.

Lövestam, E. "Jésus Fils de David chez les Synoptiques." *ST* 28 (1974) 97–109.

Luz, Ulrich. "The Disciples in the Gospel of Matthew." In *The Interpretation of Matthew,* edited by Graham Stanton, 98–128. IRT3. Philadelphia: Fortress, 1982.

———. "Die Jünger im Matthäusevangelium." *ZNW* 62 (1971) 141–71.

———. *Matthew 1–7.* Translated by Wilhelm C. Linss. CC. Minneapolis: Fortress, 1989.

———. *Matthew: A Commentary.* Translated by James E. Crouch. Vol. 2, *Matthew 8–20.* Hermeneia. Minneapolis: Fortress, 2001.

———. *Matthew: A Commentary.* Translated by James E. Crouch. Vol. 3, *Matthew 21–28.* Hermeneia. Minneapolis: Fortress, 2005.

———. "Die Wundergeschichten von Mt 8–9." In *Tradition and Interpretation in the New Testament: Essays in Honor of E. Earle Ellis for His 60th Birthday,* edited by Gerald F. Hawthorne and Otto Betz, 149–65. Grand Rapids: Eerdmans, 1987.

Bibliography

Mace, D. R. *Hebrew Marriage: A Sociological Study*. New York: Philosophical Library, 1953.

MacIver, Robert. "The Family as Government in Miniature." In *The Imprint of Roman Institutions*, edited by David W. Savage. Western Man. New York: Holt, Rinehart and Winston, 1971.

MacMullen, Ramsey. *Roman Social Relations, 50 B.C. to A.D. 284*. New Haven: Yale University Press, 1974.

————. "Women in Public in the Roman Empire." *Historia* 29 (1980) 208–18.

Malherbe, Abraham J. *Social Aspects of Early Christianity*, 3rd ed. Philadelphia: Fortress, 1983.

Malina, Bruce J. "Assessing the Historicity of Jesus' Walking on the Sea: Insights from Cross-Cultural Social Psychology." In *Authenticating the Activities of Jesus*, edited by Bruce Chilton and Craig A. Evans, 351–71. NTTS 28/2. Leiden: Brill, 1999.

————. *Christian Origins and Cultural Anthropology: Practical Models for Biblical Interpretation*. Atlanta: John Knox, 1986.

————. "Criteria for Assessing the Authentic Words of Jesus: Some Specifications." In *Authenticating the Words of Jesus*, edited by Bruce Chilton and Craig A. Evans, 27–45. NTTS 28/1. Leiden: Brill, 1999.

————. "Ελεος y la ayuda social: La utilización de las ciencieas sociales en la interpretación del Neuvo Testamento." In *Reimaginando los orígenes del cristianismo*, edited by Carmen Bernabe and Carlos Gil, 49–76. Estrella (Navarra) Spain: Verbo Divino, 2008.

————. "'Let Him Deny Himself' (Mark 8:34 and Par.): A Social Psychological Model of Self-Denial." *BTB* 24 (1994) 106–19.

————. *The New Testament World: Insights from Cultural Anthropology*. 1st ed. Atlanta: John Knox, 1981.

————. *The New Testament World: Insights from Cultural Anthropology*. 2nd ed. Louisville: Westminster John Knox, 1993.

————. *The New Testament World: Insights from Cultural Anthropology*. 3rd ed. Louisville: Westminster John Knox, 2001.

————. "Normative Dissonance and Christian Origins." *Semeia* 35 (1986) 35–42.

————. "Patron and Client: The Analogy behind Synoptic Theology." *Forum* 4 (1988) 2–32.

————. "The Social Sciences and Biblical Interpretation." *Int* 37 (1982) 229–42.

————. *The Social World of Jesus and the Gospels*. London: Routledge, 1996.

Malina, Bruce J., and Jerome H. Neyrey. *Calling Jesus Names: The Social Value of Labels in Matthew*. FF. Sonoma, CA: Polebridge, 1988.

Malina, Bruce J., and Richard L. Rohrbaugh. *Social-Science Commentary on the Synoptic Gospels*. 1st ed. Minneapolis: Fortress, 1992.

————. *Social-Science Commentary on the Synoptic Gospels*. 2nd ed. Minneapolis: Fortress, 2003.

Manson, T. W. *The Teaching of Jesus: Studies in Its Form and Content*. Cambridge: Cambridge University Press, 1967.

Marjanen, Antti. *The Woman Jesus Loved: Mary Magdalene in the Nag Hammadi Library and Related Documents*. NHS 40. Leiden: Brill, 1996.

Marquardt, Joachim. *Das Privatleben der Römer*. 1886. Reprint, Darmstadt: Wissenschaftliche Buchgesellschaft, 1975.

Bibliography

Martin, M. Kay, and Barbara Voorhies. *Female of the Species.* New York: Columbia University Press, 1975.

Matthews, Victor H., and Don C. Benjamin. *Social World of Ancient Israel, 1250–587 BCE.* Peabody, MA: Hendrickson, 1993.

McFague, Sallie. *Metaphorical Theology: Models of God in Religious Language.* Philadelphia: Fortress, 1982.

McNeile, A. H. *The Gospel according to St. Matthew: The Greek Text with Introduction, Notes, and Indices.* Grand Rapids: Baker, 1980.

McVann, Mark. "Rituals of Status Transformation in Luke-Acts: The Case of Jesus the Prophet." In *The Social World of Luke-Acts: Models for Interpretation,* edited by Jerome H. Neyrey, 333–60. Peabody, MA: Hendrickson, 1991.

Meeks, Wayne. *The First Urban Christians: The Social World of the Apostle Paul.* New Haven: Yale University Press, 1983.

Meier, John P. *A Marginal Jew: Rethinking the Historical Jesus.* Vol. 2, *Mentor, Message, and Miracles.* ABRL. New York: Doubleday, 1994.

———. *Matthew.* NTM 3. Collegeville, MN: Liturgical, 1990.

———. "Matthew, Gospel of." In *ABD* 4:622–41.

Melzer-Keller, Helga. *Jesus und die Frauen: Eine Verhältnisbestimmung nach den synoptischen Überlieferungen.* Herders biblische Studien 14. Freiburg: Herder, 1997.

Mernissi, Fatima. *Beyond the Veil: Male-Female Dynamics in a Modern Muslim Society.* Cambridge, MA: Schenkman, 1975.

Meyers, Carol. *Discovering Eve: Ancient Israelite Women in Context.* New York: Oxford University Press, 1988.

———. "Procreation, Production, and Protection: Male-Female Balance in Early Israel." *JAAR* 51 (1983) 568–93.

———. "The Roots of Restriction: Women in Early Israel." *BA* 41 (1978) 91–103.

———. "Women and the Domestic Economy of Early Israel." In *Women's Earliest Records from Ancient Egypt and Western Asia,* 265–78. Atlanta: Scholars, 1989.

Michel, Otto. "Οἰκία/Οἶκος." In *TDNT* 5 (1965) 119–59.

Minear, Paul. "The Disciples and the Crowds in the Gospel of Matthew." *ATS* 3 (1974) 28–44.

———. *Images of the Church in the New Testament.* Philadelphia: Westminster, 1960.

Morgenthaler, Robert. *Statistik des neutestamentlichen Wortschatzes.* Zurich: Gottself, 1958.

Montefiore, C. G. *A Rabbinic Anthology.* Philadelphia: Jewish Publication Society of America, 1960.

Moore, Sally F., and Barbara G. Meyerhoff, editors. *Secular Ritual.* Amsterdam: Van Gorcum, 1977.

Moxnes, Halvor. *Constructing Early Christian Families: Family as Social Reality and Metaphor.* New York: Routledge, 1997.

———. *The Economy of the Kingdom: Social Conflict and Economic Relations in Luke's Gospel.* OBT. Philadelphia: Fortress, 1988.

———. "Honor and Shame." In *The Social Sciences and New Testament Interpretation,* edited by Richard Rohrbaugh, 19–40. Peabody, MA: Hendrickson, 1996.

———. "Patron-Client Relations and the New Community in Luke-Acts." In *The Social World of Luke-Acts: Models for Interpretation,* edited by Jerome H. Neyrey, 241–68. Peabody, MA: Hendrickson, 1991.

Murdock, George Peter. *Atlas of World Cultures.* Pittsburgh: University of Pittsburgh Press, 1981.

———. *Theories of Illness: A World Survey.* Pittsburgh: University of Pittsburgh Press, 1980.

Neusner, Jacob. *From Politics to Piety: The Emergence of Pharisaic Judaism.* 2nd ed. New York: Ktav, 1979.

———. "History and Purity in First-Century Judaism." *HR* 18 (1978) 1–17.

———. *The Idea of Purity in Ancient Judaism.* SJLA 1. Leiden: Brill. 1973.

———. "Map without Territory: Mishnah's System of Sacrifices and Sanctuary." *HR* 19 (1979) 103–27.

———. *Oral Tradition in Judaism: The Case of the Mishnah.* New York: Garland, 1987.

Neyrey, Jerome H. "Clean/Unclean, Pure/Polluted, and Holy/Profane: The Idea and the System of Purity." In *The Social Sciences and New Testament Interpretation,* edited by Richard L. Rohrbaugh, 80–104. Peabody, MA: Hendrickson, 1996.

———. *Honor and Shame in the Gospel of Matthew.* Louisville: Westminster John Knox, 1998.

———. "The Idea of Purity in Mark's Gospel." *Semeia* 35 (1986) 91–128.

———. "Miracles, in Other Words: Social Science Perspectives on Healings." Unpublished paper, 1995.

———. "The Symbolic Universe of Luke-Acts: 'They Turn the World Upside Down.'" In *The Social World of Luke-Acts: Models for Interpretation,* edited by Jerome H. Neyrey, 271–304. Peabody, MA: Hendrickson, 1991.

———. "Unclean, Common, Polluted, and Taboo." *Forum* 4 (1988) 72–82.

Niditch, Susan. "Legends of Wise Heroes and Heroines." In *The Hebrew Bible and Its Modern Interpreters,* edited by D. A. Knight and G. M. Tucker, 445–64. Philadelphia: Fortress, 1985.

———. "The Wronged Woman Righted: An Analysis of Genesis 38." *HTR* 72 (1979) 143–49.

Nisbet, Robert. *Social Change and History: Aspects of the Western Theory of Development.* New York: Oxford University Press, 1969.

Nolan, Patrick, and Gerhard Lenski. *Human Societies: An Introduction to Macrosociology.* 10th ed. Boulder, CO: Paradigm, 2006.

———. *Human Societies: An Introduction to Macrosociology.* 11th ed. Boulder, CO: Paradigm, 2008.

Oakman, Douglas E. "The Countryside in Luke-Acts." In *The Social World of Luke-Acts: Models for Interpretation,* edited by Jerome H. Neyrey, 151–80. Peabody, MA: Hendrickson, 1991. Reprinted and revised in *Jesus and the Peasants,* 132–63.

———. *Jesus and the Economic Questions of His Day.* SBEC 8. Lewiston, NY: Mellen, 1986.

———. *Jesus and the Peasants.* Matrix 4. Eugene, OR: Cascade Books, 2007.

Olick, J. K. "Social Memory Studies: From 'Collective Memory' to the Historical Sociology of Mnemonic Practices." *ARS* 24 (1998) 105–40.

Olick, J. K., and J. Robbins. "Genre Memories and Memory Genres: A Dialogical Analysis of May 8, 1045 Commemorations in the Federal Republic of Germany." *ASR* 64 (1999) 381–402.

Orenstein, Henry. *Gaon: Conflict and Cohesion in an Indian Village.* Princeton, NJ: Princeton University Press, 1965.

Bibliography

Osiek, Carolyn, and David L. Balch. *Families in the New Testament World: Households and House Churches*. FRC. Louisville, Westminster John Knox, 1997.

Paige, K. E. "Virginity Rituals and Chastity Control during Puberty: Cross-Cultural Patterns." In *Menarche, the Transition from Girl to Woman*, edited by Sharon Golub, 155–74. Lexington, MA: Lexington, 1983.

Park, Robert E. "Human Migration and the Marginal Man." *AJS* 33 (1928) 831–93.

———. "Personality and Cultural Conflict." *PASS* 25 (1931) 95–110.

Parsons, Talcott. *Societies: Evolutionary and Comparative Perspectives*. FMS. Englewood Cliffs, NJ: Prentice-Hall, 1966.

Patai, Raphael. *Sex and Family in the Bible and the Middle East*. Garden City, NY: Doubleday, 1959.

Perdue, Leo G., et al. *Families in Ancient Israel*. FRC. Louisville: Westminster John Knox, 1997.

Peristiany, J. G., editor. *Honour and Shame: The Values of Mediterranean Society*. London: Weidenfeld and Nicholson, 1966.

Peristiany, J. G., and J. Pitt-Rivers, editors. *Honour and Grace in Anthropology*. Cambridge: Cambridge University Press, 1992.

Pilch, John J. "Biblical Leprosy and Body Symbolism." *BTB* 11 (1981) 108–113.

———. "Healing in Mark: A Social Science Analysis." *BTB* 15 (1985) 142–50.

———. *Healing in the New Testament: Insights from Mediterranean and Medical Anthropology*. Minneapolis: Fortress, 2000.

———. "The Health Care System in Matthew: A Social Science Analysis." *BTB* 16 (1986) 102–6.

———. "Insights and Models for Understanding the Healing Activity of the Historical Jesus." In *SBLSP* 1994, 154–77. Atlanta: Scholars, 1994.

———. "Sickness and Healing in Luke-Acts." In *The Social World of Luke-Acts: Models for Interpretation*, edited by Jerome. H. Neyrey, 181–209. Peabody, MA: Hendrickson, 1991.

———. "A Spirit Named 'Fever.'" *PACE* 21 (1992) 253–56.

———. "Visions in Revelation and Alternate Consciousness: A Perspective from Cultural Anthropology." *Listening* 28 (1993) 231–44.

Pitt-Rivers, J. *The Fate of Shechem or the Politics of Sex*. CSSA 19. Cambridge: Cambridge University Press, 1977.

———. "Honor." In *IESS* 6 (1968) 503–11.

———. "Honour and Social Status." In *Honour and Shame: The Values of Mediterranean Society*, edited by J. G. Peristiany, 19–77. London: Weidenfeld and Nicholson, 1966. Reprinted in J. Pitt-Rivers, *The Fate of Shechem or the Politics of Sex: Essays in the Anthropology of the Mediterranean*, 1–47. Cambridge: Cambridge University Press, 1977.

———. *The People of the Sierra*. Chicago: University of Chicago Press, 1961.

———. "Postscript: The Place of Grace in Anthropology." In *Honour and Grace in Anthropology*, edited by J. G. Peristiany and J. Pitt-Rivers, 215–46. Cambridge: Cambridge University Press, 1992.

Pomeroy, Sarah. *Goddesses, Whores, Wives and Slaves: Women in Classical Antiquity*. New York: Schocken, 1976.

———. *Women in Hellenistic Egypt: From Alexander to Cleopatra*. New York: Schocken, 1984.

Pomeroy, Sarah, with Ross S. Kraemer and N. Kampen. "Select Bibliography on Women in Classical Antiquity." In *Women in the Ancient World: The Arethusa Papers,* edited by J. Peradotto and J. P. Sullivan, 317–72. SSCS. Albany: SUNY Press, 1984.

Price, J. L., Jr. "Widow." In *HBD,* 1132–33. San Francisco: Harper & Row, 1985.

Rainey, A. F. "Women in Public Life." In *EncJud* 16:626. Jerusalem: Keter, 1971.

Richardson, Jacques, ed. *Models of Reality: Shaping Thought and Action.* Mt. Airy, MD: Lomond, 1984.

Riley, Matilda White. *Sociological Research 1: A Case Approach.* New York: Harcourt, Brace & World, 1963.

Ringe, Sharon H. "A Gentile Woman's Story." In *Feminist Interpretation of the Bible,* edited by Letty M. Russell, 65–72. Philadelphia: Westminster, 1985.

Robbins, Vernon K. "The Woman Who Touched Jesus' Garment: Socio-rhetorical Analysis of the Synoptic Accounts." *NTS* 33 (1987) 502–15.

Rogers, Susan C. "Female Forms of Power and the Myth of Male Dominance." *AE* 2 (1975) 727–56.

———. "Women's Place: A Critical Review of Anthropological Theory." *CSSH* 20 (1978) 123–62.

Rohrbaugh, Richard L. *The New Testament in Cross-Cultural Perspective.* Matrix 1. Eugene, OR: Cascade Books, 2007.

———. "The Pre-Industrial City in Luke-Acts: Urban Social Relations." In *The Social World of Luke-Acts,* edited by Jerome H. Neyrey, 125–50. Peabody, MA: Hendrickson, 1991

Ross, J. M. "Epileptic or Moonstruck?" *BT* 19 (1978) 126–28.

Safrai, Shemuel. "Home and Family." In *The Jewish People in the First Century,* edited by S. Safari and M. Stern. 2:728–92. CRINT. Philadelphia: Fortress, 1974.

———. "Jewish Self-Government." In *The Jewish People in the First Century,* edited by S. Safari and M. Stern, 1:377–419. CRINT. Philadelphia: Fortress, 1974.

Saldarini, Antony J. *Pharisees, Scribes, and Sadducees in Palestinian Society: A Sociological Approach.* Wilmington, DE: Glazier, 1988.

Salzman, L. F. *English Life in the Middle Ages.* London: Oxford University Press, 1929.

Sanders, H. A. "The Genealogies of Jesus." *JBL* 32 (1913) 184–93.

Sapir, J. David, and J. Christopher Crocker, editors. *The Social Use of Metaphor: Essays on the Anthropology of Rhetoric.* Philadelphia: University of Pennsylvania Press, 1977.

Schermerhorn, R. A. "Marginal Man." In A *Dictionary of the Social Sciences,* edited by Julius Gould and William L. Kolb, 406–7. New York: Free Press of Glencoe, 1964.

Schlatter, Adolf von. *Der Evangelist Matthäus: seine Sprache, sein Ziel, seine Selbständigkeit, ein Kommentar zum ersten Evangelium.* 4th ed. Stuttgart: Calwer, 1959.

Schmeller, Thomas. *Hierarchie und Egalität: eine sozialgeschichtliche Untersuchung paulinischer Gemeinden und griechisch-römischer Vereine.* SBS 162. Stuttgart: Katholisches Bibelwerk, 1995.

Schmitt, J. J. "The Gender of Ancient Israel." *JSOT* 26 (1983) 115–25.

———. "The Motherhood of God and Zion as Mother." *RB* (1985) 557–69.

———. "Virgin." In *ABD* 6:853–54.

Schottroff, Luise. *Lydia's Impatient Sisters: A Feminist Social History of Early Christianity.* Translated by Barbara and Martin Rumscheidt. Louisville: Westminster John Knox, 1995.

Schüssler Fiorenza, Elisabeth. *Discipleship of Equals: A Critical Feminist Ekklēsia-logy of Liberation.* New York: Crossroad, 1993.

————. "Luke 2:41–52." *Int* 36 (1982) 399–403.

————. *In Memory of Her: A Feminist Theological Reconstruction of Christian Origins.* New York: Crossroad, 1983.

————. "The Oratory of Euphemia and the *Ekklēsia* of Wo/man." In *Jesus, Miriam's Child, Sophia's Prophet: Critical Issues in Feminist Christology*, 3–31. New York: Continuum, 1995.

————. "The Study of Women in Early Christianity: Some Methodological Considerations." In *Critical History and Biblical Faith: New Testament Perspectives*, edited by T. J. Ryan. APCTS. Villanova, PA: College Theology Society, 1979.

Schweizer, Eduard. "Matthew's Church." In *The Interpretation of Matthew*, edited by Graham Stanton, 138–70. IRT 3. Philadelphia: Fortress, 1983. Originally published as *Matthaus und seine Gemeinde.* Stuttgart: Katholisches Bibelwerk, 1974.

Selvidge, Maria J. "Violence, Woman, and the Future of the Matthaean Community: A Redactional Critical Essay." *USQR* 39 (1984) 213–23.

Senior, Donald. "Between Two Worlds: Gentile and Jewish Christians in Matthew's Gospel." *CBQ* 61 (1999) 1–23.

————. *The Passion Narrative according to Matthew: A Redactional Study.* Gembloux: Duculot, 1975.

Sheridan, Mark. "Disciples and Discipleship in Matthew and Luke." *BTB* 3 (1973) 235–55.

Shyte, M. K. *The Status of Women in Pre-industrial Societies.* Princeton, NJ: Princeton University Press, 1978.

Sigerist, Henry E. *A History of Medicine.* 2 vols. Historical Library, Yale Medical Library 27, 38. New York: Oxford University Press, 1955–1961.

Sills, David L., editor. *The International Encyclopedia of the Social Sciences.* 17 vols. New York: Macmillan, 1968.

Sim, David C. *The Gospel of Matthew and Christian Judaism: The History and Social Setting of the Matthean Community.* SNTW. Edinburgh: T. & T. Clark, 1998.

————. "Matthew 7.21–23: Further Evidence of its Anti-Pauline Perspective." *NTS* 53 (2007) 325–43.

————. "Matthew's Anti-Paulinism: A Neglected Feature of Matthean Studies." *HvTSt* 58 (2002) 767–83.

Sjoberg, Gideon. *The Preindustrial City: Past and Present.* New York: Free Press, 1960.

Skinner, Marilyn, ed. *Rescuing Creusa: New Methodological Approaches to Women in Antiquity. Helios* 13.2. Lubbock: Texas Tech, 1986.

Smith, Dennis E. "Social Obligation in the Context of Communal Meals: A Study of the Christian Meal in 1 Corinthians in Comparison with Graeco-Roman Communal Meals." ThD diss. Cambridge: Harvard Divinity School, 1983.

Smith, Morton. *Jesus the Magician.* San Francisco: Harper & Row, 1978.

Stager, L. E. "The Archaeology of the Family in Ancient Israel." *BASOR* 260 (1985) 1–35.

Stager, L. E., and S. R. Wolff. "Child Sacrifice at Carthage—Religious Rite or Population Control?" *BAR* 10 (1984) 20–51.

Stein, S. "The Influence of Symposia Literature on the Literary Form of the Pesah Haggadah." *JJS* 8 (1957) 13–44.

Stendahl, Krister. "Matthew." *Peake's Commentary on the Bible.* London: Nelson, 1962.

Stonequist, Everett V. *The Marginal Man: A Study in Personality and Culture Conflict.* New York: Scribner's, 1937.

Strack, Hermann L., and Paul Billerbeck. *Kommentar zum Neuen Testament aus Talmud und Midrasch.* 5 vols. Munich: Beck, 1956.

Strecker, Georg. *Der Weg der Gerechtigkeit: Untersuchung zur Theologie des Matthäus.* 3rd ed. FRLANT 82. Gottingen: Vandenhoeck & Ruprecht, 1971.

Talbert, Charles H. "Miraculous Conceptions and Births in Mediterranean Antiquity." In *The Historical Jesus in Context,* edited by Amy-Jill Levine, Dale C. Allison, and John Dominic Crossan, 79–86. Princeton: Princeton University Press, 2006.

Theimann, Ronald F. "The Unnamed Woman at Bethany." *ThTo* 44 (1987) 179–88.

Theissen, Gerd. *The Miracle Stories of the Early Christian Tradition.* Translated by Francis McDonagh. Philadelphia: Fortress, 1983.

———. *Sociology of Early Palestinian Christianity.* Philadelphia: Fortress, 1978.

———. "'We Have Left Everything . . .' (Mark 10:28). Discipleship and Social Uprooting in the Jewish-Palestinian Society of the First Century." In *Social Reality and the Early Christians: Theology, Ethics, and the World of the New Testament,* 60–93. Minneapolis: Fortress, 1992.

Theissen, Gerd, and Annette Merz. *The Historical Jesus: A Comprehensive Guide.* Translated by John Bowden. Minneapolis: Fortress, 1998.

Thompson, William G. *Matthew's Advice to a Divided Community: Mt 17:22—18:35.* AnBib 44. Rome: Biblical Institute Press, 1970.

Throckmorton, Burton H. Jr. "Genealogy (Christ)." In *IDB* 2:365–66.

Thurston, B. B. "The Widows as the 'Altar of God.'" *SBLSP* 24 (1985) 279–89.

———. *The Widows: A Women's Ministry in the Early Church.* Minneapolis: Fortress, 1989.

Tidball, Derek. *The Social Context of the New Testament: A Sociological Analysis.* Grand Rapids: Zondervan, 1984.

Tilborg, Sjef van. *The Jewish Leaders in Matthew.* Leiden: Brill, 1972.

Tomson, Peter J. *Paul and the Jewish Law: Halakah in the Letters of the Apostle to the Gentiles.* Minneapolis: Fortress, 1990.

Trible, Phyllis. *God and the Rhetoric of Sexuality.* OBT. Philadelphia: Fortress, 1978.

———. *Texts of Terror: Literary-Feminist Reading of Biblical Narratives.* OBT. Philadelphia: Fortress, 1984.

Tsai, Christiana. *Queen of the Dark Chamber: The Story of Christiana Tsai as Told to Ellen L. Drummond.* Chicago: Moody, 1953.

Tolbert, Mary A. "Introduction." *The Bible and Feminist Hermeneutics. Semeia* 28 (1983) 113–26.

Trilling, Wolfgang. *Das wahre Israel: Studien zur Theologie des Matthäus Evangeliums.* 3rd ed. SANT 10. Munich: Kösel, 1964.

Turner, Ralph Edmond. *The Great Cultural Traditions: The Foundations of Civilization.* Vol. 2, *The Classical Empires.* New York: McGraw-Hill, 1941.

Turner, Terence. "Transformation, Hierarchy and Transcendence: A Reformulation of Van Gennep's Model of the Structure of *Rites de Passage.*" In *Secular Ritual,* edited by Sally F. Moore and Barbara G. Myerhoff, 53–70. Amsterdam: Van Gorcum, 1977.

Turner, Victor. *Dramas, Fields, and Metaphors: Symbolic Action in Human Society.* Ithaca, NY: Cornell University Press, 1974.

———. *The Forest of Symbols: Aspects of Ndembu Ritual.* Ithaca, NY: Cornell University Press, 1967.

———. *The Ritual Process: Structure and Anti-Structure.* Ithaca, NY: Cornell University Press, 1969.

———. "Variations on a Theme of Liminality." In *Secular Ritual,* edited by Sally F. Moore and Barbara G. Myerhoff, 36–52. Amsterdam: Van Gorcum, 1977.

Twelftree, Graham H. *Jesus the Exorcist: A Contribution to the Study of the Historical Jesus.* WUNT 2/54. Tübingen: Mohr/Siebeck, 1993.

Verner, David C. *The Household of God: The Social World of the Pastoral Epistles.* SBLDS 71. Chico, CA: Scholars, 1983.

Waetjen, Herman C. "The Genealogy as the Key to the Gospel according to Matthew." *JBL* 95 (1976) 220–25.

Wainwright, Elaine Mary. "The Gospel of Matthew." In *Searching the Scriptures,* edited by Elisabeth Schüssler Fiorenza. Vol. 2, *A Feminist Commentary,* 649–59. New York: Crossroad, 1994.

———. *Shall We Look for Another?: A Feminist Rereading of the Matthean Jesus.* Bible & Liberation. Maryknoll, NY: Orbis, 1998.

———. "Telling Stories of Healing in a Broken World." In *Transcending Boundaries: Contemporary Readings of the New Testament, Essays in Honor of Francis J. Moloney,* edited by Rekha M. Chennattu and Mary L. Coloe, 231–48. BSR 187. Rome: LAS, 2005.

———. *Towards a Feminist Critical Reading of the Gospel according to Matthew.* BZNW 60. Berlin: de Gruyter, 1991.

Weber, Max. *Economy and Society: An Outline of Interpretive Sociology.* Edited by Günther Roth and Claus Wittich. New York: Bedminister, 1968.

Wegner, Judith Romney. *Chattel or Person? The Status of Women in the Mishnah.* Oxford: Oxford University Press, 1988.

White, L Michael. "Domus Ecclesiae-Domus Dei: Adaptation and Development in the Setting for Early Christian Assembly." Ph.D. diss., Yale University, 1982.

Whyte, Martin K. *The Status of Women in Preindustrial Societies.* Princeton: Princeton University Press, 1978.

Wilkins, Michael J. *The Concept of Disciple in Matthew's Gospel: As Reflected in the Use of the Term Mathētēs.* Novum Testamentum Supplements 59. Leiden: Brill, 1988.

Williams, Ritva H. "Social Memory and the *Didachē.*" *BTB* 36 (2006) 35–39.

Wilson, Bryan R. *Magic and the Millennium: A Sociological Study of Religious Movements of Protest among Tribal and Third World Peoples.* New York: Harper & Row, 1973.

Winter, Gibson. *Elements for a Social Ethic: Scientific and Ethical Perspectives on Social Process.* New York: Macmillan, 1968.

———. *Liberating Creation: Foundations of Religious Social Ethics.* New York: Crossroad, 1981.

Wire, Antoinette C. "Gender Roles in a Scribal Community." In *The Social History of the Matthean Community: Cross Disciplinary Approaches,* edited by David Balch, 87–121. Minneapolis: Fortress, 1991.

Wolf, Eric R. *Peasants.* FMA. Englewood Cliffs, NJ: Prentice-Hall, 1966.

"Women." In *EncJud* 16. New York: Macmillan, 1971–1972.

Wong, Su-Ling, and Earl Herbert Cressy. *Daughter of Confucius: A Personal History.* New York: Farrar, Straus, and Young, 1952.

Wright, David P. "Holiness (OT)." In *ABD* 3:237–49.

Yanagisako, S. J. "Family and Household: The Analysis of Domestic Groups." *ARA* 8 (1979) 161–205.

Yarbrough, O. Larry. *Not Like the Gentiles: Marriage Rules in the Letters of Paul.* SBLDS 80. Atlanta: Scholars, 1986.

Lightning Source UK Ltd.
Milton Keynes UK
UKOW04f2302060917
308691UK00002B/329/P